Sustainable Markets for Sustainable Business

Professor Aras has tackled the very timely subject of business sustainability. She has put together a global perspective that presents best practices, discusses the role of businesses and markets, and provides examples of innovative approaches. The book will be a valuable resource not only for scholars but also for the wider business community and policy makers.

Reena Aggarwal,
Georgetown Center for Financial Markets and Policy, USA

This work demonstrates the multi-dimensional elements of sustainability, moving beyond conceptions of sustainable enterprise and industry, to ask fundamental questions regarding the sustainability of markets. Can markets be made to work towards sustainable development rather than environmental destruction? The book highlights how new modes of regulation, governance, incentives and strategic thinking are essential to reformulate the fundamental objectives and operations of economic endeavour towards sustainable goals.

Thomas Clarke,
University of Technology, Sydney, Australia

Finance, Governance and Sustainability: Challenges to Theory and Practice Series

Series Editor:
Professor Güler Aras, Yildiz Technical University, Turkey;
Georgetown University, Washington DC, USA

Focusing on the studies of academicians, researchers, entrepreneurs, policy makers and government officers, this international series aims to contribute to the progress in matters of finance, good governance and sustainability. These multidisciplinary books combine strong conceptual analysis with a wide range of empirical data and a wealth of case materials. They will be of interest to those working in a multitude of fields, across finance, governance, corporate behavior, regulations, ethics and sustainability.

Other titles in this series:

Sustainable Governance in Hybrid Organizations
Linne Marie Lauesen
ISBN: 978-1-4724-5130-9

The Changing Paradigm of Corporate Governance
Edited by Maria Aluchna and Güler Aras
ISBN: 978-1-4724-5201-6

Corporate Behavior and Sustainability
Edited by Güler Aras and Coral Ingley
ISBN: 978-1-4724-5769-1

Cosmopolitan Business Ethics
Jacob Dahl Rendtorff
ISBN: 978-1-4724-4708-1

Strategy, Structure and Corporate Governance
Nabyla Daidj
ISBN: 978-1-4724-5292-4

Sustainable Markets for Sustainable Business

A Global Perspective for Business and Financial Markets

Edited by

GÜLER ARAS
Yildiz Technical University, Istanbul, Turkey;
Georgetown University, Washington DC, USA

Routledge
Taylor & Francis Group

LONDON AND NEW YORK

First published 2015 by Gower Publishing

2 Park Square, Milton Park, Abingdon, Oxfordshire OX14 4RN
52 Vanderbilt Avenue, New York, NY 10017

Routledge is an imprint of the Taylor & Francis Group, an informa business

First issued in paperback 2019

Gower Applied Business Research
Our programme provides leaders, practitioners, scholars and researchers with thought provoking, cutting edge books that combine conceptual insights, interdisciplinary rigour and practical relevance in key areas of business and management.

British Library Cataloguing in Publication Data
A catalogue record for this book is available from the British Library.

Library of Congress Cataloging-in-Publication Data
Aras, Güler.
   Sustainable markets for sustainable business : a global perspective for business and financial markets / by Güler Aras.
        pages cm.—(Finance, governance and sustainability: challenges to theory and practice)
      Includes bibliographical references and index.
      ISBN 978-1-4724-3341-1 (hardback : alk. paper)—ISBN 978-1-4724-3342-8 (ebook)—ISBN 978-1-4724-3343-5 (epub)
   1. Social responsibility of business—Developing countries. 2. Capital market—Developing countries. 3. Sustainable development—Government policy—Developing countries. I. Title.

      HD60.5.D44A73 2015
      382.09172'4—dc23
                                                                                2014037241

   ISBN 13: 978-1-4724-3341-1 (hbk)
   ISBN 13: 978-0-367-87956-3 (pbk)

If you respect the future, you will be rewarded.
Güler Aras

Contents

List of Figures

List of Tables

Editor Biography

Güler Aras

Güler Aras is a professor of Finance and Accounting at Yildiz Technical University (YTU), Istanbul, Turkey, and a visiting professor at Georgetown University McDonough School of Business, Center for Financial Markets and Policy. She is the founding director of the Center for Finance, Governance and Sustainability (CFGS) at YTU. She is the former Dean of Faculty of Administrative and Economic Sciences, and the former Dean of the Graduate School. She served as a visiting professor at De Montfort University, Leicester, UK and at University Sains Malaysia in Penang, Malaysia. Her research focus is on financial economy and financial markets with particular emphasis on the relationship between sustainability, corporate governance, corporate social responsibility, and corporate financial performance. Professor Aras has published more than 20 books and has contributed over 200 articles in academic, business, and professional journals and magazines, including Journal of Business Ethics, Management Decision, Emerging Market Finance and Trade, International Journal of Banking Accounting and Finance, Journal of Applied Accounting Research. She also edited several book collections and conference proceedings. One of her most recent co-authored books is entitled *The Durable Corporation: Strategies for Sustainable Development*, published by Gower, and addresses the topical issue of the sustainability of corporate activity and *Governance and Social Responsibility: International Perspectives* was published by Palgrave Macmillan in 2011.

Professor Aras is the founding president of the International Financial Management Institute in Turkey (IMA, Turkish Chapter), and the Turkish Chapter of Transparency International. She has served as a board or a committee member of many national and international associations and research centers, including the Corporate Governance Association of Turkey (TKYD) where she is also an academic advisory board member, and the Institute of Internal Auditing of Turkey. She is the editor of Gower Book Series *Finance, Governance and Sustainability*: *Challenges to Theory and Practice* and the editor of Gower book series *Corporate Social Responsibility*. She has also served as an editor of *Social Responsibility Journal* and Emerald's *Development of Governance and Responsibility* book series. In addition, she is a member of a number of international editorial and advisory boards. Professor Aras has spoken extensively at professional and academic conferences, and has served as a consultant to a number of governmental and commercial organizations. She is a member of the Corporate Governance Committee of the Turkish Industry and Business Association (TÜSİAD), and a member of Certified Public Accountant (CPA-Turkey). Recently, she was elected as a member of the Specialized Committee of Minister of Development, Undersecretary of Treasury and Minister of Labour and Social Security Employment in Turkey.

Contributor Biographies

Reena Aggarwal

Reena Aggarwal is the McDonough Professor of Business Administration and Professor of Finance at Georgetown University's McDonough School of Business. She also serves as the Director of the university's Center for Financial Markets and Policy. Dr Aggarwal specializes in international stock markets, initial public offerings, and corporate governance. She has worked on major consulting projects sponsored by Credit Suisse, Wachovia, the World Bank, IMF, NASDAQ OMX Group, United Nations, and USAID. Dr Aggarwal obtained her MMS from Birla Institute of Technology and Science, India and her PhD in Finance from the University of Maryland.

Nihel Chabrak

Dr Chabrak has worked as a consultant in Business & IT in France. From 2002 until 2011 she held the position of Assistant, then Associate, Professor at Institut Mines Telecom, Paris, France. She took up several Visiting Scholar and Professor positions at the University of Wisconsin-La Crosse, USA (2007), University of Canterbury, Christchurch, New Zealand (2009), Deakin University, Melbourne, Australia (2009), University of Manouba, Tunis, Tunisia (2010), University of South Australia, Adelaide, Australia (2010) and the UAEU, Al-Ain, UAE (2011). Dr Chabrak has delivered numerous in-company courses, as well as courses and seminars in EMBA and EDBA programs in France, Morocco, and Syria on accounting (financial and management), financial analysis, and evaluation. She is currently teaching Corporate Governance in the UAEU MBA program and Corporate Social Responsibility in UAEU's DBA program. She is also involved in teaching for CMA and CIA certificate exams.

Dr Chabrak has published in international journals and conference proceedings. She was the guest editor of the special issue "The French Connection" as well as "The Global Financial Crisis" with Yves Gendron, for the *Critical Perspectives on Accounting* journal. She has been on the editorial board of *Critical Perspectives on Accounting* since January 2014. She is serving as ad hoc reviewer for journals (*Critical Perspectives on Accounting, Competition and Change Review, Journal of Business Ethics Education, Advances in Public Interest Accounting Journal,* and the *Journal of Business Ethics*). She was the co-founder and organizer of the International Critical Studies in Accounting and Finance Conference in Tunisia in 2009 and in Abu Dhabi in 2013.

Woodrow W. Clark II

Dr Clark, a long-time advocate for the environment and renewable energy, is an internationally recognized author, lecturer, public speaker, and advisor specializing in sustainable communities. He was one of the contributing scientists to the United Nations Intergovernmental Panel on Climate Change (UNIPCC) which is an organization that was awarded the Nobel Peace Prize in December 2007 along with Al Gore and his film *An Inconvenient Truth*. Clark has seven books and 50+ peer-reviewed articles that concern economics and policies for global sustainable communities, including "The Green Industrial Revolution" with Grant Cooke in 2014. His latest book is *The Next Economics* (Springer, 2012). His next book is on Smart Green Sustainable Cities and is due to be published in mid-2015. Clark is a serial entrepreneur, having started his first company at the age of 14 followed by Clark Communications in San Francisco (1980–1991) followed by Clark Strategic Partners (2004–present). Clark was a Fulbright (1994) at Aalborg University, Denmark, and a Visiting Professor there in 1999, but this was cut short when he was appointed by California Governor Gray Davis as his Renewable Energy Advisor during the state's energy crisis from 2000–2003. He earned three masters' degrees from three different universities, and his PhD at University of California, Berkeley. Clark lives with his wife and young son in California.

Thomas Clarke

Thomas Clarke is Professor of Management and Director of the key University Research Centre for Corporate Governance at the University of Technology, Sydney (UTS). Formerly, he was Chair of the Academic Board at UTS, and a member of the University Council. He was Professor of Management at China Europe International Business School (CEIBS) in Shanghai. In the UK he was a member of the Royal Society of Arts Tomorrow's Company Inquiry into the sources of sustainable business success, drafting the original position paper for the inquiry, and directing the national conference. At the Organisation for Economic Co-operation and Development (OECD) in Paris he participated in the review of the original OECD Principles of Corporate Governance. He is the author of *International Corporate* (to be published in 2015 by Routledge), and editor (with Douglas Branson) of the *Sage Handbook of Corporate Governance* (Sage, 2012). He is the corporate governance and sustainability editor of the *Journal of Business Ethics* (Springer).

Nabyla Daidj

Nabyla Daidj is an Associate Professor of Strategy at Telecom Ecole de Management (Institut Mines Telecom). Her teaching and research interests are corporate strategy, inter-organizational relationships (strategic alliances, clusters, business ecosystems, and coopetitive practices), corporate governance and corporate social responsibility (CSR). She has published in international journals and conference proceedings and, in 2008, she published a book about cooperation, game theory, and strategic management. Her current research investigates sources of value creation in international firms operating in the IT sector within the context of convergence. Her work has also been published in the *Journal of Media Business Studies*, and the *Journal of Media Economics, Communications & Strategies*.

Daniel Gorfine

Daniel Gorfine is director of financial markets policy and legal counsel in the Washington office of the Milken Institute. He focuses on financial innovation, capital access, and financial market issues. He spearheads the Institute's work on innovative capital access tools and new financial technologies. Gorfine has provided expert testimony before Congress, frequently engages with policy-makers and market participants, and is a national media contributor on these topics. Before joining the Institute, Gorfine worked at the international law firm, Covington & Burling LLP, where he advised and represented a range of business and nonprofit clients. Gorfine graduated with a BA from Brown University, a JD from George Washington University Law School and an MA from the Paul H. Nitze School of Advanced International Studies (SAIS) at Johns Hopkins University.

Coral Ingley

Coral Ingley is Associate Professor of Management at Auckland University of Technology, New Zealand and holds a PhD in Corporate Governance from

RMIT University, Melbourne, Australia. She is a professional member of the Institute of Directors, is Founder and Director of the Corporate Governance Centre in the University's Faculty of Business and Law, and teaches corporate governance and responsibility in the MBA programme as well as strategic management and research methods in the Faculty's Postgraduate degree programs. Her research focuses on various aspects of corporate governance, the outputs from which are published regularly in academic journals and presented at refereed conferences. She is also a member of editorial boards of scholarly journals and has been a regular visiting professor and researcher at universities and business schools in France, Italy, Spain, and the Netherlands.

Steve Lydenberg

Steve Lydenberg is Founding Director of the Initiative for Responsible Investment at the Hauser Institute for Civil Society at Harvard University, and Partner, Strategic Vision for Domini Social Investments LLC, New York, USA. For over three decades he has been active in responsible investment with the Council on Economic Priorities, Trillium Asset Management and KLD Research & Analytics. He is author of numerous articles on responsible investment including "Reason, Rationality and Fiduciary Duty" (*Journal of Business Ethics*) and "On Materiality and Sustainability: The Value of Disclosure in the Capital Markets" (*Initiative for Responsible Investment*). He is also author and co-author of several books on responsible investment including *Corporations and the Public Interest* (Berrett-Koehler, 2005) and *Dilemmas in Responsible Investment* (Greenleaf, 2011). He holds a Certified Financial Analysts charter and a Masters of Fine Arts from Cornell University.

Jacob Dahl Rendtorff

Jacob Dahl Rendtorff, PhD and Doctor of Administration and Social Sciences, is Professor of Responsibility, Ethics and Legitimacy of Corporations at Roskilde University, Denmark. He is also Visiting Professor in philosophy of management and ethical judgment at Copenhagen Business School. Rendtorff is head of the research group Management in Transition at Roskilde University. Rendtorff has a background in research in ethics, business ethics, bioethics, information ethics, political theory, and philosophy of law. Rendtorff has written many articles and 12 books on issues of existentialism and hermeneutics, French philosophy, ethics, bioethics, and business ethics as well as philosophy of law, and he has been co-author and editor on more than 10 other books.

Jacques Richard

Jacques Richard is Emeritus Professor at the University of Paris Dauphine. He is also a chartered accountant. He is a member of the French National Accounting Standards Board (Ministry of Finance), and a founder of the Master Sustainable Development of the University Paris Dauphine. He has published more than 100 articles in referenced journals of accounting, notably in English speaking journals such as *Accounting Organizations and Society*; *European Accounting Review*; *Critical Perspectives on Accounting*; *Accounting, Auditing and Accountability*; *Accounting in Europe*; *The Historian Accounting Review*; *Sustainability Accounting Management*; and *Policy Journal* as well as in French, German and Russian Journals. He has published more than 30 books of which 13 are in English, 14 in French, 1 in German and 2 in Russian. He has been guest professor in many universities, notably the universities of Kyoto (Japan), Moscow MGU (Russia), Sankt Petersburg (Russia), Montreal UQAM (Canada), Münster (Germany), Shanghai (China), and Vienna (Austria). He has recently won the Best Manuscript Award of the American Academy of Accounting Historians for his works on the history of accounting and management.

Dana Stefanczyk

Dana Stefanczyk is the Assistant Director of the Georgetown Center for Financial Markets and Policy. In her role Ms. Stefanczyk supports the Center's research activities and organizes events to facilitate discussion among leading scholars, practitioners, and policy makers on global finance issues. She previously worked at the Aircraft Owners and Pilots Association on the Political Action Committee. Ms. Stefanczyk holds a BA from Duke University and is currently enrolled in the MBA program at Georgetown University's McDonough School of Business.

Paul F. Williams

Paul F. Williams is Professor, Ernst & Young Faculty Research Fellow, at NC State University. He is Associate Editor of Critical Perspectives on Accounting (Associate then Editor for Accounting and the Public Interest until 2010). He served as Editorial Board Member for several journals such as *Advances in Public Interest Accounting*; *Accounting, Auditing and Accountability*; *Accounting and Business Society*' *Accounting Forum*; *Alternative Perspectives on Accounting and Finance*; *Journal of Professional Responsibility and Ethics in Accounting*; *Accountancy, Business and the Public Interest*; and *Issues in Accounting Education*.

He has published in renowned journals such as *Accounting, Organizations and Society*; *Business Ethics Quarterly*; *Critical Perspectives on Accounting*; *Accounting, Economics and Law*; *Accounting and the Public Interest*; *European Accounting Review*; *Accounting Education: An International Journal*; *The Accounting Historians Journal*, and many others. He received the Ernst & Young Outstanding Teacher Award in 1999 and the American Accounting Association's Public Interest Section Accounting Exemplar Award in 2013.

Foreword

Over the last decade, there has been a general recognition of the concept of sustainability in every walk of life, from environmental concerns to financial circles. This issue needs to be addressed at global, societal, local, as well as the personal level. Of course, it should also be addressed in terms of markets and businesses, and this is the focus of this book. The term "sustainability" has become ubiquitous in any discussions on globalization and corporate performance. Sustainability is sometimes considered a controversial issue as there are many definitions of what is meant by the term, and these will be addressed in this book. In simple terms, sustainability is a "long-termism," which is long-term thinking, "long-term strategy," and the long-term actions of corporations and the markets. In other words we should consider not only the consequences of our actions on today and tomorrow or even next year, but also on the future of the corporation, the institution, and the market.

In general, sustainability is fundamental to the healthy operation of markets and businesses, and therefore it deserves much attention. It is clearly recognized everywhere that sustainable markets and businesses are crucial to a sound global economy and sustainable development. Widespread corporate scandals, which we witnessed in the first years of the twenty-first century, and, in particular, the global financial crisis in 2008, have shown that the business world needs to operate at a different level to be immune to the devastating effects of such shortsighted operations. To alleviate these problems a fundamental rethink is required on the principles of sustainable operations by both businesses and governments.

In this book we explore the concept of sustainability in the financial markets and the business world. Moreover, we attempt to correlate and clarify the interaction and causality between markets and businesses. It is important to start this analysis by exploring what happens within markets and corporations in order to understand their approach. This book came together by doing just that: gathering experts on sustainability and exploring the crucial issues. It is hoped that the analysis presented here will be useful as it will provide realistic and practical measures to enable policy makers and corporate managers to develop sustainable strategies. We also hope that you, the reader, will find the ideas presented here equally relevant and practical, and more importantly helpful, in the development of corporate strategies and market strategies to enable sustainable development.

This book is the first of the Gower book series entitled "Finance, Governance and Sustainability: Challenges to Theory and Practice". As mentioned earlier, today's developments within the field of sustainability and governance appeal to a growing audience in many respects. While there are many studies focused on governance and finance, a focus on sustainability is missing. The convergence of the three fields of finance, governance, and sustainability, has a high potential for providing effective solutions and a wider perspective on the issues and barriers encountered about sustainability. The aim of the "Finance, Governance and Sustainability: Challenges to Theory and Practice" series is to fill this gap by bringing together recent developments in the intersection of these three fields.

This series shares the studies of those academicians, researchers, entrepreneurs, policy makers and government officers who are aiming to contribute to the progress of, and overcome the emerging barriers to, corporate sustainability and sustainable development. In addition, by linking these studies to the research and development department at the newly established Center for Finance, Corporate Governance and Sustainability at Yildiz Technical University, we will provide the most current coverage of these concepts with a global perspective. The series combines strong conceptual analyses with a wide-ranging empirical focus and a wealth of case materials. Also included are summary points, suggestions for further reading, web resources, and an extensive bibliography. The level of presentation is for graduate students, academicians, and business people as well as policy and decision makers around the world.

This book was completed during my sabbatical at the Georgetown University McDonough School of Business, Center for Financial Market and Policy, Washington, DC, USA. In completing this book, I have had very graceful and respectful support from everyone at Georgetown University, McDonough School of Business. I would like to especially thank Professor Reena Aggarwal, Founder and Director of the Center for Financial Market and Policy, for the exceptionally high quality academic atmosphere she has established. I have also benefited greatly from discussions with my academic colleagues and many finance department members. I thank Dean David Thomas for the warm hospitality and peaceful working atmosphere he provided, and Professor Lynn Doran for her kind support and friendship during my visit at Georgetown

University. Finally, I thank Dana Stefanczyk, the Center assistant director, for her graceful help.

Güler Aras
Georgetown University
McDonough School of Business
Center for Financial Market and Policy
Washington DC, USA

Introduction:
What are the Key Aspects and Challenges for Sustainability?

GÜLER ARAS

In most business circles, one of the most used words relating to corporate activity is "sustainability". Indeed it could be argued that it has been heavily overused and, with so many different meanings applied to it, it is effectively meaningless. The term sustainability currently has a high profile within the repertoire of corporate activity (Aras and Crowther, 2008). It is frequently mentioned as central to corporate activity without any attempt to define exactly what sustainable activity entails. This is understandable as the concept is problematic and subject to many varying definitions. These range from platitudes concerning sustainable development to the deep green concept of returning to the golden era before industrialization. However, it is often used by corporations merely to signify that they intend to continue their existence into the future.

Sustainability is a multidimensional and multidisciplinary concept that has three main accepted dimensions: economic growth, social responsibility, and environmental protection. Today sustainability risks and opportunities have become a global imperative and a megatrend for business. Sustainable markets are about ensuring that they contribute to positive social, environmental, and economic outcomes. The sustainability of markets is closely related to sustainable business development, market structure, environmental economics, trade and investment, tourism, and mining. Markets are one of the dominant social institutions of our time, and understanding what they are, how they work, and how they can be shaped, is essential to sustainable development. The world's markets have the potential to improve the lives of billions of people in developing countries, reduce poverty, and secure environmental quality for future generations. However, they often fail to capture the full value of natural resources, or to promote the interests of poor people. An effective public policy framework for markets is therefore required. The issue of market governance and the relationship between the market and private interests, along with political authority, remain core topics at the heart of the sustainability debate.

Many environmental problems such as climate change, pollution, land degradation, and biodiversity loss are, in part, the result of market failures. These market failures are present in most sectors of the economy including agriculture, forestry, extractive industries, manufacturing, and tourism. Those businesses having a product or service toward the end of the lifecycle chain are rarely negatively affected by the impacts their sector has on the environment and society. There is therefore little incentive to take into account these impacts (environmental or social externalities) in their decision making. As a result, the market rarely incorporates true costs of environmental or social externalities.

The right market enabling environment is essential for sustainable development. If the right conditions do not exist, however, markets may work to undermine this development resulting in the need for us to take back control. This will require civil society and the public and private sectors to work together to develop markets that will work toward sustainable development. These actions will require innovative ways to facilitate strategic thinking and execute these ideas, eventually helping us to find a solution to global problems. The benefits of free markets and economic globalization will be brought into question when local capacities and institutions are weak.

This is equally true for financial markets. The financial system needs to serve as the nervous system of the global economy rather than as its master. The current financial marketplace suffers from misplaced incentives and the invisibility of capital within the decision-making process. This leads to actions being taken despite the fact they will lead to future harm. For the financial markets to become sustainable and resilient to the challenges ahead, radical changes need to take place. A connection between money invested and where it ends up must be made, with investors becoming more aware of the social and environmental effects of their decisions. Integrated reporting, government regulation, and pension fund allocation will all be aspects of this change.

Market structures also affect the sustainability capacity of markets. Unless market structures and their impact on sustainability are understood, it is almost impossible to assess the implications of changes to the structures. Moreover, understanding the contribution of both large and small companies to sustainable development is crucial.

The questions to be asked or issues to be addressed under the heading of "market governance" will be:

- How should the market power of large companies be monitored closely, because gaining market power and supporting sustainability are conflicting concepts?

- What are the appropriate policy interventions that will enhance the sustainable development impact of both large and small companies?

- How should the power be distributed between financial corporations and governments in a sustainable market?

- What are the elements that allow better control of this balance?

- What are the success factors and technical restrictions of implementing a regulatory reform?

Businesses have the potential to contribute to sustainable markets. Their contributions can be two-fold: at the local level and at the global level. The multinational companies and their businesses can, and are expected to, play a major role in building and supporting sustainable markets. For profit and not for profit entities the business models adopted by them will affect how they contribute to sustainable development. This contribution includes how they interact with each other in procurement, sub-contracting, and other direct business arrangements. The questions that will be answered include:

- How should businesses engage with local communities and policy makers to achieve sustainable development goals?

- How can corporate social investment strategies meet community development needs?

- How can dialogue with multi-stakeholder partnerships be most effective in terms of sustainable markets?

- In what ways will business skills be revised and which new skills will be of importance?

- What kind of partnerships will have increasing importance?

- How can the private sector, civil society, and government work together to shape business models that will deliver positive economic, environmental, and social outcomes as well as business viability?

The relationship between sustainability and stability is also unclear, particularly in terms of financial markets. The two terms are often used synonymously. Nevertheless, sustainability encompasses more than just stability. In addition to pointing out the differences between these two terms, formulating certain requirements for sustainable financial markets (such as internalizing costs, ability to self-regenerate, diversity, credibility, and long-term orientation) is also crucial and will be addressed.

Benefits that are promised at a national level by sustainable development, mostly in terms of direct investments, are too often not matched by positive contributions to environmental protection, poverty reduction, or sustainable livelihoods at the local level. The questions to be asked here will include:

- What will be the new role expected from direct investment and multinational corporations in this respect?

- How can a sustainable financial market enhance and improve sustainable development?

- In short, what is the role of sustainable finance in achieving sustainable development? Is it just financing, or more?

- How do environmental, social, and governance (ESG) signals affect financial markets?

- What is the impact of institutional entrepreneurs on the viability of ESG investing?

This subject is important for the strategy planners of businesses, policy makers, and other stakeholders seeking to build more sustainable markets.

It is recognized in the financial world that a company's cost of capital is related to the perceived risk associated with investing in a particular project. In other words, there is a direct correlation between the risk involved in an investment, and the rewards which are expected to accrue from a successful investment. It is generally recognized that the larger, more established companies represent a more certain investment and therefore have a lower cost of capital. This is an established fact as far as finance theory is concerned and is recognized in the operation of financial markets around the world. Naturally a company which is sustainable will also be a more certain investment. Most large companies mention sustainability in their reporting and frequently it is featured prominently. In addition, it is noticeable that extractive industries, which by their very nature cannot be sustainable in the long term, make sustainability a prominent issue (see Aras and Crowther, 2009a).

The global financial crisis in 2008 again raised the profile of governance. Not only corporate governance but also the governance of markets, trade, and so on. Debates are taking place regarding the rules of governance, and codes around the world are being developed or amended. The focus is on the relationship between ethics and governance codes, the extension of governance procedures to all stakeholders and how widely this should be interpreted, the moderating role of culture in the operation of governance mechanisms, and the need (or not) for global mechanisms.

As a result of that financial crisis, corporate management and corporate behavior is a developing subject. There are only a few studies being conducted regarding the complex challenges of sustainable business and markets in practice. This book is intended to be largely descriptive, but also prescriptive, by providing case materials that are relevant to an international audience. To approach the problems and questions mentioned above, researchers in the field of finance and sustainability studies have been asked to write a chapter where they focus on important balancing questions. They have also been asked to present the types of answers and conclusions to the above mentioned research questions that may be drawn from their theoretical and empirical analysis.

This book is designed to address these debates in the context of business and market sustainability. The book contains three distinct parts. In the first part of the book we consider a variety of theoretical issues concerned with sustainability in the new environment. In the second part we look at these issues in the market and business practice under various guises. In the third and last part of the book, we focus on future aspects of these issues and alternative solutions.

In the first chapter of this book Güler Aras outlines the subject of the sustainability of markets and businesses, arguing that problems encountered with this led to the financial crisis in 2008. Aras shows the causality and interaction between sustainable markets and sustainable businesses. She argues that the financial crisis highlighted the importance of sustainable businesses and markets. Also, she emphasizes that this crisis showed that good governance, corporate social responsibility, and efficient risk management are essential for sustainability. Some causes of the failure of the economic system and the origins of the financial and economic crisis in 2008 show that part of the problem is caused by failures in regulation and governance. These are brought about by the nature of global markets and local governance. Attention needs to be paid not only to the development of sustainable markets and businesses but also to achieving a truly sustainable global system.

Jacob Dahl Rendtorff then explores a theoretical reexamination of sustainability in economics and business. For him the problem of sustainability in economics and business can be framed around understanding what obligations business may have with respect to environmental ethics, and what kind of philosophical theory should justify protection of the environment. The requirement to deal with this problem emerges out of the present challenges over the future of humanity on the planet. Rendtorff indicates that we are no longer passive participants in natural history. At our age, the Age of the Anthropocene, the human species has itself become a geological force that influences and changes its own natural history with the interaction of other natural forces. The connection between sustainability and ethical principles is promoted as the essence of the ethics of organizational behavior in the environment. Moreover, this leads to the difficult problem of going from ethics to law, and how to deal with environmental crime of large organizations and institutions. Finally, Rendtorff proposes the concept of the balanced company as a possible solution to the problem of how to promote international action with regard to the problem of sustainability.

We then turn our focus to the relationship between sustainable markets and sustainable development, as discussed by Woodrow W. Clark II. Clark's chapter covers current issues in sustainable development from a business and economics perspective. It is intimated that to achieve this there must be involvement from local and regional governments. Clark argues that businesses need to look at how they can also become sustainable in their daily practices. The starting point is with the local city or community governments and their regional, state and national goals. For communities to become sustainable they need to have development plans and provide resources ranging from financing to regulations. This chapter provides case studies from California in the United States to regions in Denmark in the European Union. In both government cases, there are policies and programs with financial, educational, and regulatory support. The key points are summarized into case examples.

The second part of the book examines corporate and market approaches for sustainability. It starts with a chapter from Chabrak and Richard, and focuses on the corporate world and sustainability in terms of eco-efficiency and shareholder value. They shed light on how the international community, instead of fulfilling Agenda 21, is in reality moving away from it, thus deepening the ecological crisis. They emphasize that eco-efficiency philosophy is depicted to be the corporate world initiative toward the implementation of Agenda 21. Despite its limitations in terms of natural capital conservation, a group of scholars credited eco-efficiency as the unique business solution to the environmental problem. It was endorsed as a signal of change and a win-win strategy by creating more goods and services while using fewer resources and creating less waste and pollution. In actual fact eco-efficiency has enabled the corporate world to capture the environmental debate in the belief of maximizing shareholder value. In this chapter the authors propose a new avenue toward better conservation of natural capital. A new concept of performance associated with a reformed governance model is then elaborated.

The role of small and medium-sized enterprises (SMEs) in sustainable development is then examined by Aggarwal, Gorfine and Stefanczyk. They point out that sustainable businesses create economic value and vibrant communities. The chapter authors indicate that SMEs are the engine of economic growth globally by making significant contributions to innovation, competitiveness, financial inclusion, and employment. This chapter studies the role of SMEs in sustainable development and discusses the challenges faced by these firms in raising capital. They also highlight examples of recent innovations in the United States and globally that allow SMEs easier access to finances. They discuss how both developed and emerging markets have pursued innovative approaches to making debt and equity financing available to SMEs. Several of these programs have been initiated by the private sector while others are administered by governments.

Coral Ingley then reviews the findings of two studies previously conducted among corporate boards and senior executives, which relate sustainability and corporate social responsibility. Ingley includes a short case study, which lends support to the findings from these studies and indicates a prevalent corporate mindset among boards in New Zealand companies. These studies do not appear to have moved beyond a shareholder primacy focus, having remained fixated on the compliance dimension of their governance role. These studies suggest that for more than 15 years, stakeholder relationships and a real recognition of their wider societal responsibility have not been part of directors' stream-of-consciousness with regard to their wider fiduciary duty. In this chapter

Ingley shows that there is growing evidence that, for corporations and indeed governments, sustainability is not just a fancy concept with little if any day-to-day real business relevance, but is increasingly implicated with corporate, social, and economic performance.

In the following chapter Aras and Daidj examine the sustainability issue in corporate social responsibility (CSR) and strategy, specifically in terms of sustainable or temporary competitive advantage in today's dynamic environment. Sustainable competitive advantage has traditionally been the key concept used by strategic management to explain a corporation's success. CSR contributes by developing a sustainable advantage, and is more and more considered as an opportunity and a way to develop a competitive advantage rather than as a cost. The CSR practices, as they gradually emerge, involve a higher degree of implicit forms of rules and policies. Corporations have to combine two different approaches: the maximization of short-term profitability demanded by shareholders, and the need to take into account growth over the longer term (stakeholders). CSR has an impact on value creation in the short and long term. In addition, it can be considered to be a core competency, aiming to achieve a sustainable rather than temporary advantage. Also, according to the chapter authors, the discourses of sustainability all adopt a viewpoint of the acceptability, or otherwise, of sustainable development. Equally these discourses accept that sustainability is possible, but disagree about the circumstances in which it is possible and about the resultant level of economic activity.

Although every chapter of the book contains discussion and recommended solutions, the third and final part of the book specifically focuses on future perspectives and the solution strategies for implementation of sustainability measures.

This part begins with a chapter by Thomas Clarke. Clarke analyzes the causes of the 2008 global financial crisis, with a focus on the corporate governance causes, and gauges the effectiveness of the international regulatory response. According to Clarke, the 2008 global financial crisis was a multidimensional, interconnected, and systemic crisis. Among the causes of the crisis were international macro-economic imbalances, institutional and risk management failure, corporate governance failure, and regulatory, supervisory, and crisis management failure. This global financial crisis and its aftermath consisted of multiple and compounding failures in financial markets, institutions, regulation, and governance. The long progression of financial crises around the world serves as a reminder that the system is neither self-regulating nor robust.

While the accumulated cost of the global financial crisis was being realized, the commitment to establish a new international financial regulatory framework increased. At the supra-national level sustained efforts have been made to achieve better alignment of governance institutions and practices, risk management, and remuneration with market discipline, supervision, regulation, and transparency in the international financial sector. Clarke asks: "Will the ongoing global effort at regulatory reform achieve significant change, or be marginalized by the exigencies of dealing with immediate problems such as sovereign debt, or ignored in the next dash for economic growth"? His next question is: "How resilient will this new regulatory architecture prove as new forms of systemic risk emerge, and to what extent will it be effectively enforced by national regulators, and implemented by financial institutions"?

According to Steve Lydenberg, disclosure of corporate ESG data is important for effective and sustainable systems, and disclosure of ESG data will soon become globally mandated. Lydenberg points out that such disclosure systems can potentially drive fundamental change into corporate and financial management, and help counteract today's short-termism. It does so in part because sustainability issues are often long-term in their nature and can focus money managers and corporate boards on the stability and sustainability of the systems within which they operate. Mandating disclosure of this data is driven by its increasing materiality to investment decision-making, distrust of today's financial markets, current accounting measures, the complexity of challenges in a seven to nine billion people world, private enterprise's obligations to help raise those at the bottom of the pyramid out of poverty, and strains on our environmental systems due to ever increasing commercial and private consumption. National governments and stock exchanges increasingly encourage corporate ESG disclosure. If the disclosure is to be effective and sustainable, it needs to be formulated so that users of the data can easily incorporate it into decision making. Disclosures will assist in order to clearly interpret users' decisions and alter their practices in ways that benefit themselves and users, and simultaneously align their policies with public purposes. To be sustainable over the years, these systems should also be flexible enough to expand in scope as ESG issues evolve and to improve in quality and usefulness over time.

In the next chapter, Paul F. Williams provides an argument for the rethinking of the fundamental premise that underlies the current thinking in accounting about sustainability reporting. According to the author, the current model, which has not been substantially altered in nearly half a century, is predicated on a collection of assumptions that are no longer reasonable. Corporate sustainability reporting is shaped by the belief that accounting is about producing information that is useful to individuals and firms for making rational economic decisions in a world organized around the logic of markets. In light of recent developments in the disciplines of economics, sociobiology, psychology, and anthropology this chapter argues that the premises informing accounting models of sustainability reporting are no longer sensible to hold. He mentions that the failure of effective accounting systems to develop is attributable to the false premises upon which their development has thus far been based. According to the author sustainability reporting, to be effective in contributing to the problem of sustainability, needs to provide information about accountability once again.

In the final chapter Aras outlines conclusions with a summary of the analyses and discussions.

In this book the market and business sustainability issue is discussed and is demonstrated to be vital for a sound economy and its sustainable development. We discuss what we need to create in order to support sustainable and resilient business and markets. We believe our approach to this multidimensional topic will provide the reader with a fuller understanding of the many issues and controversies involved. We are also hoping to leave the reader with the necessary background and impacts of sustainability so that we can all work together to achieve long-term market and business success.

Bibliography

Aras, G., and Kurt, D. (2012). The Effects of Stock Option Compensation on Managerial Risk Taking Behavior and Firm Financial Performance: The Global Financial Crisis from a Different Perspective. *International Journal of Economics and Finance Studies*, Vol. 4(2), 77–90.

Aras, G., Kutlu, O., and Aybars, A. (2010). Managing Corporate Performance: Investigating the Relationship between Corporate Social Responsibility and Financial Performance in Emerging Markets. *International Journal of Productivity and Performance Management*, Vol. 59(3), 229–54.

Aras, G., and Crowther, D. (2009a). Corporate Sustainability Reporting: A Study in Disingenuity? *Journal of Business Ethics*, Vol. 27, 279–88.

Aras, G., and Crowther, D. (2009b). *The Durable Corporation: Strategies for Sustainable Development*. Aldershot: Gower.

Aras, G. (2008). Corporate Governance and the Agency Problem in Financial Markets. In D. Crowther and N. Capaldi (eds), *Ashgate Research Companion to Corporate Social Responsibility*. Aldershot: Ashgate.

Aras, G., and Crowther, D. (2008). Governance and Sustainability: An Investigation into the Relationship Between Corporate Governance and Corporate Sustainability. *Management Decision*, Vol. 46(3), 433–48.

PART I
Theoretical Perspectives and
Current Issues

Chapter 1

Causality and Interaction: Sustainable Markets and Sustainable Business

GÜLER ARAS

Introduction

In recent years, sustainability has become an important topic for academics, businesses, investors, and policy makers. There has been a vast increase in the interest and concern for corporate governance, and there has been a similar growth in interest in sustainability. The growing attention of sustainability importance has created substantial interest in both markets and businesses. It is frequently mentioned as central to corporate activity without any attempt to define exactly what sustainable activity entails. However, the understanding of what sustainability means remains unclear as well as how complex this issue is for businesses and financial markets.

It is clear that sustainability is one of the main issues facing businesses at present. However, the real question is: Does the way in which the system is designed to operate actually work against its needs? The market system can be designed to control the use of scarce resources even when they are different and more concerned with environmental resources. Market mechanisms tend to do this to an extent through price. The most important issue is to create an understanding of where and how businesses can best contribute to sustainable markets and how the sustainable markets can support sustainable businesses.

Traditional accounting theory and practice assumes that value is created in the business through the transformation process, and that distribution is merely concerned with how much of the resultant profit is given to the investors in the business now and how much is retained in order to generate future profits and hence future returns to investors. This is, of course, overly simplistic for a number of reasons. Even in traditional accounting theory it is recognized that some of the retained profit is needed merely to replace worn out capital, ensuring sustainability in its narrowest sense. Accounting, of course, only attempts to record actions taking place within this transformational process, and even in doing so regards all costs as things leading to profit for distribution. This traditional view of accounting is that the only activities with which the organization should be concerned are those which take place within the organization.[1] Consequently it is considered that these are the only activities for which a role for accounting exists. Here, therefore, is located the essential dialectic of accounting: some results of actions taken are significant and need to be recorded, while others are irrelevant and need to be ignored. This view of accounting places the organization at the center of its world and the only interfaces with the external world take place at the beginning and end of its value chain. It is apparent, however, that any actions which an organization undertakes will have an effect not just upon itself but also upon the external environment within which that organization resides. In considering the effect of the organization on its external environment, it must be recognized that this environment includes the business, the local/societal, and the wider global environments at once (Aras and Crowther, 2009a).

In this chapter it is emphasized that there is a significant and natural interaction between market and business performance, and sustainability. We also try to show the causality between the market and business. Their success is important for a sound economy and sustainable development. For the markets to become sustainable and resilient, radical changes need to take place with the development of a truly thorough global sustainable system.

Markets Sustainability and Globalization

Globalization can be defined as the free movement of goods, services, and capital. Globalization is also a process which integrates world economies, culture, technology, and governance. It involves the transfer of information, skilled employee mobility, the exchange of technology, financial funds flow, and geographic arbitrage between developed and developing countries. Moreover, globalization has religious, environmental, and social dimensions. Therefore globalization affects the markets, economy, business, society, and environment in different ways:

---

1   Essentially the only purpose of traditional accounting is to record the effects of actions upon the organization itself.

- increasing competition

- technological development

- knowledge/information transfer

- portfolio investment (fund transfers between developed countries and emerging markets)

- regulation/deregulation

- international standards

- market integration

- intellectual capital mobility

- financial crisis—contagion effect—global crisis.

These are further represented in Figure 1.1 (overleaf).

It is well known that globalization, together with developments in financial markets and the ability to transfer knowledge at greater speeds, has led to an increase in the need for new international standards concerning such matters as international financial reporting, corporate governance, ethics, and corporate social responsibility. The standards have been drafted with a view to minimizing uncertainty and developing an atmosphere of confidence in a web of emerging complex relations. It is very important for financial markets, and the organizations operating within these markets, to accommodate and implement these standards because they will only be successful to the extent that they can secure this confidence. Legal provisions, control mechanisms, and sanctions are not sufficient on their own to ensure the sound operation of the system and to create confidence. Therefore, the introduction of corporate governance principles aims to increase compliance with legal provisions and create an atmosphere of confidence by giving security to stakeholders and safeguarding the interests of all parties (Aras, 2008a). The objective of sustainable financial markets is to increase trust in those markets in the context of elimination of the uncertainties, investor protection, and more efficient resource allocation.

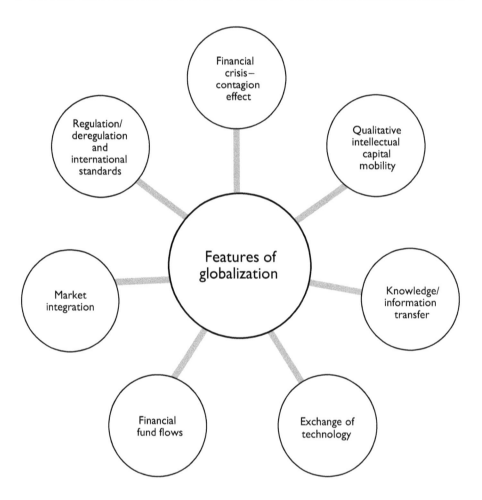

Figure 1.1   Features of globalization
Source: Aras and Crowther, 2011.

Sustainable financial institutions and markets will address such points as creating sustainable value, achieving the institutions' and markets' goals, and keeping a balance between economic and social benefits with a long-term perspective. In fact sustainability offers long-term benefits for markets and institutions, such as reducing risk and attracting new investors and shareholders.

Indicators of sustainability, therefore, tend to emphasize either stocks of wealth or, more specifically, how a portfolio of assets is managed over time. Changes in this portfolio include investments in conventional forms of produced assets (infrastructure, buildings, and machines) and human capital (via training and educational expenditures, and primary health care).

The contribution of the recent debate makes it clear that portfolio management must also take account of, for example, the depletion of non-renewable and living resources, and changes in environmental liabilities arising as a result of pollution (Atkinson et al., 2000).

For financial organizations, sustainability is much more important since they produce and provide rather intangible services in the economy. The difficulties that such a business would face when they lose their credibility in terms of their relevant circles are the numbers and types of customers. The losses they would suffer, as a result, are much higher. Financial organizations are no different from other businesses in terms of their purposes of establishment. On the other hand, confidence in management is more important in financial organizations than in other businesses. This is because gaining customers, and therefore profitability, in the financial services sector depends on the confidence built up by the organization. Financial organizations need to give more emphasis to ethical values and good governance, and the fact that their job often contains riskier and more complex relations (Aras, 2006).

When considering sustainability in financial institutions we are generally confronted with more complex problems due to the nature of finance and, therefore, of financial services and instruments. These problems are concerned with intangible services, and risky instruments and transactions. The fact that the characteristics and functions of finance, financial services, and these instruments are rather complex and, when combined with both insufficient information on the part of customers or consumers and a differentiation in their expectations, can lead to skepticism, disappointment, and extreme reactions. Often, there are suitable opportunities for abuse by financial service providers under such conditions.[2] When all these factors combine, customers can readily claim that they are deceived and this in turn contributes to the bad reputation of finance in terms of ethics and ethical behavior (Aras and Crowther, 2009a, pp.279–88). Indeed, sustainable markets should ensure that markets contribute to positive social, environmental, and economic outcomes.

These factors also imply that the financial services sector should be governed by legal regulations, and should be closely monitored. However, although most people are aware of this requirement, it is rarely fulfilled. This is particularly true in developing countries, because legal regulations have either not become fully established or their implementation has not been successful.

---

2   There are many examples of such misbehavior—in the UK, the United States and in other countries—which have received a high profile.

This leads to problems in the operation of these markets. It is evident that some of the reasons for the financial crisis in 2008 were operational and regulatory problems in these types of markets.

Analyzing Corporate Sustainability: After the Brundtland Report (1987)

There has been a significant increase in interest and concern for corporate governance; so too has there been a similar increase in interest in sustainability. A growing number of writers in the late twentieth and early twenty-first centuries recognized that the activities of an organization impact the external environment, and suggested that such an organization should be accountable to a wider audience than simply its shareholders. Such a suggestion probably first arose in the 1970s.[3] Some researchers had concerns about taking a wider view on company performance and on the social performance of a business as a member of society at large. This view was stated by Ackerman (1975) who argued that big business was recognizing the need to adapt to a new social climate of community accountability. The orientation of business to financial results, however, was inhibiting social responsiveness. McDonald and Puxty (1979) on the other hand maintain that companies are no longer the instruments of shareholders alone, but exist within society and therefore have responsibilities to the society itself. There has been a shift toward a greater accountability of companies to all participants. Implicit in this concern, with the effects of the actions of an organization on its external environment, is the recognition that it is not just the owners of the organization who are concerned with the organization's activities.

Additionally, there is a wide variety of other stakeholders who justifiably have a concern and are affected by those activities. These other stakeholders have not just an interest in the activities of the firm but also a degree of influence over the shaping of those activities. This influence is so significant it could be argued that the power and influence of these stakeholders is such that it amounts to quasi-ownership of the organization. Indeed, Gray, Owen and Maunders (1987) challenge the traditional role of accounting in reporting results and consider that, rather than an ownership approach to accountability, a stakeholder approach, recognizing the wide stakeholder community, is needed. The benefits of incorporating stakeholders into a model of performance

---

3   Although philosophers such as Robert Owen were expounding those views more than a century earlier.

measurement and accountability have, however, been extensively criticized (Freedman and Reed, 1983; Sternberg, 1997, 1998; and Hutton, 1997). Moreover, Rubenstein (1992) goes further and argues that there is a need for a new social contract between a business and its stakeholders. Central to this social contract is a concern for the future, which has become manifest through the term "sustainability". This term has become ubiquitous both within the discourse of globalization and within the discourse of corporate performance (Aras and Crowther, 2008a).

According to Aras and Crowther (2009c), the need for social responsibility is by no means universally accepted. However, evidence shows that ethical and socially responsible behavior is being engaged in successfully by a number of large corporations. This number is increasing all the time. Additionally, there is no evidence that corporations which engage in socially responsible behavior perform any worse in terms of profitability and the creation of shareholder value than other corporations. Indeed there is a growing body of evidence that socially responsible behavior leads to increased economic performance, at least in the longer term, and consequentially greater welfare and wealth for all involved. All of this means that a wide variety of activities have been classed as representing corporate social responsibility (CSR), ranging from altruism to triple bottom line reporting. Different approaches have been adopted in different countries, in different industries and corporations. Recently the agenda has shifted from a concern for CSR to a concern for sustainability, and many activities have been redesignated accordingly.

The definition and measurement of sustainability is still subject to debate. There are two broad responses to the sustainability measurement problem. The first begins with the proposition that there is little in the notion of the "sustainable business," beyond defining it as a set of pragmatic guidelines whereby a corporate entity can improve its environmental performance. The measurement issue here is to find meaningful environmental indicators that capture the flavor of the broader sustainability debate, for example, by conveying environment–economy linkages. The second response is that lessons drawn from the green national or macro accounting literature allow us to define more formally what it means for a business to be either sustainable or unsustainable. Common to both approaches is an increased emphasis on accounting for external pressures or impacts attributable to a corporate entity (Atkinson et al., 2000).

Sustainability is also a controversial topic because it means different things to different people. Nevertheless, there is a growing awareness that one is indeed involved in a battle about what sustainability means, and the extent to which it can be delivered by corporations in the easy manner they promise (as covered by the United Nations Commission on Environment and Development (Schmidheiny, 1992)). The starting point must be taken as the Brundtland Report (World Commission on Environment and Development, 1987). The Brundtland Report deals with sustainable development and the change of politics needed to achieve it. The definition of this term in the report is well known and often cited as: "Sustainable development is the development that meets the needs of the present without compromising the ability of future generations to meet their own needs." This has become part of a policy landscape being explicitly contested by the United Nations and big business through the vehicles of the World Business Council for Sustainable Development and the International Chamber of Commerce (see, for example, Beder, 1997; Mayhew, 1997; Gray and Bebbington, 2001; Aras and Crowther, 2009a).

There seems, therefore, two commonly held assumptions which permeate the discourse of corporate sustainability. The first is that sustainability is synonymous with sustainable development. The second is that a sustainable company will exist merely by recognizing environmental and social issues and incorporating them into its strategic planning. Most analysis of sustainability recognizes a two- or three-dimensional approach: environmental, social, and organizational behavior (see, for example, Dyllick and Hockerts, 2002; Spangenberg, 2004). Most work in the area of corporate sustainability does not recognize the need for acknowledging the importance of financial performance as an essential aspect of sustainability and, therefore, fails to undertake financial analysis alongside, and integrated with, other forms of analysis for the research.

Aras and Crowther (2007d) argue that this is an essential aspect of corporate sustainability and, therefore, adds a further dimension to the discussion. Furthermore, they argue that the third dimension, sometimes recognized as organizational behavior, needs to actually comprise a much broader concept of corporate culture. There are four aspects of sustainability which need to be recognized and analyzed, namely:

1.   **societal influence** which we define as a measure of the impact that society makes upon the corporation in terms of the social contract and stakeholder influence;

2.   **environmental impact** which we define as the effect of the actions of the corporation upon its geophysical environment;

3.   **organizational culture** which we define as the relationship between the corporation and its internal stakeholders, particularly employees, and all aspects of that relationship;

4.   **finance** which we define in terms of an adequate return for the level of risk undertaken.

These four elements must be considered as the key dimensions of sustainability, all of which are equally important. This analysis is, therefore, considerably broader and more complete than that of others. Furthermore, Aras and Crowther (2007b, 2007d) consider that these four aspects can be resolved into a two-dimensional matrix along the polarities of internal versus external focus, and short-term versus long-term focus. Together they represent organizational performance as seen in the model depicted below (Figure 1.2). This model provides both a representation of organizational performance and a basis for any evaluation of corporate sustainability.

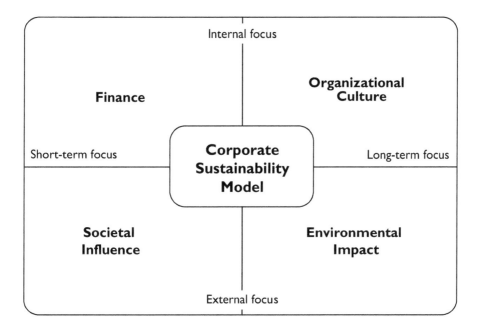

Figure 1.2   Model of corporate sustainability
Source: Aras and Crowther 2007c.

According to Aras and Crowther (2009b, pp.279–88), in order to achieve sustainable development it is first necessary to achieve sustainability. There are a number of elements to this such as economic, environmental, social, and spiritual and cultural values. What is important for sustainability is not only addressing each of these elements individually but also paying attention to maintaining the balance between them. It is the maintenance of this balance which is the most challenging and also the most essential aspect of managing sustainability.

Governance and Sustainability

MARKET GOVERNANCE AND SUSTAINABILITY

In recent decades one of the main discussion topics has been concerned with globalization. Although in theory globalization implies the free movement of capital and labour as well as the free movement of goods through trade, in practice it is the ease of movement of capital which has been primarily manifest. This liberalization of trade in financial assets is often called financial globalization meaning that globalization increases competition, increases risk, and creates new risks for business (Aras, 2007a). Financial stability and market discipline are the two main factors required to combat the inevitable uncontrolled effects of globalization. Therefore, until market discipline becomes more effective in ensuring sound financial systems, closer regulatory oversight will be key to increasing the benefits and limiting the risks of globalization. All these problems require regulation and international standards to provide financial stability and business success, and to protect the investors' and stakeholders' rights. Ultimately, the most important goal is to provide business and market sustainability.

Globalization is a multidimensional process involving economic, political, social, and cultural change. However, the most important discussion about globalization is related to the economic effect it has upon countries. Globalization in the economic and financial markets is a recognized international fact in the twenty-first century for all countries. The globalization process has dynamic, critical, and inevitable consequences for institutions, business, the environment, and especially for developing countries.

The global financial crisis has also raised several questions with respect to the corporate governance of financial institutions. Public policy makers around the world have started to question the appropriateness of the current corporate governance applied to financial institutions, and more specifically the question of how stock markets contribute to good corporate governance needs to be answered. It is relatively easy to describe what good governance is. In the *Principles of Corporate Governance*, the Organisation for Economic Co-operation and Development (OECD) acknowledges that: "Good corporate governance should provide proper incentives for the board and management to pursue objectives that are in the interests of the company and its shareholders and should facilitate effective monitoring." Effective monitoring alone will not be sufficient to ensure good governance. It should be accompanied by a comparison of results with globally accepted benchmarks to indicate any shifts away from good governance criteria and so assist institutions to stay on the right track (Aras and Yobas, 2013).

Market structures affect the sustainability capacity of markets significantly. Unless market structures and their impact on sustainability are clearly understood, it is almost impossible to assess the implications of changing market structures. Moreover, understanding the contribution made by both large and small sized companies to sustainable development is crucial and needs to be examined thoroughly. However, the market power of large companies should be closely monitored because gaining market power and supporting sustainability are conflicting concepts. Also, the need to understand and implement the appropriate policy interventions will enhance the sustainable development impact of both large and small companies.

The main objective is to reach a level of global governance. Global governance is not, of course, to imply that such a system actually exists, let alone to consider the effectiveness of its operations. It is merely to recognize that, in this increasingly globalized world, there is a need for some form of governance to deal with multinational and global issues. The term "global governance," therefore, is a descriptive term recognizing the issue and referring to concrete, co-operative, problem-solving arrangements. These may be formal in the shape of either laws or formally constituted institutions, which would manage the collective affairs through a variety of actors including states, intergovernmental organizations, nongovernmental organizations (NGOs), other civil society actors, private sector organizations, pressure groups, and individuals. Global governance may also be informal, as in the case of practices or guidelines, or temporary units, as in the case of coalitions. Thus, global governance can be considered to be a combination of formal and informal institutions, mechanisms, relationships, and processes between and among states, markets, citizens, and organizations, both inter- and nongovernmental, through which collective interests on the global plane are articulated, rights and obligations are established, and differences are mediated (Tobin, 2000; Aras and Crowther, 2009d).

In financial markets there are various areas in which problems related to sustainability and governance can arise. These areas include the agency problem and subsequent ethical issues, problems concerning insider trading, manipulation, reporting to the general public, and providing information to investors. These areas are traditional ones for conflicts of interest situations and are also referred to as "private benefits of control" (Baums and Scott, 2005). Jensen and Meckling (1976) described the problems more generally as the conflict of interest between principals (shareholders) and their agents (managers). The basic problem is that agents and managers are entrusted by principals and investors with authority over their property and capital, assuming it will advance the interests of the owners rather than be for the personal gain of the agents (Baums and Scott, 2005).

The general agency problem can be characterized as a situation in which a principal (or group of principals) seeks to establish incentives for an agent (or group of agents). The agency then takes decisions on behalf of the principal that affects them and the agent in ways that contribute maximally to the principal's own objectives. The difficulties in establishing such an incentive structure arise from either divergence of the objectives of principals and agents or from the asymmetric information between principals and agents (Vickers and Yarrow, 1988).

As stated by Lambert (2001), agency theory evaluates the impact of the conflict of interest between principals and agents because of such reasons as:

• shirking by the agent;

• diversion of resources by the agent for private consumption;

• differential time horizon of the agent and the principal;

• differential risk aversion of the agent and the principal.

Jensen and Meckling (1976) developed agency theory in the context of the conflicts of interest between corporate managers and outside equity and debt holders. Agency theory starts with the assumption that people act unreservedly in their own narrowly defined self-interest with, if necessary, guile and deceit. The firm is usually seen as a set of contracts between the various parties involved in the production process including the owners, managers, workforce, and creditors among others. Agency theory switches the center of attention from the firm to the set of contracts that define each firm. It is primarily concerned with the contracts and relationships between principals and the agents under conditions of asymmetric information (Aras, 2006).

Agency theory also suggests how to govern a modern corporation with a large number of shareholders whose collective capital is controlled and directed by separate shareholders. Miozzo and Dewick (2002) state that corporate governance is an important device as a means of reducing agency costs imposed by managers who are acting in their own interests. Jensen's and Meckling's (1976) model on agency costs and ownership structure holds a central role in corporate governance literature. As the main problem is the conflict between the principal and the agent, the focus of this theory is on determining the proxies of agency costs and the most efficient mechanisms governing the principal–agent relationship (Aras and Kutlu, 2014). Agency costs are defined as the costs associated with co-operative efforts by human beings. The agency costs within the organization occur when one entity, the principal, hires another, the agent, to act for them. According to conventional financial theory, rational shareholders will recognize the incentives facing managers to shirk, diversify, and under-invest. Therefore, the firm would suffer losses from these decisions, and these losses would represent the agency costs of outside equity financing. This is clearly related to market regulation and good governance principles.

CORPORATE GOVERNANCE AND SUSTAINABILITY

Corporate concerns increasingly focus upon two main issues, which are also important to individuals. These are good governance, and social responsibility. They are essential to reach a sustainable level of system, market, and business. We have been witness to a lot of concern that has been expressed as a result of revelations stemming from the economic and financial crisis of 2008. These exposed significant failings in governance at a corporate level, and also in markets and governments. Good governance and responsibility operate at many levels from global to corporate, and they are totally connected to sustainable behavior.

The latest economic crisis in 2008 highlighted not only the importance of governance but also showed that CSR is a central part of governance, and that both are essential for sustainability. Part of the problem is caused by failures in regulation and governance brought about by the nature of global markets and local governance. Attention needs to be paid to the development of a truly global system of governance. Good governance comprises more than regulation, laws, and some international standards. Corporate governance is necessary to protect corporations and markets from the main problems which we have already experienced.

Our question is, again: The causality between market and corporate governance: which comes first, corporate or market governance? Hugill and Siegel (2013) find that the firms' characteristics are as important as, and often meaningfully more important than, country characteristics in explaining governance ratings variances. Their results suggest that, over recent years, firms in emerging economies have had a greater capacity to rise above home-country peer firms in corporate governance ratings than has been suggested previously. However, the definition and measurement of good corporate governance is still subject to debate. Good corporate governance addresses such points as creating sustainable value, achieving the firm's goals, and keeping a balance between economic and social benefit. Also, of course, good governance offers some long-term benefits to a firm. These include reducing risk, and attracting new investors, shareholders, and more equity. It is clear that these long-term benefits are directly related to the sustainability of firms and the firms' success. We can also evaluate corporate governance from a different perspective such as general economy, companies, private and institutional investors, and banking and other financial institutions.

It is also clear that the definition of corporate governance is extended considerably beyond investor relations, and encompasses relations with all stakeholders including the environment. This is essential for the longer-term survival of a firm and is therefore a key component of sustainability. There is evidence that some firms understand this, but they are still in the minority albeit increasing in number. It is possible to say that good corporate governance addresses this, but not all firms recognize it. It is equally possible to state that a firm which has a more complete understanding of the relationship between social responsibility, sustainability, and corporate governance addresses these issues more completely. By implication, a more complete understanding of the interrelationships will lead to better corporate governance, and therefore to better economic performance (Aras and Crowther, 2011).

Good governance is important in every sphere of society whether it be the corporate environment, general environment, or the political environment. Good governance levels can improve public faith and confidence in the political environment. When the resources are too limited to meet the minimum expectations of the people, it is a good governance level that can help to promote the welfare of society. A concern with governance is also prevalent in the corporate world. Good governance is essential for good corporate performance.

Management can be interpreted as managing a firm for the purposes of creating and maintaining value for shareholders. Corporate governance procedures determine every aspect of management's role and balance the development of control mechanisms in order to increase both shareholder value and the satisfaction of other stakeholders. In other words, corporate governance is about creating a balance between the economic and social goals of companies including the efficient use of resources, accountability in the use of their power, and the impact on the social environment. The main aim of management should be creating value for shareholders. Good corporate governance includes all of the following:

- creating sustainable value;

- finding a way to reach firms' goals;

- increasing shareholders' satisfaction;

- providing efficient and effective management;

- increasing credibility;

- procuring efficient risk management;

- being an early warning system against all types of risk;

- creating responsive and accountable corporations;

- describing the role of firm units;

- developing controls and internal auditing procedures;

- maintaining the balance between economic and social benefits;

- using resources efficiently;

- establishing performance controls;

- distributing responsibility fairly;

- producing necessary information for stakeholders;

- maintaining an independent board (from management);

- ensuring compatible and sustainable performance.

Corporate governance can be very complicated and requires a long-term perspective. Good governance offers some long-term benefits for firms to maintain a sustainable business through:

- increasing corporate market value;

- increasing corporate rating;

- increasing competitive power;

- attracting new investors, shareholders, and more equity;

- achieving greater credibility;

- securing increased flexible borrowing conditions/facilities from financial institutions;

- decreasing credit interest rate/cost of capital;

- establishing new investment opportunities;

- hiring/maintaining better personnel/employees;

- reaching new markets.

These are all also highly important factors in ensuring sustainable businesses, markets, and economies. Good corporate governance should incorporate sustainability in general and deal specifically with all the major components of sustainability which are, as mentioned earlier:

- societal influence;

- environmental impact;

- organizational culture;

- finance.

From Sustainable Markets and Businesses to Sustainable Development

Sustainability implies good organizational performance, and one view of good corporate performance is that of stewardship. Just as the management of an organization is concerned with the stewardship of their financial resources, so too would management be concerned with the stewardship of environmental resources. The difference, however, is that environmental resources are mostly located externally to the organization. Stewardship in this context, therefore, is concerned with the resources of society as well as the resources of the organization. As far as stewardship of external environmental resources is concerned, then the central tenet of such an objective is that of ensuring sustainability. Sustainability is focused on the future and is concerned with ensuring that the choices of resource utilization in the future are not constrained by decisions taken in the present. This necessarily implies such concepts as generating and utilizing renewable resources, minimizing pollution, and using new techniques of manufacture and distribution. It also implies the acceptance of any costs involved in the present as an investment for the future (Aras and Crowther, 2013).

Benefits that are promised at national level for sustainable development, mostly in terms of direct investments, are often not matched by positive contributions to environmental protection, poverty reduction, or sustainable livelihoods at the local level. What will be the new role expected from direct investment and multinational companies in this respect? How can a sustainable financial market enhance and improve sustainable development? What is the role of sustainable finance in achieving sustainable development? Is it just financing a part or more? Sustainability is important for the strategy planners of businesses, policy makers, and other stakeholders seeking to build more sustainable markets.

Those toward the end of a lifecycle chain of a product or service are rarely negatively affected by the impacts their sector has on environment and society. They, therefore, have little incentive to take account of these impacts (environmental or social externalities) in their decision making. As a result the market rarely incorporates the true costs of environmental or social externalities.

Markets are one of the dominant social institutions of our time. Understanding what they are, how they work, and how they can be shaped, is essential to sustainable development. The world's markets have the potential to improve the lives of billions of people in developing countries, reducing poverty and securing environmental quality for future generations. However, markets often fail to capture the full value of natural resources or to promote the interests of poor and underprivileged people. Therefore, an effective public policy framework for markets is required. The issue of market governance and the relationship between the market (and private interests) and political authority remains a core theme at the heart of the sustainability debate.

The correct enabling environment is essential in creating sustainable markets. If the right conditions do not exist, then markets can work to undermine sustainable development. We need to take back control over these markets, which will require civil society, and the public and private sectors to work together to develop markets that will work toward sustainable development. This in turn requires finding innovative ways to address market failure, and to facilitate strategic thinking and action on those complex issues. This will eventually help us to resolve global problems. The benefits of free markets and economic globalization should be questioned when local capacities and institutions are weak.

This is equally true of financial markets. The financial system needs to serve as the nervous system of the global economy rather than as its master. The current financial marketplace suffers from misplaced incentives and the invisibility of capital within the decision-making process. These lead to actions being taken despite the fact they will result in future harm. For the financial markets to become sustainable and resilient to the challenges ahead, radical changes need to take place. A connection between money invested and where it ends up must be made, and investors should become more aware of the social and environmental effects of their decisions. Integrated reporting, government regulation, and pension fund allocation will all be important players in this change.

Model for Markets: Requirement for Sustainability

Businesses have substantial potential to contribute to sustainable markets. Their contribution can be at the local level and, due to globalization, at the global level. Multinational companies and their businesses can, and are expected to, play a major role in building and supporting sustainable markets. For profit and not for profit entities the market may contribute significantly in different ways, and they will be expected to work hand in hand.

The business models adopted by businesses affect how businesses and enterprises contribute to sustainable markets and sustainable development. These contributions include, but are not limited to, how they interact with each other in procurement, sub-contracting, and other direct business arrangements. We have to answer some questions under this heading such as: How should businesses engage with local communities and policy makers to achieve sustainable development goals? How do corporate social investment strategies meet community development needs? How can dialog with multi-stakeholder partnerships be most effective? In what ways will the business skills be revised, and which new skills will be of importance? What kind of corporation is necessary and implementable? How can the private sector, civil society, and government collaborate and work together to shape business models that deliver positive economic, environmental, and social outcomes? We have to recognize that bad business behavior is more costly than good business behavior for stakeholders, markets, society, and all economies.

To create a sustainable system both markets and businesses require regulations, standards, rules, and principles to succeed. Getting the right standards and tools in place to support and promote responsible business practices is important. Codes of conduct, ethical management systems, governance principles, and various kinds of socially and environmentally responsible standards for businesses are burgeoning.

Regulators inevitably, according to their requirements, focus upon local markets while finance escapes them through its ability to migrate around the world. Effectively, this means that any realistic form of regulation does not and cannot exist. One consequence of this regulatory failure is that contamination spreads, and the dubious practices developed in one financial market become the norm in other markets. When the inevitable crisis appears, it spreads from one country to another as all economies are affected by both the consequences of dubious lending practices and by the ensuing crisis of confidence. This calls attention to the fact that, though recognized and mostly ignored in the financial models used to legitimate financial activity, the financial market is a global market, and a corollary of this is that any regulatory regime must also be global. We have to highlight the problems with the current regime and argue for a global regulatory authority, capable of sanctioning even the most powerful actors in the market, including national and transnational governments (Aras and Crowther, 2009e).

The question of standards for sustainability activity is one which has been in existence for a long time and gradually some standards for reporting are starting to emerge. In many ways the development of sustainability reporting standards parallels the development of accounting standards. They focus upon the harmonization of common standards as being the main issue, which is a distinct contrast to ten years ago when the emergence of common standards, for either accounting or sustainability, looked no better than a remote possibility (Aras and Crowther, 2009b).

From a systemic point of view, strategies may be necessary to balance out the economic system, as both strategies produce desirable feedback loops from a sustainability perspective. For example, the reforms of the conventional system could encourage more transparency and control (anti-corruption law) so that it improves confidence in the financial system, or encourages more financial resources to become available and addresses ecological or social problems. By implementing corporate governance standards, or social and ecological standards, one can also directly have an impact on the economic system (Brunnhuber et al., 2005).

For sustainable markets and businesses there are some main requirements and strategies of focus:

- strategic and long-term approach;

- succeeding by being a good business;

- controlling market misbehavior (manipulation, insider trading, and so on);

- avoiding excessive risk;

- regulations and standards;

- good governance principles;

- socially responsible behavior;

- stakeholders' rights;

- environmental considerations.

We have to consider that misbehavior is more costly than good business behavior for stakeholders, markets, society, and all economies. It is important to create an understanding of where and how businesses can best contribute to sustainable markets, for example, in the developed, and in the middle and lower income countries. We have to ask: What are policymakers, investors, and corporations most interested in with regards to market sustainability? What are the most important issues to work on, and how should we approach these issues and create solutions?

However, in the longer term, further serious action is needed. We all know that a significant part of the problem is related to the governance of the system, markets, and business. The main part of the problem is caused by failures in regulation and governance brought about by the nature of global markets and local governance. We learned from the global crisis in 2008 that we need to focus on long-term rather than just short-term benefits. Following this financial crisis we realized just how important socially responsible behavior is in both markets and businesses. The global financial crisis raised several questions with respect to the governance and social responsibility of corporate and financial markets. It is now fairly clear that the most important components of a sustainable market and business are good governance and responsible behavior.

Conclusion

Sustainability offers long-term benefits for markets, business, and institutions. These include reducing risk, attracting new investors, protecting shareholders, and most importantly, bringing strength and longevity to markets and businesses. Sustainable markets are all about creating sustainable value, achieving the institutions' and markets' goals, and keeping a balance between economic and social benefits in a long-term perspective. Therefore, corporate and market sustainability reform is at the center of the global world. In this chapter some causes of market and business failures have been highlighted together with the significant problems that result from these failures. For markets to become sustainable and resilient to the challenges ahead, radical changes need to take place. We need to pay attention to the development of market sustainability and a truly thorough global sustainable system. This is the most important action that we need to take.

References and Bibliography

Ackerman, R.W. (1975). *The Social Challenge to Business*. Cambridge, MA: Harvard University Press.

Agrawal A., and Knoeber C.R. (1996). Firm Performance and Mechanisms to Control Agency Problems between Managers and Shareholders. *Journal of Financial and Quantitative Analysis*, Vol. 31(3), 377–398.

Aras, G., and Kutlu, O. (2015). Does Governance Efficiency Impact Equity Agency Costs? Evidence from Turkey. *Emerging Markets Finance & Trade Journal (EMFT)* (forthcoming).

Aras, G., and Yobas, B. (2013). Governance in Capital Market Institutions. *The Governance of Risk*. Emerald Book Series: Developments in Corporate Governance and Responsibility.

Aras, G., and Crowther, D. (2013). Sustainable Practice: The Real Triple Bottom Line. *The Governance of Risk*. Emerald Book Series: Developments in Corporate Governance and Responsibility.

Aras, G., Aybars, A., and Kutlu, O. (2011). The Interaction Between Corporate Social Responsibility and Value Added Intellectual Capital: Empirical Evidence from Turkey. *Social Responsibility Journal*, Vol. 7(4), 622–37.

Aras, G., Kutlu, O., and Aybars, A. (2010). Managing Corporate Performance: Investigating the Relationship between Corporate Social Responsibility and Financial Performance in Emerging Markets. *International Journal of Productivity and Performance Management*, Vol. 59(3), 229–54.

Aras, G., and Kurt, D. (2012). The Effects of Stock Option Compensation on Managerial Risk Taking Behavior and Firm Financial Performance The Global Financial Crisis From a Different Perspective. *International Journal of Economics and Finance Studies*, Vol. 4(2), 77–90.

Aras, G., and Crowther, D. (2011). Governance and the Management of Global Markets. *Governance in the Business Environment*. Emerald Book Series: Developments in Corporate Governance and Responsibility.

Aras, G., and Crowther, D. (2010a). Analysing Social Responsibility in Financial Companies. *International Journal of Banking, Accounting and Finance*, Vol. 2(3), 295–308.

Aras, G., and Crowther, D. (2010b). Sustaining Business Excellence. *Total Quality Management and Business Excellence*, Vol. 21(5), 565–76.

Aras, G., and Crowther, D. (2009a). Corporate Sustainability Reporting: A Study in Disingenuity? *Journal of Business Ethics*, Vol. 27, 279–88.

Aras, G., and Crowther, D. (2009b). Making Sustainable Development Sustainable. *Management Decision*, Vol. 47(6), 975–88.

Aras, G., and Crowther, D. (2009c). The Durable Corporation in a Time of Financial and Economic Crisis. *Economics and Management*, Vol. 14, 211–17.

Aras, G., and Crowther, D. (2009d). Introduction: Corporate Governance and Corporate Social Responsibility in Context. In G. Aras and D. Crowther (eds), *Global Perspectives on Corporate Governance and Corporate Social Responsibility*. Farnham: Gower.

Aras, G., and Crowther, D. (2009e). Towards Truly Global Markets. Discussion Papers in Social Responsibility No 0901, Social Responsibility Research Network.

Aras, G. (2008). Corporate Governance and the Agency Problem in Financial Markets. In D. Crowther and N. Capaldi (eds), *Ashgate Research Companion to Corporate Social Responsibility*. Aldershot: Ashgate.

Aras, G., and Crowther, D. (2008a). Governance and Sustainability: An Investigation into the Relationship between Corporate Governance and Corporate Sustainability. *Management Decision*, Vol. 46(3), 433–48.

Aras, G., and Crowther, D. (2008b). Evaluating Sustainability: a Need for Standards. *Issues in Social and Environmental Accounting*, Vol. 2(1), 19–35.

Aras, G., and Crowther, D. (2008c). Developing Sustainable Reporting Standards. *Journal of Applied Accounting Research*, Vol. 9(1), 4–16.

Aras, G., and Crowther, D. (2008e). The Social Obligation of Corporations. *Journal of Knowledge Globalization*, Vol. 1(1), 43–59.

Aras, G. (2007). *The Impact of the Basel II Banking Regulation on Real Industry Firms*. Istanbul: Deloitte Academy Publication, in Turkish.

Aras, G., and Crowther, D. (2007a). The Development of Corporate Social Responsibility. *Effective Executive*, Vol. X(9), 18–21.

Aras, G., and Crowther, D. (2007b). Sustainable Corporate Social Responsibility and the Value Chain. In D. Crowther and M.M. Zain (eds), *New Perspectives on Corporate Social Responsibility*, 109–28.

Aras, G., and Crowther, D. (2007c). Is Globalization Sustainable? In S. Barber (ed.), *The Geopolitics of the City*. London: Forum Press, 165–94.

Aras, G., and Crowther, D. (2007d). What Level of Trust is Needed for Sustainability? *Social Responsibility Journal*, Vol. 3(3), 60–68.

Aras, G. (2006). The Ethical Issues in the Finance and Financial Markets. *Globalization and Social Responsibility*, (eds). Cambridge, UK: Cambridge Scholars Press.

Atkinson, G., Hett, T., and Newcombe, J. (2000). Measuring 'Corporate Sustainability'. *CSERGE Working Paper, GEC 99–01*.

Baums, T., and Scott, K.E. (2005). Taking Shareholder Protection Seriously? Corporate Governance in the United States and Germany. *Journal of Applied Corporate Finance*, Vol. 17(4), Fall, 4–7.

Beder, S. (1997). *Global Spin: The Corporate Assault on Environmentalism*. London: Green Books.

Brunnhuber, S., Fink, A., and Kuhle, J.P. (2005). The Financial System Matters: Future Perspectives and Scenarios for a Sustainable Future. *Futures*, Vol. 37(4), 317–32.

Dyllick, T., and Hockerts, K. (2002). Beyond the Business Case for Corporate Sustainability. *Business Strategy and the Environment*, Vol. 11, 130–41.

Freeman, R., and Reed, D. (1983). Stockholders and Stakeholders: A New Perspective On Corporate Governance. *California Management Review*, Vol. 25, 88–106.

Gray, R.H., and Bebbington, K.J. (2001). *Accounting for the Environment*. London: Sage.

Gray, R., Owen, D., and Maunders, K. (1987). *Corporate Social Reporting: Accounting and Accountability*. London: Prentice Hall.

Hugill, A., and Siegel, J. (2013). Which Does More to Determine the Quality of Corporate Governance in Emerging Economies, Firms or Countries? *Harvard Business School Working Paper 13–055*.

Hutton, W. (1997). *Stakeholding and its Critics*. London: IEA Health and Welfare Unit.

Jensen, M., and Meckling, W. (1976). Theory of The Firm: Managerial Behavior, Agency Costs, and Ownership Structure. *Journal of Financial Economics*, Vol. 3, 305–60.

Lambert, R.A. (2001). Contracting Theory and Accounting. *Journal of Accounting and Economics*, Vol. 32, 1–87.

Mayhew, N. (1997). Fading to Grey: the Use and Abuse of Corporate Executives' 'Representational Power'. In R. Welford (ed.), *Hijacking Environmentalism: Corporate Response to Sustainable Development*. London: Earthscan, 63–95.

McDonald, D., and Puxty, A.G. (1979). An Inducement–Contribution Approach to Corporate Financial Reporting. *Accounting, Organization and Society*, Vol. 4(1–2), 53–65.

Mintzberg, H. (1983). The Case for Corporate Social Responsibility. *Journal of Business Strategy*, Vol. 4(2), 3–15.

Miozzo, M., and Dewick, P. (2002). Building Competitive Advantage: Innovation and Corporate Governance in European Construction. *Research Policy*, Vol. 31, 989–1008.

Rubenstein, D.B. (1992). Bridging the Gap between Green Accounting and Black Ink. *Accounting, Organizations and Society*, Vol. 17(5), 501–8.

Schmidheiny, S. (1992). *Changing Course*. New York: MIT Press.

Spangenberg, J.H. (2004). Reconciling Sustainability and Growth: Criteria, Indicators, Policies. *Sustainable Development*, Vol. 12, 76–84.

Sternberg, E. (1998). *Corporate Governance: Accountability in the Marketplace*. London: IEA.

Sternberg, E. (1997). The Defects of Stakeholder Theory. *Corporate Governance: An International Review*, Vol. 6(3), 151–63.

Tobin, J. (2000). Financial Globalization. *World Development*, Vol. 28(6), 1101–4.

Vickers, J.S., and Yarrow, G.K. (1988). *Privatization: An Economic Analysis*. Cambridge, MA: MIT Press.

Williamson, O.E. (1985). *The Economic Institutions of Capitalism*. New York: The Free Press.

Williamson, O.E. (1975). *Markets and Hierarchies: Analysis and Anti-trust Implications*. New York: The Free Press.

Williamson, O.E. (1970). *Corporate Control and Business Behavior*. New York: Prentice Hall.

Chapter 2

The Need for a Theoretical Reexamination of Sustainability in Economics and Business

JACOB DAHL RENDTORFF

Introduction

It is time to address the issue of sustainability and the values that should guide the interaction between organizations and the environment. This research is a development of my earlier work on bioethics and law, and my later work on business and corporate social responsibility (CSR). I argued that the basic ethical principles of respect for human autonomy, dignity, integrity, and vulnerability should be proposed as central values for biomedical and biotechnological developments. I also showed how basic ethical principles can play a role in business ethics (Kemp et al., 1997; Rendtorff, 1999; Rendtorff and Kemp, 2000; Kemp, 2000). Later on this theme was developed further in my book on business ethics *Responsibility, Ethics and Legitimacy of Corporations* (Rendtorff, 2009).

More recently, together with some colleagues, the concept of sustainability has been conceptualized with the idea of the balanced company (Rendtorff et al., 2013). The environmental challenges mean that it is necessary to view ethics from the perspective of institutions and organizations as the foundation for the discussion of values in relation to animals and nature. In particular, the threats of global warming and climate change, and environmental pollution scandals like the BP oil spill in 2010, are a challenge to the legitimacy of large organizations and institutions (Levy and Newell, 2005, p.75). We can even talk about climate change as a threat to corporate hegemony. Environmental ethics not only concern individuals but are also concerned with the relationship between different kinds of organizations and nature. Reflections on bioethics, environmental ethics, and business ethics need to be integrated. In this context, we may mention the work of the environmental scholar, Bjørn Lomborg.

In his book *The Skeptical Environmentalist* (Lomborg, 2001) he proposed a close link between ethics and economics. Lomborg's argument seems to be based on the vision that there can be good economic solutions to the most serious problems of humanity. This argument does not exclude basic ethical principles as the foundation of sustainable development; rather the argument represents a proposal for economic efficiency with regards to finding a solution for global problems.

The issue can be framed around understanding what obligations businesses may have to respect environmental ethics, and what kind of philosophical theory should justify protection of the environment (Hoffman, 1991). The argument can then be progressed to clarify how environmental ethics for organizations cannot be understood uniquely on the basis of utility and enlightened self-interest, but must be considered as a challenge to anthropocentric ethics. The connection between sustainability and ethical principles is promoted as the essence of ethics in organizational behavior in the environment. Moreover, this leads to the difficult problem of moving from ethics to law, and how to deal with environmental crime of large organizations and institutions. Finally, we can propose the concept of the balanced company as a possible solution to the problems of how to promote international action with regard to the problem of sustainability.

ECOLOGY, SUSTAINABILITY, AND CAPITALISM

Since the industrial revolution businesses have had to deal with environmental problems, but it was not until the late 1960s that these problems came to be commonly understood as severe and requiring thoughtful and efficient solutions on a global scale. There are not only problems of global warming, ozone depletion, acid rain, and depletion of air quality but also problems of water pollution (for example, toxic oil spills), temperature increases, the destructive use of ocean fishery resources, and further problems of land pollution (for example, destruction of forests, chemical or toxic substance deposits, radioactive and nuclear wastes) and deteriorating ecological conditions including the destruction of animal habitats (Velasquez, 2002, pp.269ff). In the words of the ecological ethicist Aldo Leopold: "Society has been in search of a land ethic of 'integrity, stability and beauty' in order to protect the intrinsic value and self-organization of the natural world" (Velasquez, 2002, p.290).

Until quite recently, economic markets functioned according to the idea that unlimited resources were at humankind's disposal. It was only during the second half of the twentieth century that an increasing awareness of the impossibility of naturally regulated markets began to emerge. Still, it has been extremely difficult, if not impossible, to find the correct balance between economic growth and the environment. In the late twentieth and early twenty-first centuries the view that corporations should focus on gaining economic profit without concern for the environment has been strenuously challenged. Today there is even more awareness of the fact that environmental concerns in business might contribute to good business and that good environmental policies pay (Hoffman, 1991). The problem of global climate change may, because of its serious impact on global life, be one of the drivers for increased awareness of the need for action relating to environmental degradation (Levy and Newell, 2005, p.85). Corporations and institutions facing this problem start to be aware that they need to take environmental problems seriously in order to obtain social respect and appear as good corporate citizens.

Joseph R. Desjardins, ([1999] 2002a, pp.280 and 286) emphasizes that the idea of sustainable development implies a new kind of environmental business responsibility. Environmental issues represent a challenge to the concept of growth that is central to neoclassical mainstream economics. When dealing with CSR to the environment, business ethics has to rely on the development of a theory of sustainable economics. In this way, the concept of sustainability implies a redefinition of economics that moves away from the concept of endless growth regardless of limited natural resources. Hermann Daly has tried to reformulate economic theory by focusing on environmental concerns not only as a side constraint but as essential to all kinds of economic action. Daly argues that there are ecological limits to economic growth, and that the economic system of the world is dependent on the natural world which functions as the basis for economic resources and energy (Daly, 1996). In order to deal effectively with the environmental problems of the world, we would have to develop a "steady-state" (in other words, sustainable economics) using renewable resources that do not damage the carrying capacity of the natural system or destroy the planet's life-conditions for future generations (Desjardins, [1999] 2002a, p.288). Natural resources should be treated as capital for developing sustainable economic relations, rather than as goods for unlimited use.

The need for a theoretical reexamination of the notion of sustainability is due to the present crisis of the world economy. We can mention the financial crisis in 2008 that can be considered as an environmental crisis indicating that there are limits to growth and that the present model of expansion, credits, and profits does not help to solve the problems of the environment (Nielsen, 2013). The environmental crisis implies that there are limits to a system based on a non-sustainable fossil economy that has resulted in the climate crisis and the CO_2 problem of global warming. Accordingly, the environmental crisis in combination with the financial crisis can be deemed to be a world crisis. The solution of green growth as an alternative concept of growth has been criticized by many as a kind of "having your cake and eating it too" economy. From this perspective, it is argued that we need an economy of scarcity where we need to move from the era of plenty to an era of scarcity. It is in this context that we can talk about the need for a new ecological economics and the need for a "great transition" that challenges the myth of eternal growth and helps to solve the financial, food, and climate crises (Nielson, 2013). Indeed, we want to develop sustainable business strategies for such a green transition of large businesses. This strategy should go beyond the concept of growth toward a sustainable combination of business and green growth. Such a sustainable economy would be an economy that acknowledges that the Earth is not an infinite growth system. The proponents for a new economics argue for the transition toward an economics where the environment is not just a resource and an externality, but where economic sustainability implies sustainable limits to consumption and a move beyond pure economic growth toward a sustainable and green economy.

Sustainable economics describes the effort to develop a framework for economic theory that not only searches for regulations in terms of pragmatic utility but also recognizes deontological concerns for the rights of animals and nature. Sustainability implies that issues of biodiversity, ecology, and global warming are included in economic considerations. In such a holistic approach to economics, nature is viewed from the perspective of many different historical, aesthetic, or spiritual values. These values are integrated into an economic business strategy that respects nature and animals as expressions of intrinsic value and the search for the common good of humanity. It is the task of an alternative ecologically oriented economic model to make these concerns explicit and concrete. Daly's book *Beyond Growth* (1996) has contributed to this framework for economics by emphasizing that the economy is just a subsystem of the Earth's biosphere (Desjardins, 2002b). With its abstract concept of growth, neoclassical economics ignores this dependence on the biosphere and is not able to develop an economic system that is based on recycling its limited resources. It is the task of business strategy to comply with the recognition of such biophysical limits to growth and provide models for sustainable development within the firm. This is particularly so for the world's industrial, agricultural, and service-oriented corporations who have their fair share of responsibility for global environmental problems.

The common understanding of the legitimate responsibility of corporations has definitely been changing. All the stakeholders in environmental issues—

not only owners and shareholders but other groups, such as consumers, employees, and the local community—should be consulted when determining the values and strategic goals of the company. It may be worth reiterating the stakeholder philosopher Edward R. Freeman's definition of a stakeholder as: "any group or individual who can affect or is affected by the corporation" (Freeman, 1984; Elkington, [1997] 1999, p.298). In a stakeholder economy, the firm is open to these groups and, most importantly, has learned to listen. This search for a moral dimension to the economy is based on the idea that companies, in order to be successful, must have good relations with the community and the social environment (Elkington, [1997] 1999, p.234). Social capital and goodwill are considered as conditions for economic success.

Indeed, the problem of our failing ecological consciousness does not only concern these accidents but can be shown to be a part of our general understanding of the world. Just look at the social and psychological barriers for solving the climate change issue (Kemp and Nielsen, 2009). Socio-economic barriers and ideological barriers in business are constructed by society and we need to overcome them in order to create a balanced relative to climate change. The barriers are not only local but global. Among socio-economic barriers for efficient ecological action we can mention egoism and opportunism; nosism (collective egoism); institutional isomorphism and path-dependency; limited utilitarianism—privilege of present generations; limited resources—prioritization of use of resources; nationalism or patriotism, in other words US argumentation); and lack of global consciousness (cosmopolitanism).

Among physical or epistemological barriers we can mention invisibility of climate change; complexity of climate change—it is nearly impossible to foresee the results of climate change and the effects of certain actions; the imperceptibility of climate change—it is very difficult to experience climate change; subjective or ideological barriers; the complex of insignificance; fatalism; and shortsightedness. We need to understand the barriers to climate change consciousness in order to make corporations able to contribute in a responsible manner to solve climate change issues. This is necessary in order really to solve global problems of sustainability and climate change.

There are also many examples of environmental disasters due to wrong or careless actions by companies, for example, the 1979 Three Mile Island nuclear accident in the United States, the 1986 reactor meltdown in Chernobyl, Ukraine, the catastrophe of the Union Carbide Fertilizer operations in Bhopal, India in 1984 where more than 2,000 people died from gas explosions, the 1989

Exxon Valdez Oil Spill, and more recently in 2010 the Mexican Gulf BP oil spill (Hoffman et al., 1990; Fisher and Lovell, 2006, pp.469–73).

Together with our limited mindset and conceptual barriers for action these are just a few cases demonstrating that ecologically responsible action is necessary if corporations want to survive in the long run. This action should involve, among other things, examining new technological possibilities of waste management, recycling, and good use of resources. It may also involve principles of environmental auditing, green marketing, and public relations, as well as policies of values for environmental investments, such as establishing environmental mutual funds that have criteria for screening environmentally sound investment objectives. The strategy of respect for the biophysical limits of economics and corporate activities, biodiversity, and environmental protection must be based on the triple bottom line if companies want to have good relations with stakeholders in the social and economic development of the twenty-first century (Elkington, [1997] 1999, p.20).

The Ethical Basis of Sustainability

What are the ethical implications of the search for a concept of sustainable economics as the basis for the triple bottom line? The ethical ideas of autonomy, dignity, integrity, and vulnerability that I developed together with Peter Kemp in *Basic Ethical Principles in European Bioethics and Biolaw* (Rendtorff and Kemp, 2000), may be values for understanding sustainability as a bridge between humans and non-humans. This implies that the ethical principles may not only function as the foundation for ethics between human beings in organizations but also constitute basic values for the interaction between organizations and corporations, and animals, plants, and our biosphere as a whole.

The basic ethical principles may be considered within the framework of socially and environmentally responsible businesses. Responsibility signifies that there is somebody, an agent with intentional actions, who takes, or is attributed, responsibility for something or someone. Traditionally, this responsibility has been attributed to people, however, power over the whole living world has changed the extension and scope of human responsibility (Jonas, 1979). Corporations should be made responsible for natural entities. What is needed is a meaningful concept of organizational responsibility for animals, nature, and the whole biosphere. This is necessary because humanity, with the help of biotechnology, can change agriculture and food production in a way that would lead to profound social change and possibilities for life on Earth.

Due to modern technology and science, industrial society takes more and more risks. This requires business organizations, among others, to be responsible for the distribution of the dangers and disadvantages of these risks.

The basic ethical principles are essential to the idea of sustainable development if we consider them as hermeneutically emerged out of the human social and political discourse of protection of the environment. Even though they are not explicitly discussed in the important report of the United Nations World Commission on the Environment and Development (WCED) *Our Common Future* (1987), they can be considered as the ethical foundation of the message of the WCED's report. The starting point, according to this view, is the reality of humanity's global responsibility for the survival of future generations. The report emphasizes the close connection between global issues of poverty and environmental problems. It is important to remember that environmental problems are also social problems. Sustainable development implies a close connection between social development and environmental protection. Sustainability is a common ideal for society and nature in which both human rights and ecological stability must be secured. Sustainability is only possible when it is based on ethical, cultural, and aesthetic concerns (WCED, 1987, p.9).

Even though it is not directly analyzed in the report, one might say that the concept of humanity's political and moral autonomy in the context of democratic political development is very important. Sustainability, it is argued, is not really possible without democracy and human rights. Moreover, the report explicitly states that sustainability strategies imply securing a dignified life for human beings (ibid., p.13). In particular, problems of population density and poverty manifest the need to protect human dignity. The result is that basic education and health are central aspects of sustainability, because of the close link between ecosystem stability and social carrying capacity in establishing social stability and sustainability (ibid., p.97).

The notion of integrity is very present in the concept of sustainability. In *Our Common Future* (ibid., p.34) the integrity of ecosystems is given major importance. The report is concerned with protecting forests from destruction, water pollution, or other types of destruction, such as nuclear disaster which are based on the need to save the ecosystem for future generations. The problem of increased destruction of species is an indication of the international responsibility to preserve the integrity of ecosystems (ibid., p.67). Society and corporations should contribute to the preservation of the general integrity of ecosystems not only for future generations but also because of aesthetic, ethical, and cultural concerns which should precede strict economic market calculations.

In addition, the notion of vulnerability can be mentioned as an important presupposition of sustainable development. It is often stated in the report (ibid., p.61) that economic development should not lead to increased critical vulnerability. Agriculture should, for example, avoid exploiting resources. Agricultural production should be based on long-term security and quality, rather than quantity. Moreover, *Our Common Future* speaks about the need to protect vulnerable populations. Sustainable developments include the important work of empowering vulnerable groups (ibid., p.114). This means that local communities should gradually be integrated into larger communities in a way that protects their traditional culture and lifestyle. Put another way, the marginalization of vulnerable groups is a symptom of unsustainable development.

Finally, the concepts of responsibility and solidarity can be said to be highly significant for the principle of sustainable development (ibid., p.114). The notion that we have a responsibility to future generations, which is implicit in sustainability, also forges a close connection between responsibility and solidarity, implying an equitable distribution of risks among all nations (ibid., pp.61–2). The aim of sustainable world politics is to provide equality among countries in order to provide a decent standard of living for all with integrity and dignity, and in harmony with the ecosystem.

BEYOND ANTHROPOCENTRIC ENVIRONMENTAL ETHICS

This interpretation of sustainability is a response to the many people who have criticized the notion of sustainable development for being anthropocentric, but it is also a critique of those who think that the basic ethical principles imply a holistic conception of ethics which cannot be valid in a post-metaphysical worldview. Among the many conceptions that attempt to go beyond anthropocentric ethics, a general theme is the threat of the destruction of living conditions on Earth. Moreover, this kind of thought is marked by strong criticism of technological culture and capitalist economics. Such critical philosophical movements argue for a new understanding of the relationship between humankind and nature. Other positions go further, and argue from the viewpoint of universalism, endowing nature and animals with the same moral status as humans. This is often combined with the deep ecology approach which posits a unique moral status for nature. These arguments propose to overcome the anthropocentric limits of ethics, so that ethics is no longer based on rational individual subjects. Non-anthropocentric positions point to a close relationship between nature and the human life-world. This is also the case in *Our Common Future* (WCED, 1987) when it emphasizes the close connection between nature and culture. These propositions for alternatives to anthropocentric ethics are based on a bridge between person, body, and nature.

The necessity of a non-anthropocentric point of view becomes even more important when we consider that we live in the age of the *Anthropocene* (Crutzen, 2002, pp.143–5). The concept of the age of the Anthropocene is a geological concept signifying that the impact of humanity on the environment on the planet has become more serious. Because of climate change and other modifications of the natural environment by humanity, geologists have started to characterize the present geological period as the Anthropocene age where human beings as a species contribute to the geological situation of nature. The age of the Anthropocene may have started in the eighteenth century when human beings started to act as a collective force of evolution that modifies their natural environment. Since that time, the expansion of the global geography with the increase of human beings on Earth has contributed to this modification of the natural environment of humanity. As a result of its impact on nature and climate through its thermo-industrial revolution, humanity is a new geological force that changes its own natural environment. One of the founders of the concept of the Anthropocene, the Russian geologist Vladimir Vernadsky who visited Sorbonne in 1922–3, even cited the French philosopher Henri Bergson's concept of *l'évolution créatrice* to determine the concept of the Anthropocene in the thermo-industrial development of humanity (Grinevald, 2012). It may be argued that the concept of human responsibility as an indication of what it really means to be human has become particularly important in the age of the Anthropocene, because we need to go beyond ourselves to non-anthropocentric responsibility. It is implicit in the concept of responsibility as the key notion, in order to understand the ethical duty in a modern technological civilization. We can indeed observe a moralization of the concept of responsibility going beyond a strict legal definition in terms of just being responsible for an action that can be casually imputed.

Non-anthropocentric positions often rely on a phenomenological conception of human beings seeking to overcome a contradictory idea of the relationship between subject and object, between internal experience and external material (Kemp et al., 1997). What matters is the intrinsic value, richness, and diversity of nature (Velasquez, 2002, p.289). Moreover, these movements of thought want to avoid oppositions between mechanical and teleological conceptions of nature. Humans are simultaneously considered to be living organisms taking part in an ecosystem, and spiritual beings with the freedom and autonomy to transcend this bond. We experience nature through our bodily incarnation in time and space in our everyday life-world.

The perspective can be taken as the basis for an ethical position bridging the gap between humans and ecosystems. Ethics is, in this context, based on human rationality, a vision of the good life, and reflective judgment. Concrete action and the capacity to practically judge ethical principles are the driving forces in this process. The ethical principles may, therefore, be founded on the presupposition that human beings participate in nature, but at the same time that we can transcend this participation and manifest ourselves as different from nature.

Even though environmental ethics starts from anthropocentrism, it transcends a conception of nature only viewed from the perspective of human relations. Illustrating this from the perspective of deep communication theory, it might be argued that nature speaks to us (von der Pfordten, 1986). But such a communicative relation is rather problematic because we can never communicate totally with nature, even if some animals have simple rules of language. We can open ourselves to nature, but communication is determined by human reality. Although only human beings can talk, it might be possible for animals and nature to be a part of this communicative community as objects that we talk about. In such a communicative perspective human beings and their actions and responsibilities determine ethics, but this does not mean that animals and nature cannot be included in ethical reflections.

This privileged participation of human beings in nature might therefore be considered as the theoretical and meta-ethical foundation of a non-anthropocentric normative ethics. Kant's *Critique of Judgment* ([1794] 2004) and *Foundations of Metaphysics of Morals* ([1785] 1999) may be mentioned here as important references for the foundation of ethical principles as the basis for the idea of sustainability. Kant considered human beings as moral agents with an intrinsic inviolable moral status. Through participation in categorical imperative and moral law, we come to recognize other human beings as *ends in themselves*. Animals and nature are not directly seen as moral entities, but this does not imply that Kant should not recognize the need for the ethical protection of nature and animals.

In Kant's philosophy, the ideas of purpose and of teleological self-organization of living systems are central aspects of the foundational contribution of moral status to animals and non-human nature (Harste, 1994). Moreover, this is based on the human capacity of moral reasoning, and not primarily on the independent moral status of nature. In this weak anthropocentric foundation the status of human beings as moral depends on how we treat animals and nature. There is a close connection between the beauty of society and of nature. At the same time, the particular position of nature as a system of self-organizing, auto-poetic organisms, as well as its position as an object of human aesthetic enjoyment, might be emphasized. However, in general, the Kantian argument represents ethical justification on the basis of human reality, even though it clearly attributes important independent moral significance to animals and nature. It is this bio-humanism, or the idea of human and civilization's concern for nature, that is the basis of the proposed relationship between sustainability and ethical principles.

Determining the relationship between ethical principles, sustainable development, and the different interests of different stakeholders, including environmental stakeholders, can be proposed as the basis for understanding organizational and institutional behavior in relation to the environment (Starik, 1995, p.216). It can be considered as an argument for stakeholder management, in other words, including the environment as a stakeholder. Nature and the environment must be included among the stakeholders of the firm, even though it is not easy to identify these interests. It must be admitted that they are an important part of the future actions of organizations (Society for Business Ethics, 2000). Being aware of the environment as a stakeholder encourages corporations to extend their perspective on deliberation. Such an intensified ethical sensibility can be illustrated by four basic concerns (Starik, 1995, p.216):

1. **panoramization**—extending the perspective of analysis;

2. **prioritization**—including environmental complexity in decision-making;

3. **politicization**—including the environment in formulating the organization's political priorities;

4. **particularization**—which aims to make the organization increasingly aware of dimensions of environmental ethical concerns.

The ultimate concern of sustainability strategies for environmental management in institutions and corporations is that—echoing Hans Jonas's ethical language of responsibility—in the future there will still be human beings on Earth (Jones, 1979). There is a link between stakeholder management and the idea that the corporation should serve the triple bottom line of people, planet, and profits (social, environmental, and economic bottom line). The triple bottom line also implies concerns for distributive justice and equality between generations in order to secure effective and responsible use of resources in the daily practices of the business. It is important to emphasize that these concerns for environmental values are only relieved when a code of values is accomplished with effective structures of decision-making, including dialogue with stakeholders and open environmental audits that integrate ethical principles, sustainability, and transparency. These codes should be forward-looking in order to make environmental issues, protecting nature, and action to deal with climate change and global warming an integrated part of long-term strategic planning.

From Ethics to Law

The discussion about ethical principles and sustainability now moves from ethics to law (Rendtorff and Kemp, 2000; Kemp et al., 1997). How can we punish or sentence a corporation and who is really responsible when a corporation does not respect the environment? Issues of environmental protection not only focus on utility and efficiency but also on distributive justice and fairness toward future generations (Velasquez, 2002, p.310). The immediate legal problem is, nevertheless, how to judge or sentence corporations who have been found guilty of committing environmental crime, for example, as is the case with BP and the pollution of the Mexican Gulf in 2010. Today, legislation about environmental issues has become more efficient in many countries. However, there still remain problems regarding just sentencing, how to prevent further environmental crime, or make corporations proactive in their activities in order to prevent environmental crime.

But can a corporation really be forced to be environmentally responsible? It could be argued that if corporations could meaningfully be considered as persons, they could then be held morally responsible. Moral responsibility would, thus, be the basis for legal punishment. The liberal tradition, on the contrary, has—since John Locke—argued that one cannot be responsible for one's own waste since it is no longer one's property. This tradition also does not recognize individual responsibility beyond death. Moreover, corporations are considered as legal fictions: artificial units of individuals which cannot have a particular moral responsibility (French, 1991, p.4). It is a difficulty for environmental law that it is necessary to consider the corporation as a responsible person in order to attribute moral responsibility to it. The solution may be found in a corporation as a collectively responsible entity that can be considered responsible for its actions, also in relation to future generations. This is not impossible, according to French (ibid., p.7), who argues that a corporation, like a person, is capable of rational agency. We have to admit that ethical principles and values of sustainability also apply at the collective and institutional level.

If we look at the predominant legal traditions in the West, there has, however, been a judicial tendency to exclude the environment as an entity for human concern. In the classical natural law tradition, the relationship between human beings, the cosmos, justice, and the nature of things has played an important role in the view that human beings are integrated in a natural teleology of goodness and harmony with the world (Strauss, 1953, 1964). When modern theories of the social contract separated the subject and object, wrenching humankind from nature, they neglected to define *nature*. It is practically nonexistent among the subjects constituting legal and political community. This omission had a powerful effect on the modern conception of the relation between human beings and nature, and had an important impact on our willingness to respect the environment. For Jean-Jacques Rousseau, the social contract is a result of the general will among free human subjects (Rousseau, [1762] 2001). Rawls's theory of justice also seems to have little room for nature or animals as participants in the community of the original position, who have to decide the structure of future society behind the veil of ignorance (Rawls, 1971).

However, a modified sustainability position might also be proposed as the basis for judicial regulation. This is the position of sustainability that I have proposed. It is open to a bio-centric perspective, without the metaphysical implications of the deep ecology position. Michael Hoffman provides an illustrative example: "If you were the last human being on Earth after a nuclear disaster and there only was one tree left. . . [assuming that] you would not be harmed by the existence of the tree, you would be likely to agree that it would be wrong to destroy the tree, that it had its own right to live, and that its existence would make a difference on Earth independent of you" (Hoffman, 1991). This position implies a bio-humanism which is compatible with the proposed sustainability perspective, and results in corporations having an obligation to work for the improvement of the environment independently of their own interest in economic benefit. This is also the argument for formulating legal regulation of the ethical and moral responsibility of corporations in relation to the environment. Indeed, the symbolic nature of criminal law may respond to public demands for correct and just punishment of organizations perpetrating criminal damage against the environment.

The Balanced Company

We can propose the idea of the business ethics of the balanced company as a business reply to the challenges of redefining the concept of sustainability (Rendtorff et al., 2013, pp.33–59). The balanced company is a company that follows the international recommendations of sustainability and respect for nature. According to this approach the corporation follows the Brundtland Report and the Global Compact with increased focus on the ethics of sustainability and respect for the cultural and aesthetic resources. The balanced company is a company that is built on a strategy of business ethics, as I proposed in my book *Responsibility, Ethics and Legitimacy of Corporations* (2009). From this point of view the corporation needs to be a good corporate citizen that assumes its fundamental responsibility for society and the environment.

This company also takes into account the requirement to deal with the problem of climate change. Moreover, business corporations need to work in relation to the new concept of sustainability. In this context we may see the idea of the balanced company as a third way that combines sustainability and growth in a new manner that overcomes the tensions between growth and non-growth in the debate about business and the environment.

Recently, from the research Management in Transition at Roskilde University, we have proposed the concept of the "balanced company" as the basis for dealing with the global problems of sustainability. This approach to sustainable development is published in our book *The Balanced Company: Organizing for the 21st Century* (Rendtorff et al., 2013).We emphasize that the concept of balance in the sense of business ethics is concerned with internal and external justification of values, and in relation to the function of the business it is concerned with society, integrity and stakeholder management. Indeed we can integrate concern for climate change in this business strategy. The struggle against climate change and global warming is an important part of CSR, because the problem of climate change has become so urgent for our efforts to preserve the Earth. Managing the balanced company means relating business practice to the new and redefined concept of sustainability. This allows the business to obtain greater harmony with the environment, taking into account the triple bottom line of balancing the corporation. The balanced company searches ethical and ecological integrity in relation to the environment.

Conclusion

How can we integrate value-driven management with CSR and sustainability in the framework of the concept of the balanced company? Here we need to combine responsibility with concern for balance. Responsibility signifies that there is somebody, an agent with intentional actions, who takes, or is attributed, responsibility for something or someone. Traditionally, this responsibility has been attributed to people. However, power over the whole living world has changed the extension and scope of human responsibility so we move from individual to organizational responsibility. In this responsibility we can focus on the triple bottom line and stakeholder management as the foundation of long-term environmental business ethics when we develop business strategies on this foundation. The balanced company manages according to the triple bottom line of simultaneous economic, social, and environmental concerns.

We can also consider the balanced scorecard as constituting a concrete strategy for balance in the firm. When the founders of the concept of the balanced scorecard, Kaplan and Norton, defined the balanced scorecard, they emphasized that a strategy-focused organization includes a balanced scorecard that measures the relationship between different kinds of non-material performance that can also be related to ethical, social, and environmental issues.

The triple bottom line and the balanced scorecard do not only show economic performance but they also express the social and environmental performance of the company that should be taken into account when it concerns the equilibrium of the balanced company in relation to the environment. In this way the integrity of the balanced company also includes stakeholder management and concern for the different constituencies of the firm. With this focus on integrity and stakeholder management we can say that reporting on the basis of the triple bottom line cannot be reduced to being empty and meaningless, as it is stated by criticism of the triple bottom line principle. It can be stated that it is untrue that the triple bottom line cannot express the content of CSR.

We can instead emphasize that the triple bottom line is a practical way to relate to the realization of integrity and stakeholder management as an expression of CSR and green corporate citizenship in relation to the daily practice of the corporation. How do we move from the concept of the triple bottom line to the concept of the balanced company? The answer is that with business ethics we can experience a formulation of the concern for the triple bottom line as a kind of communication and interaction with stakeholders and the environment. In this sense, business ethics and CSR and values in business have significance as central for the organization and management of the corporation as a balanced company. Accordingly, business ethics is relevant for understanding the legitimacy of the corporation in relation to the balanced company with a sense of global responsibility for sustainable development.

References and Bibliography

Crutzen, P.J. (2002). Geology of Mankind. *Nature*, 3 Janvier 2002, 23; French translation: La géologie de l'humanité: Anthropocène, *Ecologie et Politique*, Vol. 34, 143–5, addendum par Jacques Grinevald: L'Anthropocène et la révolution thermo-industrielle, *Sources et Fondements, Ecologie et Politique*.

Daly, H. (1996). *Beyond Growth*. Boston: Beacon Press.

Desjardins, J.R. ([1999] 2002a). Business's Environmental Responsibility. *A Companion to Business Ethics*, Blackwell Companions to Philosophy, R.E. Frederick, ed. Oxford: Blackwell Publishers.

Desjardins, J.R. (2002b). Environmental Responsibility, in N.E. Bowie *The Blackwell Guide to Business Ethics*, Oxford: Blackwell Publishers, 258.

Elkington, J. ([1997] 1999). *Cannibals with Forks. The Triple Bottom Line of 21st Century Business*. Oxford: Capstone.

Fisher, C., and Lovell, A. (2006). *Business Ethics and Values. Individual, Corporate and International Perspectives*. Essex: Pearson Education, Prentice Hall, Financial Times, 469–73.

Freeman, E.R. (1984). *Strategic Management: A Stakeholder Approach*. Boston, MA: Pitman Publishing Inc.

French, P. (1991). Terre Gaste. *The Corporation, Ethics and the Environment*, Hoffman, Frederick and Petry eds. New York, Westport, Connecticut, London: Quorum Books.

Grinevald, J. (2012). Le concept d'Anthropocène, son contexte historique to scientifique. *Entropia*, Vol. 12, 22–38.

Harste, G. (1994). *Kompleksitet og Dømmekraft*. Aalborg: Nordic Summer University.

Hoffman, W.M. (1990). R. Frederick and E.S. Petry (eds), *The Corporation, Ethics and the Environment*. Westpoint, Connecticut, London: Quorum Books, New Port.

Hoffman, W.M. (1991). Business and Environmental Ethics. *Business Ethics Quarterly*, Vol. 1(2), 169–184.

Jonas, H. (1979). *Das Prinzip Verantwortung*. Frankfurt: Insel Verlag.

Kant, I. ([1785] 1999). *Grundlegung zur Metaphysik der Sitten*. Hamburg: Felix Meiner Verlag.

Kant, I. ([1794] 2004). *Kritik der Urteilskraft*. Frankfurt am Main: Suhrkamp Werkausgabe.

Kemp, P. (2000). Bæredygtighedens etik. *Dansk naturpolitik i bæredygtighedens perspektiv*. Copenhagen: Naturrådet.

Kemp, P., Lebech, M., and Rendtorff, J.D. (1997). *Den bioetiske vending*. Copenhagen: Spektrum.

Kemp, P., and Nielsen, L.W. (2009). *The Barriers to Climate Awareness. A Report on the Ethics of Sustainability*. Copenhagen: Ministry of Climate and Energy.

Levy, D.L., and Newell, P.J. (2005). *The Business of Global Environmental Governance*. Cambridge, MA: MIT Press.

Lomborg, B. (2001). *The Skeptical Environmentalist*. Cambridge: Cambridge University Press.

Nielsen, J.S. (2013). *Den store Omstilling*. Copenhagen: Informations Forlag.

vd Pfordten, D. (1986). *Ökologische Ethik*. Hamburg: Rowolt Taschenbuch Verlag.

Rawls, J. (1971). *A Theory of Justice*. Boston, MA: Harvard University Press.

Rendtorff, J.D. (1999). *Bioetik og Ret, Kroppen Mellem Person og Ting*. Copenhagen: Gyldendal.

Rendtorff, J.D. (2009). *Responsibility, Ethics and Legitimacy of Corporations*. Copenhagen: Copenhagen Business School Press.

Rendtorff, J.D. (2013). A Business Ethics Approach to Balance. In J.D. Rendtorff, I. Jensen and J.D. Scheuer (eds), *The Balanced Company: Organizing for the 21st Century*, (Corporate Social Responsibility). Farnham: Gower, 33–59.

Rendtorff, J.D., and Kemp, P. (2000). *Basic Ethical Principles in European Bioethics and Biolaw*. Copenhagen and Barcelona: Center for Ethics and Law.

Rendtorff, J.D., Jensen, I., and Scheuer, J.D. (2013). (eds). *The Balanced Company: Organizing for the 21st Century*. Farnham: Gower Publishing Ltd.

Rousseau, J-J. ([1762] 2001). *Du Contrat Social*. Paris: Flammarion.

Society for Business Ethics, Philosophy Documentation Center. (2000). *Environmental Challenges to Business*, special ed. Bowling Green: The Ruffin Series, No 2.

Starik, M. (1995). Stakeholder Status for Non-Human Nature. *Journal of Business Ethics*, Vol. 14, 207–17.

Strauss, L. (1953). *Natural Right and History*. Chicago: University of Chicago Press.

Strauss, L. (1964). *The City and Man*. Chicago: University of Chicago Press.

Velasquez, M.G. (2002). *Business Ethics. Concept and Cases*. 5th ed. New Jersey: Prentice Hall.

World Commission on Environment and Development, (1987). *Our Common Future*. Oxford: Oxford University Press.

Chapter 3

The Relationship between Sustainable Markets and Sustainable Development

WOODROW W. CLARK II

Overview

Economics is not a science, but it must become one. The significance for a science of economics is the core factor for connecting sustainable markets and development. Otherwise, only fallacious numbers, percentages, and figures influence the development of land, communities, and regions for the special financial interests of those who control the numbers—and money.

The Next Economics (Clark, 2012b) makes the argument that economics needs to become a science, and then illustrates this with contributions from other authors. By changing economics from a field of study another book, *Qualitative Economics* (Clark and Fast, 2008), identifies the issue in the subtitle: "How economics needs to become a science." Political leaders and decision-makers as well as most academics should look at the definition and meaning of science itself.

The objective and scientific review of modern economic theory documents its failure to be a science and means that the field of economics must find a new paradigm and philosophical roots. For policy makers and elected officials to quote economic statistics as if it is science is both incorrect and dysfunctional for all communities. *The Economist* made that point and more in a special issue (*The Economist*, 2009) almost ten months after the global economic collapse in October 2008. The cover showed a Bible melting with the title "Modern Economic Theory". Why? Because economists did not predict the western and hence global economic depression that started before October 2008.

Science follows a proven line of thinking. In order to discover something or investigate an idea, there must be a set of hypotheses, with each being investigated using qualitative and quantitative data. Then the evidence needs to be replicated. If not, then science tries another set of hypotheses with another set of rules. Even when the results are proven, it is also critical to replicate those hypotheses and test them again, and again, and again.

A very strategic application of economics is concerned with the environment and the impact of climate change around the world. This is part of what is called "social capitalism", under which is "natural capitalism" (Clark and Li, 2004). All forms of societal concerns ranging from the environment to groups, families, businesses, and governments need the science of economics. Social capitalism is one economic format in which economics can become a science. The focus on the environment is significant because dramatic climate change, whether due to hot or cold weather, can cause storms and damage to communities around the world.

For economics to become a science, it must also help redefine capitalism. With Professor Xing Li we published several peer reviewed papers on social capitalism (Clark and Li, 2012; 2013) where we concluded that there is nothing wrong with making money, rather the issue is within what context: environmental, natural, social, or societal issues ranging from health to retirement and pensions. Economics can help solve and reverse climate problems through sustainable communities with the financing of new technologies that do not depend on fossil fuels, nuclear energy, and other dangerous forms of power generation for our infrastructures of buildings, homes and transportation systems.

The Roles of Public and Private Sectors

Collaboration must become the norm, not the use of public partnerships which are often advocated by companies who may only be interested in profit for themselves, as will be seen below. Both government and industry need clear, concise, and consistent market rules, standards, codes, and operating protocols in order to achieve the goals of society in the civic market (Clark and Lund, 2001). In the book *Agile Energy Systems* (Clark and Bradshaw, 2004) five principles are outlined for the framework of a civic market which combines the public and private sectors in the energy sector:

GOVERNMENT OVERSIGHT OF EXISTING UTILITIES

The traditional regulatory framework is close to micro-management as all aspects of the utility are regulated, for example, prices are set, and specific technologies are mandated. A new model of oversight would not replace existing utilities or micro-manage them, but would help them move toward being agile systems through the right combination of incentive and mandate. An example is favorable contracts by the state for renewable power and distributed power. Another is working on helping intermittent power producers use the grid for back-up connections and intermittent power.

STRATEGIES FOR TRANSITIONAL COSTS

The transition from regulated systems to the agile system requires tools for dealing with unknowns and negative unintended consequences. The energy crisis in California from 2000–2004 cost the state at least $40 billion because it had signed long-term energy contracts at inflated prices which legally could not be rewritten. Innovation is more difficult when there are outlandish costs.

JOINT PUBLIC–PRIVATE INVESTMENT

Public ownership is not the best solution; rather investments from public sector pension funds would allow public influence in the utility. Another example is government and public sector leadership in green power for public buildings. In short, capitalism must be concerned also with societal issues.

INNOVATIVE RENEWABLE TECHNOLOGICAL SYSTEMS

Governments can develop market mechanisms to direct the market to innovative technologies through new regulations, codes, and standards. For example, sustainable building codes need to factor into energy conservation and material efficiencies ranging from LED lighting to smart meters that measure and control energy usage daily.

SYSTEMATIC AND REGIONAL IMPLICATIONS FOR THE POWER SYSTEM

Opportunities for energy include economic development, such as jobs and business development from emerging technologies, as well as environmental solutions such as green renewable energy technologies.

Integrated Systems

The following is an illustration of the agile energy system using both central power plant and on-site distributed energy systems.

Consider agile energy systems as a combination of local or regional energy systems (including on-site and self-generation) and central grid systems. In the future the central grid is used primarily for redundancy and back-up purposes. Hence these agile systems are flexible and do not have just one set of particular technologies or market mechanisms, rather a new paradigm which combines central power systems generating power miles from the end-user with on-site or distributed power from intermittent power such as solar, wind, and run-of-the-river hydropower, along with storage devices such as flywheels, fuel cells, and the central grid itself. As summarized in a book review of agile energy systems by Professor Henrik Lund in 2004, they have the following features:

- **Diversity**. Using diversified and renewable energy sources make agile systems less vulnerable to disruption and more reliable especially because they are less reliant on distant suppliers who are dependent on declining fossil fuels. This diversity also builds in needed redundancy.

- **Balance**. Agile systems emphasize the best use of energy not just the amount. Balance involves promoting conservation, encouraging the shifting of use to non-peak times, and reducing consumption, not just selling power.

- **Interdependence and interconnection**. Agile systems find ways to avoid bottlenecks in delivery and integrate energy, two areas which are traditionally separated. For example, co-generation integrates electricity and heat systems. Hydrogen paired technologies, for example wind-produced electricity, can be stored in hydrogen fuel cells and can then be used to transport fuel.

- **Spatially appropriate**. Agile energy systems are smaller and located close to where energy is needed, and coupled with renewable resources. Building specific or on-site generation is critical. Neighborhood scale systems (or distributed generation) are ideal because they recognize environmental costs and can be linked to the grid.

- **Regional**. An agile system links the community to other levels such as regional, national, and even global.

- **Public good**. Agile systems have the public good as a primary goal. Hence they are called the "civic core needs" for all communities of any size.

European Union (EU) Cases: Especially Germany and Nordic Countries

Agile sustainable communities are smart networks of public organizations and private companies that include energy producers, generators, transmission lines, and distributors who focus on specific local consumers such as colleges, shopping malls, walking streets, residential and retirement communities, and office complexes. Energy plans are one of the key roles in all communities regardless of size. Often ignored or taken for granted, energy is a critical infrastructure in any community, region, or nation. The EU addressed the same issues as Bachrach (2001) and provided a definition of sustainable smart communities in the spring of 2007 as five strategies under the Written Declaration 16/2007 from the President of the EU:

> *Written Declaration on establishing a distributed green hydrogen economy and advancing a third industrial revolution in Europe through a partnership with committed regions and cities, SMEs, and civil society organisations.*
> *The European Parliament,*
> *Having regard to Rule 116 of its Rules of Procedure,*
> A. *Because of the rising cost of fossil fuels and warming of the Earth's climate,*
> B. *Whereas a post-fossil fuel and post-nuclear energy vision should be the next important project of the European Union,*
> C. *Whereas, the five key factors for energy independence are: maximizing energy efficiency, reducing global warming gas emissions, optimizing the commercial introduction of renewable energy, establishing hydrogen fuel cell technology to store renewable energies, and creating smart power grids to distribute energy.*

Sustainable smart communities are therefore those that can be self-sufficient because they set public policy goals in order to generate local renewable power, and conserve water and waste that are controlled for reuse and safe disposal (Clark and

Lund, 2006). These communities are smart because they use efficiency technologies (software, metering, and equipment) to both save and conserve energy when it is not needed, and also to interconnect the buildings to create a smart campus. Even more critically, smart campuses allow students, staff, faculties, and families to connect with one another while not leaving their home. Working for third parties can be done without daily travel, thus reducing the need for vehicles and the use of fossil fuels and infrastructures like roads, bridges, and so on.

In many countries sustainable communities are known as "central plants" for heating and cooling. In the United States this system is known as distributed generation (DG) or on-site renewable power generation, and companies have been created to install such systems that service multiple buildings. The central plant is illustrated below in Figure 3.1 and has been the standard for most countries for the last 100 years using primarily fossil fuels and hydroelectric (dams and water) power systems. In Europe and other parts of the world they are known as combined heat and power systems (Clark et al., 2004; Lund, 2000, 2005; Clark, 2004a; Hvelplund, 2006; Lund and Munster, 2006a, 2006b).

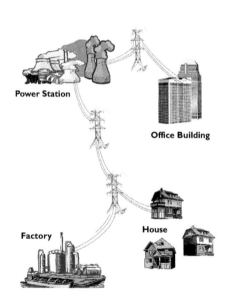

Energy Systems are the Changing Nature of Power Generation

Conventional Electrical Power Grid (left)
Centralized power stations generate electricity and transmit via power lines, pipelines or other means over long distances to customers in their homes, and businesses in factories, offices, and public buildings such as fire stations, city, county state city offices, court houses, and others like hospitals, colleges, and so on.

The New Agile Energy System
Many small on site generating facilities, including those based on renewable (green) energy sources such as wind, bio-mass and solar power, are efficiently utilized and coordinated using real time monitoring control systems along with power generation and storage.
    Offices, hospitals, shopping malls, campuses, and other facilities generate their own power and sell the excess back to the grid. Electric and hydrogen-powered cars can act as generators when not in use. Energy storage technologies provide base-load in supply from intermittent wind and solar power generation sources.
    Agile "green" power generation provides energy security while it reduces transmission losses, operating costs, and the enviromental impact on global warming.

Figure 3.1   Energy systems are the changing nature of power generation
Source: Clark Strategic Partners, 2010.

Energy Systems are the Changing Nature of Power Generation

The problem has been that energy systems rely upon fossil fuel technologies such as coal, natural gas, and nuclear. This Second Industrial Revolution source of energy (Rifkin, 2004) has been replaced with the Third Industrial Revolution (Rifkin, 2011) which uses renewable energy and is far more environmentally friendly, if not a significant part of the solution to global warming. Agile systems and now the Green Industrial Revolution (Clark and Cooke, 2011, 2014; Clark, 2012a) represent the use of renewable (sustainable) on-site power generation with the grid as a back-up system, hence the ability of communities to reduce and eliminate their need for fossil fuels (Cooper and Clark, 1996). Japan (Adams, 2009) and Germany (Morris, 2014; Borden and Stonington, 2014) are two nations that have created sustainable communities that are less dependent on fossil fuels.

Some journalists have characterized new energy infrastructures as the *energy internet* (*The Economist*, 2004). Agility is the key. It means flexibility for a state or region such that communities generate their energy from local on-site renewable energy sources, for example, solar, water, waste, wind, geo-thermal, and biomass which can also be backed up by storage technologies for a firm base-load. The more advanced renewable systems have storage systems that make them hybrid energy generators much like the popular low emission hybrid cars on the highways.

The basic issue is to reduce society's demand for and use of carbon. Rifkin contrasts the issue between the Second and Third Industrial Revolutions and illustrate the basic differences and what comprises agile sustainable communities (Clark, 2006).

However, global concern came about only recently with the recognition by the Intergovernmental Panel on Climate Change (IPCC) (IPCC, 2007) and Mr Al Gore being awarded both a Nobel Peace Prize and Academy Award in 2007. Now the United States is finally apparently ready to take action. Even green economics, and hence the need for education, has started. Porter and van der Linde (Porter and van der Linde, 1995) made this point in the mid-1990s as to how green businesses could be competitive. In 2003 the California Governor's Office predicted that its *Next Economy* would be in large part based upon sustainable development (Clark and Feinberg, 2003). Research and development in new technologies like fuel cells (Clark and Paolucci, 1997), and green economic development (California Infrastructure Commission, 2002) are all critical. However, there remains a need to be careful, as with

ENRON (Clark and Demirag, 2002, 2005), around policy makers who rush to find popular solutions which are ones advocated by lobbying business and finance organizations.

There are three basic concerns surrounding sustainable and smart communities that need to be addressed locally, particularly starting on the political level, in order to establish policies and goals for the entire community (Bradshaw and Winn, 2000). As a result, three components typically make up sustainable and smart communities (EU, 2004, 2007; American Association of Sustainable Higher Education (AASHE), 2007).

First, smart and sustainable communities need a strategic master plan for infrastructure that includes energy, transportation, water, waste, and telecommunications that complement the traditional academic areas of research, curricula, outreach, and assessments (Clark, 2009, 2010, 2014).

Second, there is the array of issues pertaining to the siting of buildings and overall facility master planning which must be addressed from the green perspective. In other words, renewable energy, as well as recycling and conservation concerns, and energy efficient orientation are designed for multiple use by the academic and local community (US Green Building Council, 2006). Developing dense, compact, walkable campuses that enable a range of transportation choices leads to reduced energy consumption and environmental protection (Leadership in Energy and Environmental Design (LEED), 2007). Historically, college campuses were often like towns and villages that were self-sustaining for education, family, business, and recreational activities (Grist, 2007).

Third, a sustainable smart campus is part of both an educational network and community itself (Jin, 2010; Lo, 2011). It draws students, faculty, and staff from a broader region (Los Angeles Community College District (LACCD), 2006–2014). This is also true of an office cluster of buildings, residential housing developments, government offices, and shopping malls. All these buildings and areas require communication and transportation along with the need for water, waste, and energy (Clark, 2009). Each of these construction and building infrastructures in any community require recycling and reuse of waste, and act as a vibrant, "experiential" applied educational model that catalyzes creative learning among community members and broader regional and national areas.

Starting Point: A Public Policy (Government) Plan with Financing

The place to start is with a plan that should be directed at small, relatively self-contained communities or villages within larger cities and regions. The issue is to eliminate the dependency on central grid connected energy by communities, for example college campuses, since most of these power generation sources come from fossil fuels like coal, natural gas, and nuclear power. Local on-site power can be more efficiently used and based on the region's renewable energy resources such as wind, solar, biomass, and storage devices, among other technologies (Clark and Eisenberg, 2008).

One model is now being accomplished in Denmark where many communities are generating power with wind and biomass combined in order to provide base-load. Denmark has a goal of 50 per cent renewable energy generation, primarily from on-site and local resources by 2020 (Lund and Østergaard, 2010; Carlson, 2005; Lund, 2009). The country is well on its way to meeting that national goal (Lund and Hevelplund, 2012). What needs to be done first is to start with the political decision-makers with public policy leadership, financial rewards, or assistance, and specific programs including education and training. Otherwise communities and everyone in them are not compelled or motivated to change. People become comfortable in their life styles and behavior patterns.

Smart Green Communities (Cities)

College campuses represent how this paradigm shift from central grid to local on-site power generation can take place (Clark and Eisenberg, 2008). Jeremy Rifkin called it: "The shift from the Second to the Third Industrial Revolution" (Rifkin, 2011). The Written Declaration from the EU Commission (European Union, Written Declaration 16/2007, 2007) declared that the member states would start to create smart grid communities on the local level that would be connected to a larger national and regional energy system. The basis for the program would be the EU Third Industrial Revolution with its roots in both renewable energy and local smart grids. Small towns and communities like colleges are logical places to start. The EU committed two billion euros in 2007, with a matching three billion euros over the next five years.

Leaders of institutions of higher education need to understand the connection between their growth and development, and their impact on the environment. Leaders of all kinds of institutions (public and private) need to be equipped to analyze their actions or inactions on infrastructure issues such as building design/construction, expansion, maintenance, energy use, and so on and to understand how they will impact the natural resources around them.

Many decision-makers are expanding their built footprint in efficient ways. Other leaders are addressing the environmental issues associated with energy, transportation, water, waste management, and relationships with local communities from a variety of perspectives. However, colleges and universities are critical in that they provide the training and education for future leaders in the public and private sectors. They must do this in a way that ensures their primary products, graduates, are prepared to help societies make the transition from unsustainable to sustainable development economics, new ventures, and social patterns.

In addition to adopting smart growth strategies in development projects, which in themselves yield better environmental outcomes, colleges and universities can and should pursue site-specific strategies to increase sustainability on and off campus. Sustainable practices not only provide beneficial environmental outcomes, they can be cost-efficient in an increasingly competitive recruitment environment. Colleges and universities are finding that campus sustainability initiatives can provide them with a competitive edge. Sustainable development is now becoming both acceptable and sought after in terms of economic growth and job creation.

Cases of Agile Integrated Smart Sustainable Systems

California has a long and proud tradition of advancing from one innovative wave to another. Some scholars would say that the state simply experiences business cycles in reaction to markets. Economists and industrial and political leaders, however, provide a far more compelling explanation: innovation in the form of creativity and experimentation which are the historical roots and assets of California. The state is a draw or even Mecca for people with fresh and new ideas. The American Indians experienced this spiritual pull to the region as did the Spaniards and later the European and Asian immigrants drawn by the 49er Gold Rush.

Silicon Valley was built in the 1950s and 1960s upon the discovery of, not industrial demand for, the electronic transistor that then led to the development of microprocessors and semiconductors. Other regions, states, and countries throughout the world attempt to mimic the Valley, but none has done so successfully (Henton and Waldhom, 1998). The key question for California in the early twenty-first century is: "What is next on the technology horizon?" (Henton, 2001).

The key to the Next California is the synergy, combination, or integration of the following technologies, rather than their isolation or segmentation (California Energy Commission, 2001):

- bioscience/biotechnology (including stem cell research and bioinformatics);

- computing technologies/micro-electronics;

- digital media, Hollywood, and technology;

- energy and environmental technologies;

- nanoscience;

- new infrastructure economy;

- space and sea;

- telecommunications, wireless, and broadband.

Today there is a Synergic California Economy in products that combine the old and the new. Stereos now commonly incorporate record player, tuner, audiotape, CD, and DVD components in one small consumer package—yet they lack a product name. Similarly, some retail outlets have incorporated new IT and other advanced technologies that continuously use innovative information technologies in its retail business to maximize productivity and profits (Clark, 2003). These are just two examples of the state's vast opportunities to augment its major industries, including manufacturing, agriculture, and services, with innovative technologies.

Governor Gray Davis (Governor from 1999 to 2003) formed a Commission for the Building of the 21st Century, enhanced our public educational system, produced a sustainable building road map, and created four research and development programs throughout the University of California System that reflect the Next California Economy in bioscience, nanotechnology, informatics, and other areas (California Hydrogen Highway, 2004–2008). While the next Governor, Arnold Schwarzenegger (Governor from 2004 to 2010), tried to set plans he did not provide state funding and so they did not happen, one such plan being the California Hydrogen Highway (Clark and Feinberg, 2003; Clark, 2004c). The current Governor, Jerry Brown, is doing just that and succeeding with a balanced budget despite cutbacks in some funding (Clark, 2012b).

Business and Economics for Sustainable and Smart Communities

Given the social capitalism that provides a framework for the private sector and government, it is important to realize that a state can be a major player in redirecting an economic downturn into a period of vitality. California is experiencing a time that will require efforts from all major entities that collectively comprise the state. The recommendations made toward achieving the Next California Economy (Clark and Feinberg, 2003) are organized according to seven major themes (A–G):

A) INNOVATION AND CREATIVITY ARE INTELLECTUAL PROPERTY AND KNOWLEDGE CAPITAL

- **Form new emerging technology consortia, especially in nanotechnologies, bioscience, and stem cell research.** Businesses can go far when all systems, which are connecting networks from the Governor down to the implementers, are intact. For example, a successful example of a private/public consortium for flat panel displays was formed in California in the early 1990s.

- **Establish an Advisor and Office of Science and Technology to the Governor.** This position would ensure that the emerging industries receive the proper attention from state officials. The federal government has such an office, as well as several states. Also, the office could serve to coordinate the state's resources serving the emerging technology industries. This would help ensure the efficient allocation of state efforts, especially given the state budget.

- **Mine technologies through the creation of a California Intellectual Property Exchange one-stop shop for all intellectual property in California.** Some work group members believe that thousands of available technologies and products are shelved somewhere because of insufficient means of commercialization. Moreover, some advisors felt that knowledge transfer should not take years, that many innovative ideas are ready to be funded with risk capital, and a significant number can be commercialized today.

- **Guide investment capital according to the best interests of businesses, the state, and the public at large, as well as help investors learn state/public sector guidelines and rules governing such funding through workshops and seminars, and establish a State Financial Resources website**. The groups felt that there are no similar efforts currently being undertaken by the state. Such activities are an easy and cost-effective means of developing desired industries and infrastructure.

- **Encourage the universities and business schools to commercialize emerging technologies through incentives and state support**. For example, create science parks for the commercialization of R&D, and develop programs that match students with start-up and growing companies for preparing business or strategic plans. Such activities will help stimulate the unshelving of patents and technologies.

- **Help strengthen the state's emerging technology areas by fostering communication between existing entities**. For example, the Silicon Valley has numerous resources, but it did not know how to collaborate until Joint Venture Silicon Valley was formed and helped to leverage these resources for the maximum benefit of everyone. One of the key successes of Silicon Valley is that everyone now knows each other through social and business networks, and collaboration has increased.

- **Connect California's traditional industries with new and innovative technologies and industries to help leverage both**. Many retail companies are the most innovative in the United States for implementing new technologies in traditional businesses. In other words, what really matters is innovation in existing industries not just the emerging technology fields alone. Moreover, such a symbiotic relationship will help the competitiveness of current California industries, for example, agriculture, manufacturing, entertainment, tourism and so on, while helping to stimulate market demand for the state's emerging technologies.

B) COMMERCIALIZATION TURNS INTO LOCAL BUSINESS DEVELOPMENT

- **Review and redefine small businesses**. Defining a small business is surprisingly difficult. Many opinion leaders from corporate America, to the federal government, to the state, to local municipalities, have independently developed their own unique small business definitions. California, which currently has numerous definitions for small businesses, contributes to the confusion. One requirement is that universal definitions should be adopted. Moreover, additional state benefits should be provided to gazelle and micro-sized businesses.

- **Form a support advisory group consisting of both state and local governments to facilitate and fast track growing businesses through government processes, including site selection, capital generation, workforce development, permitting, and licensing**. This recommendation is designed to decrease the time from idea to business start-up and to make compliance easier and more cost-efficient while simultaneously satisfying the intent of regulations. As the city of Sunnyvale has proven, entities that take start-ups by the hand and walk them through permitting and benefits will achieve greater success.

- **Examine, and where feasible, model state efforts to rebuild the local economy through matching local communities with new industries and workforces**. The Los Angeles Mayor's Office tried to attract the international fuel cell community to fill the dot.com void through a retrained workforce and good living conditions. The same is being done in the Central Valley. The premise of these efforts is that new technologies significantly stimulate job growth. The state can assist by facilitating and brokering local with regional and state concerns when necessary.

- **Create small business Task Forces throughout the state, nationally, and internationally to retain and attract businesses**. This recommendation incorporates the theme of "red teams" which was a similar concept previously employed by the state to help retain businesses threatening to move out of state. This recommendation, however, also incorporates the attraction of existing businesses to the state. It could also create teams to help mediate local disputes in key technology-focused regions. It is important to note that some in the work group felt that the state should not pursue dinosaur businesses, but should aggressively attract new and emerging businesses especially in the bioscience, nanotechnology, and information technology disciplines.

- **Target businesses to relocate to California by aggressively promoting resources businesses outside the state**. Such resources include knowledge capital, research institutions, and creative workforces. Target businesses should be selected based on the state's regional needs and in conjunction with local entities.

- **Review and improve the efficiency of the state's ability to actively help new and emerging businesses open new markets nationally and internationally**. The ability to do so in today's global economy is paramount to growth, and therefore survival, of most emerging technology businesses. Without more expansive markets, many emerging technologies will be unable to stimulate enough demand to provide a cost-effective product and/or service.

- **Organize, administer, disseminate, and promote data and informational programs to assist start-up businesses in establishing themselves**. Taxes, consulting agreements, technology protections, and copyrights are not part of the entrepreneurial thinking process. Many businesses are using money to get companies going rather than using the expertise of attorneys and CPAs. The long-term implications are proving disastrous. Small businesses, however, are unaware that they are available and/or how to access them.

- **Research and disseminate the market tax credits offered by the US Department of Treasury**. Some advisors felt that this might be a viable tax credit for California to offer as well.

- **Increase emerging technology-related businesses' participation in state procurement opportunities**. In order to maximize the state's procurement benefits among the emerging technology community, the pool of certified small businesses needs to continue to be increased. In addition, the state should encourage the community to participate in procurement opportunities. Possible implementation tools include coordinated and focused outreach, state procurement demonstrations designed to educate potential businesses about participating, and state goals for procurement dollars going to emerging businesses.

C) FINANCING AND FUNDING LEVERAGED INTO GROWING BUSINESSES

- **The reduced revenue received from capital gains tax was a major contributor to the state's budget difficulties in 2012.** From the emerging technology standpoint, the state needs to ensure that current and future funding is allocated efficiently, and to entities that will help yield a return on investment. The state should explore alternative means of providing funding.

- **Market funds benefited by recent bond measures.** Various local and special interest public sector districts: affordable housing, public schools, and community colleges, passed a number of bond measures (totaling over $40 billion) in 2002 that provided for new building and construction in the state. These bond measures provided contracts and procurement mechanisms for small businesses, many of which included markets for emerging and growing businesses.

- **Identify the recipients of current state research funding and analyze the effectiveness of such spending,** in particular how it compares with other entities still requiring funding.

- **Encourage state entities to leverage state funds with federal dollars.** The US Department of Transportation, the US Department of Defense, and the US Department of Energy are among the entities with whom such relationships should be explored, as the federal government implements homeland security measures, organizations and institutions. California clearly should be a major public and private sector recipient of these funds.

- **Aggressively solicit federal dollars earmarked for homeland security**. It is important to note that California is already home to most of the related businesses. Therefore, securing such funding could support existing state businesses if a coordinated effort to obtain the funding is launched.

- **Support investment in the Next California industries, including leveraging dollars from the California public employee funds—**

the California Public Employment Retirement Scheme and the California State Teachers Retirement Scheme—with private equity funds and federal dollars, or develop a system of guarantees at the local level that targets intellectual property and helps small, start-up and/or entrepreneurial businesses to be pulled safely across the valley of death. This could be part of the Treasurer's Office or the Insurance Commissioner's and be known as credit enhancement, guarantees, or forming pre-competitive strategic alliances.

- **Create a California Information Technology Group whereby businesses compete by presenting their ideas in the hope of securing funding.** Many in the group stated that this could be an instant source of job growth and help the entrepreneurial businesses that die because they are unable to fund growth.

- **Require the Department of Finance to use life cycle analysis for all agencies and departments.** Financing a project is critical and is usually done with a cost–benefit analysis that rarely considers high initial costs for new technologies and the related benefits to society—known as externalities such as health benefits. The other approach is life cycle analysis which takes these externalities into account over the useful life of a project. An inter-agency working group revised the project finance manual, known as the Standard Practices Manual, for the California Public Utility Commission and other agencies and departments and this should become state policy through the California Department of Finance.

D) REGULATIONS TURNED INTO COMPETITIVE STANDARDS AND BENCHMARKS

- **Lead the nation and the world in emerging technologies such as nanotechnology and biosciences, for example, stem cell research.** Create professional protocols, standards and codes which, rather than inhibit, are industry-encouraging and stabilizing. The state should establish such standards and goals preemptively and pre-competitively. Waiting to determine the course taken by the federal government is likely to be counterproductive to the state's interests, especially given the federal trend to be slow, focusing on the lowest common denominator and becoming politicized. Furthermore, such protocols and codes enable the state to ensure that any imposed federal standards do not establish more red tape, and that they are marketed and developed in the best interests of California.

- **Create and promote industry friendly regulations**. Create industry and state working groups to revise and implement new regulations and standards. This was done with the California Independent System Operators (CAISO) in 2001–2 when a team of over 40 industries met with CAISO staff under the Governor's Office facilitation to create new rules and tariffs for intermittent resources, for example, wind and solar energy that were ultimately approved by the Federal Energy Regulatory Commission in March 2002 and set the standards for the nation. Stigmas surrounding new technologies have created fear and uncertainty. To the extent that this fear and uncertainty is inaccurate, the state should take strides to form collaborations with the private sector to protect the emerging industry. This will help dissipate unnecessary apprehension and the resulting drive for over-regulation.

- **The state should market the positive regulations**. Some small business owners, especially those in emerging technologies, want very little government interaction. Many of these owners, however, do not know that government procurement, and research and development have given rise to the technologies on which their businesses are founded. Conversely, the state should make sure it removes itself from regulation, where feasible, once the technology has transferred/commercialized. In short, the state should continue to encourage innovation and remove itself from involvement at the appropriate time, but it should also acknowledge the successful use of public funds.

E) INFRASTRUCTURES BUILT FOR THE FUTURE

- **Build existing infrastructures for the future that are clean and integrated**. In 2003 Governor Gray Davis signed the AB #857 (Environment Goals Policy Report) which empowered his Office of Planning and Research to develop plans for the state's future. The law started from the Governor's *Commission For The Twenty-first Century* (California Infrastructure Commission, 2002) which provided a vision for the future of California in eight infrastructure areas. The need to rebuild California provided the market demand for both newly emerging technologies and the growth of existing companies for the future of the state.

- **Sustainable public and commercial and residential buildings are a growing market for emerging technologies and industries.** Growing industries to satisfy the demand in the building sector was a result of the Consumer Agency leadership and its report in December 2001 for the *Sustainable Public Buildings Road Map*. State government leadership in sustainable building leads directly to commercial and residential sustainable buildings. These are new private sector markets for emerging technologies and growing businesses.

- **Assure that future infrastructure improvements include emerging technology industries.** Currently, the work group does not believe that the state decisions regarding infrastructure funding reflect the interests of the emerging technology industries. This is a major oversight, especially given the rapid nature of progression experienced by these industries. It is essential that the state is able to support these industries starting in the immediate future, or they are likely to move out of state where such infrastructure efforts are underway. Other states include Texas, New Mexico, Massachusetts, and North Carolina.

F) WORKFORCE TRAINED FOR THE NEXT ECONOMY JOBS, CAREERS, AND NEW ENTERPRISES

- **Convene University of California campuses, California State University campuses, Community Colleges and Local Workforce Investment Boards to form Regional Advisory Groups whereby select business interests and unions influence the degrees, programs, and courses offered in their area.** California businesses are using more H-1B visa holders because the workforce is deficient in demand skill sets. Many attribute this problem to the failure of the California higher education system to provide key training programs including new technologies, regulatory matters, Food and Drug Administration compliance, quality issues, good manufacturing practice, technology management, project management, data management, interdisciplinary aspects of product creation, and development and approval.

- **In addition, current education and other workforce development programs need to be expedited due to the speed of the industries' evolution.** The availability venue for skill upgrading, which is key to the rapidly evolving industry, is not sufficient.

Finally, some emerging industries demand individuals with interactive and team skills, customer focus, and leadership and management, but the US education institutions tend to promote individualism, independence, and self-motivation. This recommendation is designed to create an adequate supply of workers for the emerging industries. Some innovative ideas might be:

- Business demands—job fairs could be established throughout the state.
- CEO "Adopt a School" has been tried in some communities very successfully.
- Data bank and centralized or one-stop location for data would be invaluable to businesses and government procurement programs.
- Target teams could be established for certain communities for focused activities and events.
- Mentors for young people, as well as growing firms, need to be established at the local and regional level drawing on the expertise of experienced business leaders.

• **Entice K-12 students into the sciences and engineering fields.** The California Council on Science and Technology claims that students in California's K-12 schools are not sufficiently interested or aware of science and technology career paths, and not enough graduates are sufficiently trained to attend college, particularly in science and mathematics.

• **Explore means of improving housing availability and pricing.** Emerging technology industries currently have an insatiable demand for technician-level engineers and scientists. The locations, such as San Francisco, San Diego, and Los Angeles, and employee pay for these positions, however, are inconsistent with housing availability and pricing. As a result, the affordable housing shortage is compounding the difficulty for emerging industries to attract and retain the in-demand positions which are mostly the younger, more recently educated workforce. Similarly, it also adds to the difficulties in attracting and retaining employees from other areas.

• **Promote California's positive international image.** For example, many Europeans believe that personal safety is an issue in California. This is another obstacle to attracting and retaining in-demand workers from outside the state.

G) COMMUNITIES BECOME SUSTAINABLE (VIABLE AND CLEAN): RENEWABLE ENERGY

- **Encourage businesses to incorporate energy efficient technologies into their products.** In the past, energy costs were a comparatively trivial aspect of building projects, but there is now more interest in the wake of the energy crisis. Today innovative companies can couple energy efficiency with other products more in demand. This, in turn, will help stimulate the demand for such technologies. More demand helps the cost competitiveness of our existing and emerging technologies.

- **Convene a Pacific Rim summit of leaders focused on the renewable energy environment with the outcome that the countries embrace or adhere to the Kyoto Accords.** California has made its mark internationally as the first nation state to sign aggressive reduction greenhouse gas legislation through the setting of standards. The California Air Resources Board has responsibility for development and implementation of these standards which include clean fuels, new infrastructures, and the demand for emerging technologies.

- **Move toward a hydrogen renewable energy economy.** Hydrogen is the key as long as it is from renewable energy and watercourses, both in terms of infrastructure and fuel use in transportation, and energy storage. The creation of a task force to strategize, plan, and partner with the private sector worldwide on the creation of hydrogen and new advanced technologies for all sectors in California and the western region of the United States.

- **Green Credits—Emissions' Market.** Government can establish, monitor, and regulate a carbon tax or incentive. Discussions internationally and nationally now are around forming green taxes such as the feed-in-tariff or just a carbon tax, albeit called an incentive as the funds go back into sustainable business creation. Rather than leave the market creation to the private sector, which has already resulted in Enron-type market structures via Cap and Trade, states should take the lead in both public policy and market oversight through the most direct manner: taxes known as incentives. Market forces in climate and emissions trading should *not* be left to their own devices as profits and personal benefits can take control.

- **Value Added Tax**. Create legislation for the California Public Utilities Commission to provide a percentage of rate reductions which will be given for green building in the future. Use of tax (incentive) policy can be shifted from one area to another, for example, from sales to value added as in Europe, and created for the public good. Basically that is what the state did with its smoking policies and taxes to make California smoke free. Now other states and nations are following the California lead.

Conclusions and Next Steps for all Smart Green Communities

VISION OF GREEN ENERGY STRATEGY SYSTEMS

Energy strategy research, development, and implementation encompass the analysis, planning, decision making, and practical steps required to go from a current energy system to a future energy system. The system may be studied in local, regional, national, or global context so as to meet certain aspirations: security of supply, access to affordable and reliable energy, limiting environmental impacts of energy use, and creating sustainable communities. Various perspectives can be taken by energy system modelers, corporate strategists, governments, and energy end-users.

PRESENT, NEAR AND FUTURE GREEN ENERGY SYSTEMS

An informed energy strategy recognizes the need for fundamental transformation in our energy systems to respond to changing societal needs, perceptions, choices, and emerging planetary boundaries. Energy strategy research is a holistic discipline which strives to effectively combine technology solutions, business principles, economics, and political and social sciences in order to achieve more informed, accurate, measurable, and effective strategies that can be evaluated for future energy solutions. To optimize future energy systems, the development of new and improved system options, and their implementation strategy, must take into account progress in data analysis, foresight methods, science, and technology as well as the uncertainties related to the input parameters, in other words regulations, financing and technology issues, and future conditions, for example changing markets, depletion of fossil fuels, climate change, and revised regulations. Studying the possible options for directing the dynamics of the energy transition process is a core part of energy strategy research.

STRATEGY CASES OF IMPLEMENTATION AND LESSONS

Energy strategy modelers and analysts need to be connected with policy-makers who are concerned with implementing these models in both the public and the private sectors. Personal accounts of energy strategy decision-making processes by senior and major decision makers are part of energy strategy knowledge development. Dissemination of human ingenuity to develop and implement sustainable energy solutions is an essential part of energy strategy research that includes both models and practitioner insights. Forward-looking energy strategy research leverages insights and understandings gained from past strategy choices that have been operationalized. Measured and verified analyses of the outcomes from previously implemented energy strategies provide a solid foundation for the formulation of new strategies which is why the assessment of historic energy evolution and choices is part of energy strategy research.

GREEN ENERGY MODELS AND PLANS FOR ACTUAL CASES

From an energy system modeler perspective a range of energy resources and technology solutions may be considered for the energy strategy development process. Energy system models and energy strategy models go hand in hand. The former have an academic emphasis, and the latter include an additional aspect of practical application. Advances in the efficacy and/or efficiency of a particular energy system are part of the core topics studied by energy strategy as a discipline. However, such studies should not have too narrow a scope. The best energy solutions should reflect system analyses that take into account a wide range of societal boundary conditions: leverage of economics, availability of resources and technologies, and environmental footprint reduction.

CORPORATE AND BUSINESS GREEN ENERGY VISIONS

We recognize the reality of partisan energy strategies. Energy strategies developed by companies and professional societies are commonly dedicated to a particular subset of energy systems. An energy strategy and the associated project options for its realization can be classified as partisan when aimed at promoting maximum market penetration of one particular or limited set of energy technology options, with individual groups competing to grow market share and create profits for one or more subsets of the energy system at the expense of other subsets. Hence the biased perspective may address and investigate the broader question of what optimization parameters are viable from a corporate perspective. Informed comparisons of corporate energy strategies—integrated and hybrid analyses, economics, funding, and technology, together with the highlighting of synergies and antagonisms—are part of energy strategy research. Companies and their affiliated partners are not necessarily acting alone in their preferential choices to promote one or more energy system options.

GOVERNMENT AND NONGOVERNMENT ORGANIZATION (NGO) GREEN ENERGY PLANS AS SOLUTIONS

From a government perspective an energy strategy may be based on the full range of primary energy resources and related technology solutions. Optimization criteria are important to better understand the highest utility or lowest cost for energy, and choices should be supported by energy system models and life cycle analyses that assess optimization possibilities based on established or new boundary conditions, for example, expansion of energy infrastructure, cartelization, embargoes on technology transfer, market penetration, and the commercialization of end-use technologies, greenhouse gas emission reduction targets, and more general targets for the reduction of the environmental footprint. A national energy strategy may include the development of a portfolio of balanced solutions as a way of hedging against future uncertainties which explains why energy strategy research is concerned with the management of risk and uncertainty.

NATIONAL AND GLOBAL GREEN ENERGY STRATEGIES AND PLANS

A national energy strategy plan can be partisan, in other words the optimization of national energy, without due consideration for other nations, can occur and may lead to global tensions. Energy strategy development and implementation include a fair component of energy policy making. Energy strategy research seeks to be alert to national energy strategies, policies, and regulations that inappropriately facilitate choices based on populist demand, antiquated public perceptions, special interest groups, and vested interests of providers of ineffective energy systems. Political rhetoric and manipulating markets for the benefit of specific companies, governments, and NGOs should not be mixed in with energy system analysis, but could be an area of critical appraisal particularly when assessing their impact on energy system development and choices. Energy strategy research develops and documents knowledge that is in the best interests of local and global communities, and the planet's sustainable future.

ECONOMICS OF GREEN ENERGY SYSTEMS

Research on energy market behavior and assessments of the societal needs, environmental impact, and economic implications of current energy systems and future energy strategy scenarios are part of the energy strategy development process, and represent a significant area for research. Penetration rates of new technologies, their limitations, and potential evolution in a regional or global context are part of energy strategy research and require an open-minded approach that includes energy solutions with multifaceted and multidisciplinary aspects. Sustainable energy solutions that reduce and reverse their impacts on the environment should be based upon measurable results and require networking with all relevant disciplines ranging from the natural sciences, quantitative and qualitative economics, behavioral economics, applied mathematics, engineering, and social sciences.

EMERGING AND IMPLEMENTATION OF TECHNOLOGIES

Technology tools that support and improve energy system and strategy models are considered part of the core topics studied by energy strategy as a discipline. Research into algorithms and optimization methods for system control are not part of energy strategy's disciplinal core focus unless they touch upon topics that affect strategy choices such as transitioning from regular to smart grid systems, and explicitly address the strategic dimensions.

References and Bibliography

Adams, L., and Funaki, K. (2009). Japanese Experience with Efforts at the Community Level toward a Sustainable Economy. In W.W. Clark II (ed.), *Sustainable Communities*. New York: Springer Press.

American Association of Sustainable Higher Education (AASHE). (2006). Climate Neutral Policy and Summit (2007), adopted by Leadership Council, October 2006. Arizona: Temple.

Bachrach, D. (2001). Comparison of Electric Industry Restructuring Across USA.

Berkeley and California Energy Commission, Governor Davis, Building for the 21st Century Infrastructure Commission, Sacramento, CA, August 2001, Appendix. Sacramento, CA.

Borden, E., and Stonington, J. (forthcoming). Chapter 15: Germany's Energiewende. *Global Sustainable Communities Design Handbook: Green Design, Engineering, Health, Technologies, Education, Economics, Contracts, Policy, Law and Entrepreneurship*. Elsevier Press, Oxford, UK.

Bradshaw, T.K., and Winn, K. (2000). Gleaners, Do-Gooders, and Balers: Options for Linking Sustainability and Economic Development. *Journal of the Community Development Society*, Vol. 31(1), 112–29.

Brundtland Report (1987). United Nations World Commission on Environment and Development. New York, NY.

California Bio-Mass Collaborative. (2013). http://biomass.ucdavis.edu. Last accessed October 23, 2013.

California Energy Commission (CEC). (2001). *Future Energy Plans for California Report*. Sacramento, CA.

California Hydrogen Business Council. http://www.CaliforniaHydrogen.org. Last accessed September 15, 2014, Sacramento, CA.

California Hydrogen Highway. http://www.hydrogenhighway.ca.gov. Last accessed September 15, 2014, Sacramento, CA.

California Infrastructure Commission for the 21st Century, (2002). Invest in California. http://www.ltg.ca.gov/programs/cb21/index.asp. Last accessed October 23, 2014. Sacramento, CA.

California Wind Consortium, http://cwec.ucdavis.edu. Last accessed January 27, 2014.

Carlson, S. (2005). An Engineering Building as 'Green' as Possible. UC Santa Cruz.

Chronicle of Higher Education, *Campus Architecture*, March 25, Section B: B1–32.

Clark, W.W. II. (2014). *Global Sustainable Communities Design Handbook: Green Design, Engineering, Health, Technologies, Education, Economics, Contracts, Policy, Law and Entrepreneurship*. Oxford, UK: Elsevier Press.

Clark, W.W. II., and Cooke, G. (2014). The Green Industrial Revolution. *Global Sustainable Communities Design Handbook: Green Design, Engineering, Health, Technologies, Education, Economics, Contracts, Policy, Law and Entrepreneurship.* Oxford, UK: Elsevier Press.

Clark, W.W. II., and Li, X. (2013). The Political-Economics of the Green Industrial Revolution: Renewable Energy as the Key to National Sustainable Communities. *Renewable Energy Governance,* Chapter 22. Oxford, UK: Elsevier Press.

Clark, W.W. II. (2012a). The Green Industrial Revolution. *The Next Economics: Global Cases in Energy, Environment, and Climate Change.* New York: Springer Press.

Clark, W.W. II. (2012b). *The Next Economics: Global Cases in Energy, Environment, and Climate Change.* New York: Springer Press.

Clark, W.W. II., and Li, X. (2012). Social Capitalism: China's Economic Rise. *The Next Economics: Global Cases in Energy, Environment, and Climate Change.* New York: Springer Press.

Clark, W.W. II., and Cooke, G. (2011). *Global Energy Innovation.* Santa Barbara, CA: Praeger Press.

Clark, W.W. II. (2010). *Sustainable Communities Design Handbook.* Oxford: Elsevier Press.

Clark, W.W. II. (2009). Ed. and author. *Sustainable Communities.* New York: Springer Press.

Clark W.W. II., and Eisenberg, L. (2008). Agile Sustainable Communities: On-site Renewable Energy Generation. *Utility Policies,* Vol. 16(4), 262–74.

Clark, W.W. II., and Fast, M. (2008). *Qualitative Economics: Toward a Science of Economics.* Oxford, UK: Coxmoor Press.

Clark, W.W. II. (2006). Partnerships in Creating Agile Sustainable Development Communities. *Journal of Clean Production,* December. Oxford, UK: Elsevier Press.

Clark, W.W. II., and Isherwood, W. (2006). *Energy Infrastructure for Inner Mongolia Autonomous Region: Five Nation Comparative Case Studies.* Asian Development Bank, Manila, PI and PRC Government, Beijing, PRC.

Clark, W.W. II., and Lund, H. (2006). Sustainable Development in Practice. *Journal of Clean Production*, December. London, UK: Elsevier Press.

Clark, W.W. II., and Demirag, I. (2005). US Financial Regulatory Change: The Case of the California Energy Crisis. Special Issue: *Journal of Banking Regulation*, Vol. 7(1/2), 75–93.

Clark, W.W. II. (2004a). Distributed Generation: renewable energy in local communities. *Energy Policy*, Fall. London, UK: Elsevier Press.

Clark, W.W. II. (2004b). Innovation for a Sustainable Hydrogen Economy. *Boosting Innovation from Research to Market*, pp. 65–7. New York: Springer Press.

Clark, W.W. II. (2004c). Hydrogen: the Pathway to Energy Independence. *Utilities Policy*. London, UK: Elsevier Press.

Clark, W.W. II., and Bradshaw, E. (2004). *Agile Energy Systems: Global Lessons from the California Energy Crisis*. Oxford, UK: Elsevier Press.

Clark, W.W. II., Isherwood, W., Aceves, S., and Berry, G. (2004). Distributed Generation: Public Policy on Local Communities. *Utilities Policy*, Oxford, UK: Elsevier Press.

Clark, W.W. II., with W. Isherwood, J.R. Smith, S. Aceves, and G. Berry. (2004). Distributed Generation: Remote Power Systems with Advanced Storage Technologies. *Energy Policy*, Vol. 32(14), 1573–89.

Clark, W.W. II., and Li, X. (2004). Social Capitalism: Transfer of Technology for Developing Nations. *International Journal of Technology Transfer and Commercialization*, Vol. 3(1), 1–11.

Clark, W.W. II., and Rifkin, J. (2004). Co-Chairs, Green Hydrogen Science & Technology Team Composed of Leading Experts Including Nobel Laureates, www.foet.org. Last accessed April 2014.

Clark, W.W. II. (2003). California Energy Challenge: Solutions for the Future. *Energy Pulse: Insight, Analysis and Commentary on the Global Power Industry*, January. http://www.energypulse.net. Last accessed October 23, 2013.

Clark, W.W. II., and Feinberg, T. (2003). *California's Next Economy*. Governor's Office of Planning and Research. Local Government Commission website at http://www.lgc.org January 2003, 1–56. Last accessed July 2013.

Clark, W.W. II., and Demirag, I. (2002). Enron: the Failure of corporate Governance. *Journal of Corporate Citizenship*, Vol. 8, Winter, 105–22.

Clark, W.W. II., and Lund, H. (2001). Civic Markets in the California Energy Crisis. *International Journal of Global Energy Issues. Interscience*, Vol. 16(4), 328–44.

Clark, W.W. II., and Paolucci, E. (1997). An International Model for Technology Commercialization: Fuel Cells into Vehicle Process and Design Manufacturing, *Journal of Technology Transfer*, July.

Cooper, J., and Clark, W.W. II. (1996). Zinc/Air Fuel Cell: An Alternative to Clean Fuels in Fleet Electric Vehicle Applications. *International Journal of Environmentally Conscious Design & Manufacturing*, Vol. 5(3–4), 235–52.

Economist. (2009). Collapse of Modern Economic Theory. Cover page and Special Section. 16 July.

Economist. (2004). Building the Energy Internet. Electronic version, May 11, 2004 www.economist.com. Last accessed October 29, 2013.

Emerald Cities: The Promise of Green Development. *The American Prospect*. Special Section. January 2007.

Energy's Future: Beyond Carbon. *Scientific American Special Issue*. December 2006.

Energy Policy Act. (2005). US Congress, October.

Executive Order S–20–04 (2006). *Green Building Action Plan*, Department of Finance Budget Letter 06–27 under Public Utilities Code Section 388. 18 September.

European Union (EU) Parliament Rule (#116), Smart and Sustainable Communities. May 2007. Brussels, Belgium.

Green Universities (GU) http://www.grist.org/news/maindish/2007/08/10/colleges/. Last accessed October 31, 2007.

Hebel, S. (2005). The Hard Birth of a Research University. UC Merced. *Chronicle of Higher Education*, April 1: section A: A1–25.

Henton, D. (2001). Next Silicon Valley: Riding the Waves of Innovation. *Silicon Valley*, December.

Henton, D., and Waldhorn, S.A. (1998). California: The Megastate Economy. In R.S. Fosler (ed.), *The New Economic Role of American States*. Oxford, UK: Oxford University Press, 204–47.

Hvelplund, F. (2006). Renewable Energy and the Need for Local Energy Markets. *Energy*, Vol. 31(13), 2293–302.

Intergovernmental Panel on Climate Change (IPCC), United Nations Environmental Programme (UNEP) and the World Meteorological Organization (WMO) established the IPCC in 1988. Four Reports (Assessments on Climate Change) were given in 2007. http://www.ipcc.ch. Last accessed October 2014.

Isherwood, W., Smith, J.R., Aceves, S., Berry, G., and Clark, W.W. II., with R. Johnson, D. Das, D. Goering and R. Seifert. (2000). Remote Power Systems with Advanced Storage Technologies for Aaskan Villages. (University of Calif., Lawrence Livermore National Laboratory, UCRL-ID-129289: January 1997), *Energy Policy*, Oxford, UK: Elsevier Press.

Jin, A.J. (2010). Transformational Relationship of Renewable Energies and the Smart Grid. In W.W. Clark, II. (ed. and author), *Sustainable Communities*. New York: Springer Press, 217–32.

LEED for Neighborhood Development: Rating System. With Congress for the New Urbanism and Natural Resource Defense Council (NRDC), June 2007. Washington, DC.

Lo, V. (2011). China's Role in Global Economic Development: A Plan. Speech by Chairman of Shui On Land, given at Asian Society, Los Angeles, CA, April 25.

Los Angeles Community College District (LACCD) www.laccd.edu. Last accessed November 2013.

Lovins, A. (2001). *The Economic Renewal Guide: A Collaborative Process of Sustainable Development*. Denver, CO: Rocky Mountain Institute.

Lund, H. (2009). Chapter 10, Sustainable Towns: The Case of Frederikshavn, Denmark. W.W. Clark, II. *Sustainable Communities*. New York: Springer Press.

Lund, H. (2005). Large-scale Integration of Wind Power into Different Energy Systems. *Energy*, Vol. 30(13), 2402–12.

Lund, H. (2000). Choice Awareness: Decision Making at the Local Level. *Journal of Energy Policy*, Vol. 2, 249–59.

Lund, H., and Hvelplund, F. (2012). The Economic Crisis and Sustainable Development: The Design of Job Creation Strategies by Use of Concrete Institutional Economics. *Energy*. September.

Lund, H., and Munster, E. (2006a). Integrated Energy Systems and Local Energy Markets. *Energy Policy*, Vol. 34(10), 1152–60.

Lund, H., and Munster, E. (2006b). Integrated Transportation and Energy Sector CO_2 Emission Control Strategies. *Transport Policy*, Vol. 13(5), 426–33.

Lund, H., and Østergaard, P.O. (2010). Climate Change Mitigation from a Bottom-up Community Approach: A Case in Denmark, in W.W. Clark, II. *Sustainable Communities Design Handbook*. Oxford, UK: Elsevier Press.

Marcus, W., and Hamrin, J. (2001). *How we got into the California Energy Crisis*. Paper given at National Renewable Laboratory, March 2001. San Francisco, CA: Center for Resource Solutions.

Morris, C. (2014). Energiewende—Germany's community-driven since the 1970s. *Global Sustainable Communities Design Handbook: Green Design, Engineering, Health, Technologies, Education, Economics, Contracts, Policy, Law and Entrepreneurship*. Oxford, UK: Elsevier Press.

Porter, M.E., and van der Linde, C. (1995). Green and Competitive. *Harvard Business Review*, September–October, 120–34.

Rifkin, J. (2011). *The Third Industrial Revolution: How Lateral Power is Transforming Energy, the Economy, and the World*. New York: Palgrave Macmillan Press.

Rifkin, J. (2004). *The European Dream: How Europe's Future is Quietly Eclipsing the American Dream*. New York: Tarcher/Penguin.

University of California, Los Angeles (UCLA) (2014). Smart Grid Conferences. SMERC, School of Electrical Engineering. Los Angeles, CA.

US Green Building Council, http://www.usgbc.org. Last accessed January 2014.

Young, R. (2007). An Epiphany. *Chronicle of Higher Education* and ASSHE. August.

PART II
Corporate and Market Approaches

Chapter 4

The Corporate World and Sustainability: Eco-efficiency and the Doxic Shareholder Value

NIHEL CHABRAK AND JACQUES RICHARD

Introduction

In June 1992 the United Nations Conference on Environment and Development (UNCED), also known as the Earth Summit, was held in Rio de Janeiro. During the Summit, leaders set out the principles of sustainable development elaborated in *Our Common Future*, a report that was published by the World Commission on Environment and Development (WCED) in 1987, known as the Brundtland report. Composed of 21 members, mostly from the developing countries and chaired by former Norwegian Environment Minister Gro Harlem Brundtland, the commission set out to highlight the crises in development and the environment, and to seek ways forward. The Brundtland report defines sustainable development as: "development which meets the needs of the present without compromising the ability of future generations to meet their own needs" (WCED, 1987, p.43). This classic definition was given a political salience by the Earth Summit. Besides the agreement on the Climate Change Convention, which had led to the Kyoto Protocol, other binding agreements were opened to signature during the conference such as the Convention on Biological Diversity and the United Nations Convention to Combat Desertification. But the major overall document coming out of Rio is a nonbinding international partnership action plan entitled "Agenda 21" which was devised for the twenty-first century with regard to sustainable development and environmental protection worldwide.

In September 2002 The World Summit on Sustainable Development (WSSD), known as Rio+10, was held in Johannesburg to recognize sustainable development as an overarching goal for all United Nations agencies, programs and funds, and for national, regional, and international institutions. The Johannesburg Plan of Implementation has affirmed commitment to the full application of Agenda 21 that was issued by the 1992 Earth Summit. It was also intended to help in achieving the Millennium Development Goals. This Summit was marked by the absence of an official delegation from the United States, an absence that was acclaimed by 30 conservative activists including Fred L. Smith Jr., president of the Competitive Enterprise Institute, Paul M. Weyrich of Coalitions for America, Grover Norquist of Americans for Tax Reform, and David A. Keene of the American Conservative Union.[1]

Twenty years after the Earth Summit, the United Nations Conference on Sustainable Development (UNCSD), known as Rio+20, was again held in Rio de Janeiro, in June 2012, following the UN General Assembly Resolution A/RES/64/236 on 24 December 2009. A total of 192 UN member states, private sector companies, NGOs, and other groups participated in this conference. Rio+20 was intended to revamp political commitment for sustainable development, assess progress toward meeting previous commitments since the first Summit, and address new challenges. The UN wanted Rio to endorse a "green economy roadmap". The major outcome of that Summit was a nonbinding document entitled *The Future We Want*. However, the absence of key leaders to the conference like US President Barack Obama, German Chancellor Angela Merkel, and United Kingdom's Prime Minister David Cameron was interpreted as a sign of negligence by their administrations in prioritizing sustainability issues.

Since the Brundtland report and the first Rio Summit, sustainable development has become a desirable goal for which implementation has proven difficult. In his 2002 report on implementing Agenda 21, United Nations Secretary General Kofi Annan raised the undoubted gap in enactment and confirmed that: "progress toward reaching the goals set at Rio has been slower than anticipated" (United Nations Economic and Social Council, 2002, p.4). The main reason behind this gap is the difficulty of conceiving the move from theory to practice. Obviously, the elusive definition of sustainable development has led to this dilemma. The universal adoption of sustainable development is undoubtedly due to this vagueness. Sustainable development has gained currency within governments, NGOs, and prominent international organizations including the World Bank, the International Monetary Fund, and the World Trade Organization. It was also celebrated by the private sector in the form of a corporate social responsibility (CSR) agenda. Voluntary initiatives

---

1   http://news.google.com/newspapers?nid=110&dat=20020815&id=3-ZOAAAAIBAJ&sjid=_ UsDAAAIBAJ&pg=3178,5534673. Last accessed October 22, 2014.

including the World Business Council on Sustainable Development (WBCSD), the OECD Round Table on Sustainable Development, United Nations Global Compact (UNGC), Caux Round Table (CRT), Equator Principles (EP), Global Reporting Initiative (GRI), Young Global Leaders—Global Business Oath, Extractive Industries Transparency Initiative, CERES principles, Business Leaders Initiative on Human Rights (BLIHR), and many others have proven the unequivocal interest of the private sector in this new trend but not necessarily for sustainability. The flexibility of the sustainable development concept has enabled many actors to adapt it to their own purposes. Its suppleness has consequently led to various interpretations and confusion that has compromised the effectiveness of its implementation.

It is in this very specific context that the concept of "eco-efficiency" was introduced in the field of environmental management, along with the concept of the Triple Bottom Line. The purpose of this chapter is to present a new reading of the eco-efficiency philosophy in order to uncover the hidden agenda of its advocates, and to propose a radical change toward better conservation of natural capital. For that purpose, firstly, we expose the context in which eco-efficiency came to be settled and disseminated. Secondly, in the light of the context of its upsurge, we portray a new understanding of eco-efficiency, its tenets, and its limits. Thirdly, we expose another mainstream environmental management school of thought based on the concept of the triple bottom line. And fourthly, we argue for a new approach to discard the triple financial, ecological, and human crises. A new concept of profit along with a reformed governance model is portrayed.

The Origins and Dissemination of Eco-efficiency: How the Ecological Debate was Captured by the Shareholder Value Imperatives

The Earth Summit held in Rio in 1992 came in response to an increasing pressure relayed by public debate on the future of the globe and humanity. Thereupon a group of multinational companies, supported by renowned scholars, started elaborating a new management conception that takes into account ecological considerations without impairing the doxic philosophy of shareholder value. This new approach of management is based on a fundamental concept that came to be known as eco-efficiency, which later became a new environmental management philosophy. Before we scrutinize the socio-historical context to understand the climate of opinion in which eco-efficiency was fashioned and the institutional apparatus that has led to it becoming dominant, we portray the doxic shareholder value ideology.

THE DOXIC SHAREHOLDER VALUE IDEOLOGY

For Greek philosophers doxa is the opposite of knowledge (truth), since it encompasses the idea of error. In Plato's allegory of the cave, truth for the prisoners was nothing but the shadows of images appearing on a wall, images which were projections of unreal objects carried behind them. When the prisoners were bound to look straight at the light of the sun, they turned their eyes away and instead focused on the shadows to which they were more accustomed. For Bourdieu (1977) doxa refers to something taken for granted. Doxa makes its own arbitrariness seem natural, and produces a committed and unconscious adherence to the established order. Doxa has endless capacity to set misrecognized limits (what is commonly called a sense of reality), in the dialectic between objective chances and agents' aspirations (Bourdieu and Passeron, 1977). It is fundamental in the constitution of habitus gifted with the objectivity secured by consensus on meaning, and by repeated similar and unified experiences within a group. These homogeneous and hysteresis habitus engender the internalization by individuals of objective social structures through their mental schemes and perceptions (their ethos). Individuals' mental schemes and cognitive structures are variants of, and reproduce, the group habitus. Thus, the world is rendered as comprising objective order and tradition, and as closed, natural, self-evident, and undisputed: "[it] goes without saying, because it comes without saying" (Bourdieu, 1977, p.167). What happens is that the world goes unquestioned; there is nothing to do except what is done; and what is done is right—and what should be done. Bourdieu (1977, p.164), calls this experience doxa: "so as to distinguish it from an orthodox or heterodox belief implying awareness and recognition of the possibility of different or antagonistic beliefs."

The very idea of shareholder value maximization has always been more of a political statement than a factual reality. The shareholder value is an ideology that was disseminated to legitimate governance by markets. Since Berle and Means ([1932] 1982) outlined the separation of control and ownership in large US corporations, a new form of capitalism without capitalists has occurred (Dahrendorf, [1957] 1972). Dispersed shareholding structures have given rise to the accession to power of the "organization man" (Dahrendorf, [1957] 1972) and to the ascendancy of what came to be known as the "technostructure" (Galbraith, [1967] 2007) in charge of ensuring the best allocation of resources. However, the financial difficulties of US conglomerates in the 1960s and 1970s have provided excuses to the economists from the *Chicago School* to elaborate and promote an outsider governance model by markets, and the doctrine of shareholder value maximization (SVM). Their argument was that SVM is the only alternative to improve the performance of the economy as a whole consistently with the neo-classical theory of market economy (Fama and Jensen, 1983a, pp.327–49; 1983b, pp.301–25). This shift from the insider model of governance that dominated the glorious thirties was strengthened by the increasing role of institutional investors in markets. Since boards are required to ensure managers delivered value (Cadbury Report, 1992), the possibility of corporate resistance was undermined, and companies came to be harassed by activist investors (Erturk et al., 2008). This has led corporate America to largely endorse this doctrine without even questioning its assumptions. It is against this backdrop of false choice offered to managers that the corporate world answer to sustainability should be analyzed.

THE BIRTH AND DISSEMINATION OF ECO-EFFICIENCY

If the concept of eco-efficiency was first described by Schaltegger and Sturm (1990), its broad use has been induced through the WBCSD founded by the Swiss business entrepreneur, Stephan Schmidheiny. Obviously, the eco-efficiency movement was developed in Switzerland in the 1990s with a dissertation by Stefan Schaltegger and Andreas Sturm on environmental management at the Swiss University of Basel (Schaltegger and Sturm, 1992, 1994). Since then other mainly German scholars, including Roger Buritt, Frank Figge, Tobias Hahn, Holger Petersen, Terje Synnestvedt and Marcus Wagner have actively contributed to promoting eco-efficiency. Major academic publications, such as *An Introduction to Corporate Environmental Management: Striving for Sustainability* (Schaltegger et al., 2003) were to provide eco-efficiency with the required scientific justification for its global dissemination. Simultaneously, representatives of big multinational companies such as Stefan Schmidheiny, Federico Zorraquin, Livio DeSimone and Frank Popoff started considering the concept of eco-efficiency as the best solution for a new green management. At the Earth Summit, the private sector took a keen interest and wanted to be involved to be sure that what was to come out of it would be business-friendly and able to cope with the imposed doctrine of shareholder value. Their activism culminated in the Business Council for Sustainable Development (BCSD) forum, and the WBCSD association, both initiated by Stefan Schmidheiny.

Following his appointment as chief advisor for business and industry to the secretary general of the 1992 Earth Summit, Maurice Strong, Stefan Schmidheiny invited some 50 business leaders to become members of the BCSD forum. Their objective was to present a global business perspective on sustainable development, and to stimulate the interest and the involvement of the international community (Schmidheiny, 1992: Preface IX). This forum was transformed into a book entitled *Changing Course* (Schmidheiny, 1992) during the 1992 United Nations Earth Summit, and popularized the concept of eco-efficiency for the business sector which has led to large-scale adoption. Meanwhile, the International Chamber of Commerce (ICC) was also required to prepare business input for the same conference. In 1993 a group of ICC member companies formed the World Industry Council for the Environment (WICE) which, at the beginning of 1995, merged with the BCSD to form the WBCSD, based in Geneva, Switzerland with an office in Washington, D.C. The WBSCD is now a coalition of more than 120 international companies having a common commitment to the principles of economic growth and sustainable development, in other words to a new management approach based on eco-efficiency which is allegedly branded as having nothing in common with traditional management, that is concerned only with shareholder value—the infamous "business as usual".

The WBCSD rapidly became involved in many other initiatives such as the Round Table on Sustainable Development established in 1998 by the OECD Secretary General, Simon Upton. Founded to provide an informal setting through which ministers as well as international business and civil society leaders can engage without prejudice in negotiating issues related to sustainability, the Round Table's sole donor is the WBCSD.[2] The chairman and founder of the Round Table, Simon Upton, is a former New Zealand politician and member of Parliament serving from 1981 to 2001 and representing the National Party. He worked as a part-time consultant for several years at PriceWaterhouseCoopers.

Among the very first participants in the WBCSD, were Federico Zorraquin, Argentinean entrepreneur; Livio De Simone,[3] Chairman and Chief Executive Officer of 3M Cardiovascular Devices, Inc. from November 1991 to January 2001; and Frank Popoff, a Bulgarian American businessman who has served as the Chairman of Chemical Financial Corporation since April 2004.[4] Together, they published several books such as *Financing Change: The Financial Community,*

---

2   http://www.oecd.org/sd-roundtable/donors. Last accessed October 22, 2014.
3   DeSimone serves as a Director of Cargill, Milliken & Company Inc., and American Express Funds. He serves as Trustee of the University of Minnesota Foundation. He served as a Director of General Mills, Inc., Legacy Vulcan Corp., and Nexia Biotechnologies Inc. He served as an Independent Trustee of RiverSource Managers Series Inc. and RiverSource Partners Small Cap Equity Fund (http://investing.businessweek.com/research/stocks/people/person.asp?personI d=289196&ticker=TGT&previousCapId=398625&previousTitle=GOLDMAN%20SACHS%20 GROUP%20INC. Last accessed October 22, 2014.
4   Popoff served as the Chairman and Chief Executive Officer of The Dow Chemical Company from December 2000 to April 2004, and Chairman of the Board from 1995 to November 2000. He has served as Director of American Express, Qwest Communications International Inc., United Technologies Corp. and Shin-Etsu Chemical Co. Ltd. Director Emeritus, and the

Eco-efficiency, and Sustainable Development (Schmidheiny and Zorraquin, 1998), and *Eco-efficiency: The Business Link to Sustainable Development* (DeSimone and Popoff, 2000)[5] which includes a laudatory preface by Maurice Strong where he affirms that the concept of eco-efficiency would be born with the 1992 Earth Summit (1997, p.vii). In these publications, Schmidheiny, Zorraquin, DeSimone and Popoff advocate for deregulation if the international community is determined to build a sustainable world.

The WBCSD argues for deregulation because any delay in implementing sustainability is due to the lack of leadership and to each sector waiting on the others to start moving. Holliday et al. (2002, p.18) note that: "politicians tend not to run for office on promises of making the price of goods reflect their real (higher) costs for the sake of sustainable development; consumers tend not to demand to pay such higher costs; business tends not to lobby lawmakers for higher prices." In *Changing Course* Schmidheiny states: "The world is moving toward deregulation. This requires corporations to assume more social, economic, and environmental responsibility in defining their roles" (Schmidheiny, 1992, p.xii). He adds: "We must expand our concept (of responsibility) to those who have a stake in our operations to include not only employees and shareholders but also suppliers, customers, neighbors, citizens' groups, and others. Appropriate communications with these stakeholders will help us to refine continually our visions, strategies, and actions" (ibid., p.xii). For him: "prosperous companies in a sustainable world will be those that are better than their competitors at 'adding value' for all stakeholders, not just for customers and investors" (ibid., p.86).

Among the other members of the WBCSD who signed the declaration of commitment to promoting an international partnership in changing course toward a common future, is Alex Krauer, Präsident des Verwaltungsrates, Ciba-Geigy AG, Switzerland. It is interesting to recall that the seminal work of Schaltegger and Sturm on eco-efficiency, published in 1990, was grounded in an applied research project conducted within that specific Swiss firm, Ciba-Geigy.

In this section we will shed light on the institutional apparatus that was devised to enable the corporate world, governed by the doxic shareholder value doctrine, to capture the environmental debate through the concept of

---

Indiana University Foundation. He is also a member of the American Chemical Society (http://en.wikipedia.org/wiki/Frank_Popoff. Last accessed October 22, 2014.

5 This book presents case studies of the application of eco-efficiency from a number of international companies, including 3M and the Dow Chemical Company where DeSimone and Popoff had served.

eco-efficiency. The notion of sustainable development has lost credibility since the recommendations of the Earth Summit became subjugated to the dominance of the economic growth agenda. If the United Nations initiated and led the international debate and interest in sustainable development, it was never the major instigator to implement this concept. The WBCSD is the main international forum to concretely design management approaches to deal with environmental problems. The huge expectations that came out of the Earth Summit were quickly tempered because of the capturing of the ecological debate by the corporate world that perpetuated the same neo-liberal economic paradigm which celebrates the doxic shareholder value ideology. Rather than sustaining the global eco-system, the corporate world imposed its philosophy on how to sustain economic growth with a slight ecological touch. As a result, the sustainable development movement has been subsumed within the shareholder value paradigm. In the light of the connections between the corporate world and academia that paved the way for eco-efficiency to be largely adopted, a new reading of this concept must be achieved.

The Concept of Eco-efficiency and its Limitations: The Rhetoric of Change

The concept of eco-efficiency was designated by BCSD (1993) to be a corporate response to the global goal of sustainable eco-efficiency development. Coined in its report *Changing Course*, written by Schmidheiney for the 1992 Earth Summit, the term eco-efficiency describes those corporations that are already producing economically valuable useful goods and services, while continuously reducing ecological impacts, in other words resource consumption and pollution. It was intended to be a practical approach for companies to contribute to green growth through the pursuit of long-term profits, though incorporating activities that respect the carrying capacity of the Earth. The success of this new approach is due to its being considered as a practical tool for enhancing both economic and environmental benefits, and which was then celebrated by hundreds of companies around the world (United Nations, Economic and Social Commission for Asia and the Pacific (ESCAP), 2009).

To better understand the tenets of this concept, we prefer returning to its original account in the academic writings by Schaltegger and other scholars. In *An Introduction to Corporate Environmental Management: Striving for Sustainability* Schaltegger et al. (2003) identify four types of rationalities: socio-cultural, technological, economic, and political to distinguish two types of efficiency in the field of environmental management: the environmental efficiency and eco-efficiency. According to Schaltegger and Sturm (1990), if environmental efficiency relates to the technical realm, eco-efficiency is what belongs to the economic realm.

ENVIRONMENTAL EFFICIENCY

Since there is no value creation without environmental impact being added, environmental efficiency is defined as a specific example of technical efficiency that examines the relationship between environmental inputs (impacts) and outputs (value). One relative measure of performance is to compare the two factors as a ratio. In a specific environmental way, efficiency is measured by a technical ratio of productivity that compares a quantity of production during a period of time (to consider value) with the quantity of environmental impacts added during the same period of activity (Schaltegger and Sturm, 1992, 1994). Schaltegger et al., (2003) consider these impacts as the total environmental effects or influences of corporate activities. These effects can be weighted with regard to their relative harm on the environment (Schaltegger and Sturm, 1990).

$$Environmental\ efficiency = \frac{Quantities\ produced}{Created\ impacts\ (quantities)}$$

The following example is intended to explain environmental efficiency for a farmer over a period of two years. For simplification purposes we assume the quantity of chemical fertilizers injected into the soil to be the sole environmental impact for consideration.[6] Also, local conditions such as the type of soil, the local climate, the type of culture, and the agricultural practices the farmer is employing are to be neglected. Table 4.1 shows the environmental efficiency for the farmer over a two-year period.

Table 4.1   The farmer environmental efficiency over two years

	Year 1	Year 2
Quantity produced	50 units	150 units
Quantity of chemical fertilizers (created impacts)	50 kilos	100 kilos
Environmental efficiency	1	1.5

6   This indirect measure is to replace the true direct impacts as measured by the change in eutrophication, acidification, human toxicity, climate changes, and so on.

Our farmer is considered to have improved the environmental efficiency, because he produced 1.5 units instead of 1 unit for each kilo of chemical fertilizer used. Yet, this progress does not translate into better conservation of natural capital since the global consumption of chemical fertilizers used in the same parcel of soil has doubled. Consequently, an environmental degradation due to chemical fertilizers' overuse is expected. This phenomenon is known as the rebound effect. Rebound effect occurs when improving the efficiency of resource-use per unit is outstripped by the absolute increase in demand for the goods and the deterioration of resource efficiency in consumption. The rising production is expected to cause an absolute increase in the chemicals used which are detrimental to the environment (Dyckhoff, 2000, pp.2583–90). In their seminal work, Schaltegger and Sturm (1990) consider a product to be ecological only if it implies the conservation of the ecological system. Schaltegger et al. (2003) seem to be aware of the problematic character of environmental efficiency as a performance measurement, but they tend to underestimate it. For Schaltegger et al. (2003) environmental efficiency, even if it seems to be rather about effectiveness, is a necessary condition toward measuring environmental performance. However, they state that resource productivity (minimizing the resources used in producing a unit of output) should be completed by another indicator that measures the efficiency of economic activities in generating added value from the use of those resources. The new indicator is to be designed with additional consideration for the relationship of the environment to the economy.

ECO-EFFICIENCY

For Schaltegger and Wagner (2006) CSR definitions, based on Carroll (1979, pp.497–505; 1999, pp.268–95) are not appropriate to account for the general economic relevance of corporate societal engagement. CSR should not lead to the establishment of a parallel organization to the existing one in order to deal with non-economic issues separately from other business issues and to measure a non-economic performance alongside the economic one. This argument constitutes the departure point toward establishing a business case for CSR and sustainability. As defended by Edvardsson and Enquist (2009) and Vogel (2005), CSR needs to be a proactive approach and a business model for values-based companies.

For Shaltegger and Sturm (1992, 1994) the environmental view of efficiency is informative, but not enough for corporate decisions about environmental impacts. What is necessary is to know how to solve business problems in an environmentally and economically efficient way. Hence, another economic view is required to frame environmental management. According to Holliday Jr. et al. (2002) the WCED's key concept of sustainable development has informed environment and development discussion since 1987, but it has never quite caught on to become a rallying cause because the term is not appealing. With eco-efficiency, things are more tempting primarily for the corporate world.

Eco-efficiency is stated to be the efficiency of economic activities in generating added value from the use of resources with lower adverse environmental impacts owing to technological innovation. In other words, while creating value for shareholders, managers should assume the responsibility of systematically reducing environmental damages and risks (Schaltegger et al., 2003). For Schmidheiny (1992) it consists of maximizing added value while minimizing resource and energy use. According to DeSimone and Popoff (1997), it is a matter of more output being obtained from a given resource input or environmental effect. According to the WBCSD (2000) fundamental to eco-efficiency is the adoption of a new management philosophy that stimulates the search for environmental improvements which yield parallel economic benefits. Finally, to solve the problem of opposition between both the ecological and the economic spheres, Schaltegger and Sturm (1990) seem to suggest that managers need to maneuver in the political and socio-cultural spheres and to make compromises with stakeholders including ecologists.

A measure of the greatest environmental net income per unit of capital expenditure (profitability) has to be determined in order to account for the new efficiency concept labeled "economic and ecologic efficiency" by Schaltegger and Sturm (1992, 1994) or simply eco-efficiency:

$$Eco\text{-}efficiency \quad \frac{Economic\ value\ creation}{Environmental\ impact\ added\ (quantity)}$$

The concept of eco-efficiency is not about internalizing what companies used to externalize, since it does not affect financial accounting concepts. It does not require a change in the way profit is measured. Eco-efficiency is simply a ratio comparing two constructs taken from conventional financial accounting to measure profitability (numerator) and from a system of management accounting like the one required by GRI (2010, 2011), to give a measurement of environmental impacts (denominator). Table 4.2 portrays the eco-efficiency calculation for our farmer over the two-year period.

Table 4.2   The farmer eco-efficiency over two years

	Year 1	Year 2
Conventional financial accounting net income	100	630
Quantity of chemical fertilizers (created impacts)	50 kilos	100 kilos
Eco-efficiency	2	6.3

Greater eco-efficiency occurs generally when environmental impact added is reduced for the same level of expenditure and net economic value created. Similarly, better eco-efficiency arises when, for the same environmental impact added, the lowest level of expenditure is incurred and the net economic value created is increased. This could be the result of an improved competition or an increase in prices. In this case, companies are stimulated to increase their activity to gain higher net economic value added. In our example the farmer's net income was multiplied by 6.3 while his chemical fertilizers' consumption has doubled. Hence, his eco-efficiency indicator has multiplied by 3.15. This result simulates him to keep using more and more chemical fertilizers despite its effect on the environment. Eco-efficiency can be improved even when companies are not directly focused on environmental protection.

Despite the limit of eco-efficiency in terms of natural capital conservation, Shaltegger et al. (2003) seem convinced that it is the only way for the business world to think environmentally by bringing them to solve environmental problems in an economic way. Schmidheiny (1992), BCSD (1993), DeSimone and Popoff (1997), and the WBCSD (1996) share the same creed. In the last three publications, it is obvious that the conservation of natural capital (considering the absolute effect on the environment) is a matter of concern. According to BCSD (1993), eco-efficiency is: "achieved by the delivery of competitively priced goods and services that satisfy human needs and bring quality of life, while progressively reducing ecological impacts and resource intensity throughout the life cycle to a level at least in line with the Earth's estimated carrying capacity." However, this statement is empty and does not offer tools to implement natural capital conservation. Since it does not challenge the tenets of eco-efficiency and its partial solution to environmental problems dictated by economic imperatives of the business realm, the BCSD is suspected of being engaged in an exercise in style.

To conclude this section, eco-efficiency became dominant in academic and professional writings because it is appealing for the business world to have a CSR attitude while sustaining economic performance (Callens and Tyteca, 1999). The words "change" or "changing" are used by the WBCSD in several reports (Changing Course; CSR meeting: changing expectations; a changing future for paper; signals of change; business progress toward sustainable development, and so on) to portray this philosophy as a new trend in doing business is only rhetoric and an act of communication used for persuasive strategy (Hunter, 1990). In the next section we portray another mainstream environmental management school of thought that proposes different tools for the same objective of capturing the ecological debate.

The Triple Bottom Line (TBL) School of Thought

Popularized by Elkington (1998), the TBL approach is a variant of socially responsible capitalism. What distinguishes this approach from the previous one is the concern for natural conservation. Elkington (1998) seems to be advocating for two new lines to be added to the conventional financial bottom line, and an aspiration to decrease absolute environmental impacts accordingly. The TBL School is more concerned with environmental effectiveness compared to the eco-efficiency approach. However, like eco-efficiency, it remains a win–win strategy that consists of permitting the reduction of ecological and human impacts while preserving a financial return in line with the constraint of the cost of capital. In fact, since the major preoccupation of financial capitalism is to maximize shareholder value, any ecological decision that might decrease financial return is to be forsaken.

To illustrate this new philosophy of environmental management, let's imagine that our farmer has decided to reduce the environmental impact of chemical fertilizer use during the second year of activity. He decides to use a new technology that permits a rational spreading of the chemical fertilizer and a reduction of the quantity used to 40 kilos (instead of 50) for the same level of production. If the rent of the special machinery to be used for spreading the chemical fertilizer is 170, and if the price of a kilo of fertilizer is 20, then his environmental net income amounts to 30 (20 × 10 kilos − 170). The profit and loss statement will show the following income:

Conventional management income	100
Environmental income	30
Total income	130

The second line of income shows the environmental performance of the farmer (a third line is to be associated with human capital management, if applicable). The total income is an increase, because the cost of the machinery is less than the savings from chemical fertilizer optimal use. If the cost of the new technology is more than 200, then the farmer would not have taken the ecological decision because he is driven by financial capital maintenance imperatives. Maintaining natural capital in this case would be akin to schizophrenic behavior. Like eco-efficiency, the TBL approach fails in solving the ecological issue in a systematic way since it does not question the SVM ideology.

In the last section we argue for new environmental management approaches (the eco-balances approach as well as the Cost Accounting for the Renewal of Environment (CARE) model), intended to deal with ecological problems in a systematic way to better achieve natural capital conservation. Both models require a fundamental transformation of the financial accounting system.

Toward New Approaches of Environmental Management

The first approach to be exposed in this section is developed by Dyckhoff (2000) while the second is elaborated by Richard (2012).

ECO-BALANCES APPROACH

The concept of eco-efficiency was elaborated by Schaltegger in association with other scholars, and then promoted by the WBCSD. Dyckhoff's (2000) central concept in his book "Umweltmanagement" is integrated management— "Integriertes Management". He was influenced by the work of Sankt Gall School, Switzerland, from one side and Ayres and Simonis (1994), two Americans who developed the principles of management around the so-called "industrial metabolism", from the other. Dyckhoff's writings are also influenced by ecological economists such as Costanza, Cumberland, Daly, Goodland, and Noorgard. He was also influenced by the work of two Swiss environmental business accountants, Müller-Wenck (1972) and Braunschweig (with Müller-Wenck, 1988), to whom belong the paternity of eco-balances.

Unlike the concept of eco-efficiency, Dyckhoff (2000) considers the approach he adopts to not be influenced by "economicity" ("Wirtschaftlichkeit"). In line with ecological economists like Daly (1994), Dyckhoff's (2000) sustainable management approach respects "circularity" ("Kreislaufprinzip") that is the basic ecological principle of conservation. He asserts that the economic activity is to be in the mode of circular economy ("Kreislaufwirtschaft") that is an economic system close to the functioning of any ecological system based on circularity. Also, sustainable management is to respect three rules:

1.   The extraction of nonrenewable resources is conditional upon their future replacement by renewable ones. This is possible only if profits from nonrenewable resources are to be invested to produce renewable ones.

2.   The exploitation of renewable resources is to be in respect of the limits of their regeneration.

3.   Pollution and waste emissions must occur within the limits of their absorption by nature.

For Dyckhoff, environmental impacts should be in line with the absorption capability of nature. The eco-balances approach requires a business to identify the nature of its environmental impacts and to compare it with the limits of absorption estimated by experts, with the objective of not infringing them. To illustrate this approach, let's consider that the eco-balance of the farm reveals that 50 kilos of nitrogen have been incorporated into the soil during the first year. If experts estimate 20 kilos is the maximum of nitrogen that can be absorbed without contaminating the groundwater, then the farmer is required to reduce the quantity of nitrogen by 30 kilos. The model to be exposed in the last section is intended to improve Dyckhoff's environmental management approach by introducing an accounting system that permits natural capital conservation.

THE CARE MODEL

The first serious attempts to design an accounting model that tends toward the conservation of natural capital were by Bebbington and Gray (2001) and Howes (2002). In this section we refer to a new attempt by Richard (2012) to achieve both natural and human capital conservation. In this attempt, an environmental balance sheet is proposed along with an environmental profit and loss statement. This new accounting approach is called CARE. CARE is based on four main successive stages. In the first stage, following Dyckhoff's concept of eco-balances and the principle of circularity, it is proposed to identify environmental and social gaps. Any human and ecological impact is to be compared with the limits fixed by independent experts under the supervision of stakeholders' representatives. If the gaps are negative, measures to restore or renew the ecological and human capitals altered by economic activity are to be identified and its cost calculated in the second stage. This does not require a valuation of the altered capital, or the cost of damage to be internalized as defended by the neo-classical approach of Pigou.[7] We do not need to incorporate a compensation cost. The purpose is only to maintain natural and human capitals in the same way as the financial one using different technical measures and adjustments. In the third stage, the restoration costs will be recorded in the profit and loss statement as depreciation expenses of natural and human capitals, which counterpart will be in the balance sheet as a credit in a contra-asset account (natural or human asset) or in a liability one. The CARE model is then characterized in terms of Three Depreciation Lines (TDL) instead of TBL.

To illustrate this new approach, let's imagine that our farmer has decided at the end of the first year to comply with the principles of circular economy and has reduced his consumption of chemical fertilizer by 30 kilos. For that purpose, he used a new type of farming based on semi-direct vegetal covering. The cost incurred in this new management method amounts to 670. Since savings from using less chemical fertilizer is 600 (30 kilos × 20), the net cost of this shift toward better conservation of natural capital is only 70. This cost is to be recorded as a depreciation expense of the soil in the profit and loss statement of the first year. The first year's profit and loss statement shows the following:

Net sales	1100
Cost of fertilizers (50 × 20)	1000
Depreciation expense of the soil	70
Net ecological income	30

Our ecological farmer must content himself with a small profit of 30 while the other financial farmers show an income of 100. If the income is totally distributed, the ecological farmer would have 1,070 at the beginning of the second year to buy 20 kilos of chemical fertilizers for 400 and the remaining 670 to be invested in new ecological management to preserve natural capital. The same reasoning will be applied to preserve human capital by considering any cost for a decent life, as expressed by Perroux (1952) and Passet (2000) as an expense to be recorded as a depreciation of human capital in the profit and loss statement.

---

7   In his book *The Economics of Welfare* (1938) A.C. Pigou states that companies should be taxed for the damage they cause to the environment. For him this is the way to internalize the cost they have been externalizing.

The fourth stage assures that the accumulated depreciation will be used for the only purpose of natural and human capital conservation. This step is fundamental for a real sustainability approach and strong conservation of capitals.

The CARE model is intended to assure a systematic maintenance of human and natural capital in the same way as traditional accounting was to assure the maintenance of financial capital. The first consequence of the model is the calculation of a new profit after considering depreciation of three main types of resources. This profit is the only real performance that results from a diligent management to deal with the depletion issue of human and natural capital. CARE profit corresponds to a true conception of capitalism which seriously encompasses all forms of capitals. The second major consequence is related to a new power distribution between representatives of the three types of capital in the governance process. The new power distribution is suggested to be proportional to the size of each capital or, in an equal way, in compliance with the principle of environmental co-determination (Richard, 2012). Contrary to the eco-efficiency and TBL approaches, the TDL of the CARE model is based on new concepts of profits and governance moving toward a strong conservation of all forms of capital.

Conclusion

The concept of eco-efficiency is portrayed in this chapter as an instrument used by the corporate world to capture the ecological debate within the boundaries of SVM ideology. The business community, with the help of a number of scholars, introduced in a proactive way an environmental initiative as a driving force to not undermine the doxic shareholder value creed. Eco-efficiency is a way to paint environmentally destructive practices green, and a scientific excuse for economic growth without due concern for environmental or social imperatives (Corporate Watch, 2006; Greenpeace, 2010). The destiny of the Earth and the whole eco-system is too important to be left to the corporate world imprisoned in the doxic SVM thinking. Friedman's (1970) argument against business responsibilities to factors other than the responsibility to maximize the profits for shareholders is no longer sufficient. The emergence of new guidelines to comprehend the effects of business activities on the society and the environment, as well as new management and governance approaches leading to sustainability, have become an emergency.

References and Bibliography

Ayres, R.U., and Simonis, U.K. (1994). *Industrial Metabolism: Restructuring for Sustainable Development.* Tokyo: United Nations University Press.

Business Council for Sustainable Development. (1993). *How Can Business Contribute to Sustainable Development? Getting Eco-Efficient.* UNEP.

Bebbington, J., and Gray, R. (2001). An Account of Sustainability: Failure, Success and a Reconceptualisation. *Critical Perspectives on Accounting,* Vol. 12(5), 557–605.

Bourdieu, P. (1977). *Outline of a Theory of Practice.* Cambridge: Cambridge University Press.

Bourdieu, P., and Passeron, J.C. (1977). *Reproduction in Education, Society and Culture.* London: Sage Publications Ltd.

Business Council of Sustainable Development (BCSD). (1993). *Getting Eco-efficient – Report of the Business Council for Sustainable Development,* First Antwerp Eco-efficiency workshop. Geneva. November.

Berle A. Jr., and Means, G.C. ([1932] 1982). *The Modern Corporation and Private Property.* New York: W.S Hein. Original edition published by Macmillan.

Braunschweig, A., and Müller-Wenck, R. (1988). *Ökobilanz für Unternehmungen. Ein Wegleiter für die Praxis.* Paul Haupt Verlag Ed.

Cadbury Report. (1992). http://www.ecgi.org/codes/documents/cadbury.pdf. Last accessed October 22, 2014.

Callens, I., and Tyteca, D. (1999). Towards Indicators of Sustainable Development for Firms: A Productive Efficiency Perspective. *Ecological Economics,* Vol. 28, 41–53.

Carroll, A.B. (1999). Corporate Social Responsibility: Evolution of a Definitional Construct. *Business and Society,* Vol. 38(3), 268–95.

Caroll, A.B. (1979). A Three-dimensional Conceptual Model of Corporate Performance. *Academy of Management Review,* Vol. 4(2), 497–505.

Corporate Watch Report. (2006). What is wrong with CSR: http://www. corporatewatch.org/sites/default/files/CSRreport.pdf. Last accessed October 22, 2014.

Daly, H.E. (1994). Operationalizing Sustainable Development by Investing in Natural Capital. In AnnMari Jansson et al. (eds), *Investing in Natural Capital: The Ecological Economics Approach to Sustainability*. Washington, DC: Island Press, 22–37.

Dahrendorf, R. (1972). *Classes et conflits de classes dans la société industrielle*. Paris: Mouton. Original edition (1957) *Soziale Klassen und Klassenconflik in der industriellen Gesellschaft*. Stuttgart: F. Enke.

De Simone, L.D., and Popoff, F. (2000). *Eco-efficiency. The Business Link to Sustainable Development*. Cambridge, MA: MIT Press.

Dyckhoff, H. (2000). The Natural Environment: Towards an Essential Factor of the Future. *International Journal of Production Research*, Vol. 38(12), 2583–90.

Edvardsson, B., and Enquist, B. (2009). *Values-based Service for Sustainable Business—Lessons From The Retailers IKEA, Starbucks, H&M and Bodyshop*. New York: Routledge.

Elkington, J. (1998). *Cannibals with Forks: The Triple Bottom Line of 21st Century Business*. New Society Publishers.

Erturk, I., Froud, J., Johql, S., Leqver, A., and Williams, K. (ed). (2008). *Financialization at Work: Key Texts and Commentary*. New York: Routledge.

Fama, E.F., and Jensen, M.C. (1983a). Agency Problems and Residual Claims. *Journal of Law and Economics*, Vol. 26(2), 327–49.

Fama, E.F., and Jensen, M.C. (1983b). Separation of Ownership and Control. *Journal of Law and Economics*, Vol. 26(2), 301–25.

Friedman, M. (1970). The Social Responsibility of Business is to Increase its Profits. *New York Times Magazine*, September 13.

Galbraith, J.K. ([1967] 2007). *The New Industrial State*. Princeton, NJ: Princeton University Press.

Global Reporting Initiative (GRI). (2010–11). *GRI: Inside (and) out.* https://www. globalreporting.org/resourcelibrary/GRI-Sustainability-Report-2010-2011.pdf. Last accessed October 22, 2014.

Greenpeace Annual Report. (2010). http://www.greenpeace.org/international/ Global/international/publications/greenpeace/2011/GPI_Annual_Report_ 2010.pdf. Last accessed October 22, 2014.

Holliday, Jr. C.O., Schmidheiny, S., and Watts, P. (2002). *Walking the Talk: The Business Case for Sustainable Development.* http://www.wbcsd.org/Pages/ EDocument/EDocumentDetails.aspx?ID=198andNoSearchContextKey=tr ue. Last accessed October 22, 2014.

Howes, R. (2002). *Environmental Cost Accounting: An Introduction and Practical Guide.* London: The Chartered Institute of Management Accountants.

Hunter, A. (1990). Introduction: Rhetoric in Research, Networks of Knowledge. In Hunter, A. (ed), *The Rhetoric of Social Research Understood and Believed.* Piscataway, NJ: Rutgers University Press.

Müller-Wenck, R. (1972). *Ökologische Buchhaltung. Eine Einführung.* St Gallen: Mimeo.

Passet, R. (2000). *L'illusion neo-liberale.* Paris: Fayard.

Perroux, F. (1952). *Les coûts de l'homme, Economie appliquée.* Janvier–mars.

Richard, J. (2012). Accounting and Sustainable Development (In French). *Economica.* Paris.

Schaltegger, S., Burritt, R., and Petersen, H. (2003). *An Introduction to Corporate Environmental Management: Striving for Sustainability.* Sheffield: Greenleaf Publishing.

Schaltegger, S., and Sturm, A. (1992/1994). *Environmentally Oriented Decisions in Firms.* Ökologieorientierte Entscheidungen in Unternehmen. Bern, Switzerland: Haupt-Verlag.

Schaltegger, S., and Sturm, A. (1990). Ökologische Rationalität: Ansatzpunkte zur Ausgestaltung von ökologieorientierten Managementinstrumenten. *Die Unternehmung*, Vol. 44(4), 273–290. Available only in German.

Schaltegger, S., and Sturm, A. (1989). Ökologie-induzierte Entscheidungsprobleme des managements. *Ansatzpunkte zur Ausgestaltung von Instrumenten.* (Ecology induced management decision support. Starting points for instrument formation). Discussion Paper No. 8914. Basel, Switzerland.

Schaltegger, S., and Wagner, M. (2006). Integrative Management of Sustainability Performance, Measurement and Reporting. *International Journal of Accounting, Auditing and Performance Evaluation,* Vol. 3(1), 1–19.

Schmidheiny, S. (1992). *Changing Course: A Global Perspective on Development and the Environment.* Cambridge, MA: MIT Press.

Schmidheiny, S., and Zorraquin F. (1998). *Financing Change: The Financial Community, Eco-efficiency, and Sustainable Development* (with the World Business Council for Sustainable Development). Cambridge, MA: MIT Press.

United Nations, ESCAP. (2009). *Eco-efficiency Indicators: Measuring Resource-Use Efficiency and the Impact of Economic Activities on the Environment:* http:// sustainabledevelopment.un.org/index.php?page=view&type=400&nr=785& menu=1301. Last accessed October 22, 2014.

United Nations Economic and Social Council. (2002). *Implementing Agenda 21: Report of the Secretary-General.* Commission on Sustainable Development acting as the preparatory committee for the World Summit on Sustainable Development, Second preparatory session, 28 January–8 February 2002.

Vogel, D. (2005). *The Market For Virtue: The Potential And Limits Of Corporate Social Responsibility.* NW, Washington DC: The Brookings Institution.

World Business Council for Sustainable Development (WBCSD). (2000). *Eco-efficiency: Creating More Value with Less Input.* Geneva.

World Business Council for Sustainable Development (WBCSD). (1996). *Eco-efficient Leadership for Improved Economic and Environmental Performance:* http://oldwww.wbcsd.org/Plugins/DocSearch/details.asp?DocTypeId=25&Obj ectId=Mjk5&URLBack=%2Ftemplates%2FTemplateWBCSD2%2Flayout.asp%3 Ftype%3Dp%26MenuId%3DODU%26doOpen%3D1%26ClickMenu%3DRight Menu%26CurPage%3D1%26SortOrder%3Dpubdate%2520ASC. Last accessed October 22, 2014.

World Commission on Environment and Development, United Nations. (1987). Our Common Future: http://conspect.nl/pdf/Our_Common_Future-Brundtland_Report_1987.pdf. Last accessed October 22, 2014.

Chapter 5

The Role of Small and Medium-sized Enterprises in Sustainable Development

REENA AGGARWAL, DANIEL GORFINE, AND DANA STEFANCZYK

Introduction

Sustainable businesses create economic value and vibrant communities. Small and medium sized enterprises (SMEs) are the engine of economic growth globally, making significant contributions to innovation, competitiveness, financial inclusion and employment. This paper examines the role of SMEs in sustainable development and discusses the challenges faced by these firms in raising capital. We also highlight examples of recent innovations in the United States and globally that allow SMEs easier access to finance.[1]

Role of SMEs Globally

The International Finance Corporation (IFC) describes SMEs as: "firms whose financial requirements are too large for microfinance, but are too small to be effectively served by corporate banking models" (IFC, 2010).

A strict definition is hard to find, however. The World Bank gives a classification under which firms must meet two of three requirements related to the number of employees, assets, or annual sales (see Table 5.1). The World Bank further defines businesses with fewer than ten employees as Micro Small Enterprises, and refers to the entire grouping of businesses as Micro Small and Medium Enterprises (MSMEs). In the United States official statistics typically refer to

1 We acknowledge the exceptional research assistance and contributions of Jackson Mueller. Aggarwal acknowledges financial support from the Robert E. McDonough endowment.

small businesses as being those with fewer than 50 employees and medium-sized enterprises as those with fewer than 500. Other criteria frequently used to identify SMEs include annual sales, assets, and size of outstanding loans or investments.

Table 5.1   **World Bank micro, small and medium enterprises (MSME) classification, 2005**

Firm size	Max Employees	Max Assets	Max Annual Sales
Micro	10	$10,000	$100,000
Small	50	$3 million	$3 million
Medium	300	$15 million	$15 million

Source: Significantly adapted from Ayyagari, Beck, and Demirgüç-Kunt (2003).

Though the strict definition can vary, fostering development of SMEs is a priority for both developed and emerging economies. SMEs are a primary driver of job creation and GDP growth. For example, in the United States SME activity contributes to nearly half of US private non-farm GDP, SMEs employ nearly 50 percent of the US private sector workforce,[2] and they are responsible for creating 67 percent of net new jobs in the economy from the end of the financial downturn in mid-2009 through to the end of 2011 (US Small Business Administration, 2012). Globally, SMEs contribute to economic diversification and social stability, and they play an important role in private sector development. A strong SME sector is seen as an indicator that the economy as a whole is healthy and dynamic.

SMEs also fill an important middle ground in an economy: more efficient than microenterprises, but more nimble and innovative than large firms. Moreover, they provide an important bridging function: frequently doing business with large corporations, as well as providing links to the formal sector for microenterprises. They are active at nearly every point in the value chain as producers, suppliers, distributors, retailers, and service providers, often in symbiotic relationships with larger businesses.

Critically, SMEs are also key drivers of innovation, and ensure that an economy remains dynamic and vibrant. For example, before innovator Cisco

2   http://www.sbecouncil.org/about-us/facts-and-data/.

Systems became the multibillion dollar tech giant it now is, it spent the better part of the early 1990s on the Forbes list of America's Best Small Companies.[3]

SMEs and Sustainable Development

In emerging economies, SMEs help to provide a strong base for economic activity. SMEs make up 30 to 35 percent of the business landscape, with multinational firms and large enterprises comprising only 1 percent (IFC Advisory Services, 2010). The SME sector is important to national economies because it contributes significantly to employment and GDP, and because its growth is linked with the formalizing of an economy. The following are key data points that highlight the role of SMEs.

ECONOMIC CONTRIBUTION

SME contribution to GDP in high-income countries, and in some middle-income countries, accounts for over half of national output. Ayyagari, et al. (2003) report that the median contribution to GDP of SMEs increases, based on country income. In low-income countries, on average, the SME sector contributes 16 percent to GDP. By contrast, in high-income countries, the SME sector contributes 51 percent.

EMPLOYMENT

Globally, SMEs employ more than one-third of the population (Kushnir et al., 2010). In 2009 the SME share of employment in lower-income countries such as the Middle East and North Africa (MENA) region was approximately 30 percent. For the upper-middle and high-income countries of the Organisation for Economic Co-operation and Development (OECD), SMEs represented nearly half of formal employment in 2009, demonstrating their increased contribution in more developed economies.

---

3   http://www.forbes.com/best-small-companies/.

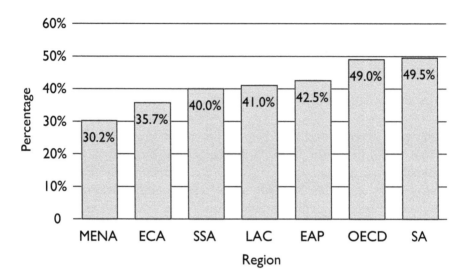

Figure 5.1   SME employment as a percentage of total private employment
Source: Adapted from Nasr, Sahar; Rostom, Ahmed. 2013. *SME Contributions to Employment, Job Creation, and Growth in the Arab World.* World Bank, Washington, DC. © World Bank. https://openknowledge.worldbank.org/handle/10986/16897 License: CC BY 3.0 IGO.

Beyond total employment, SMEs are also seen as a strong source of job creation, indeed smaller firms have higher employment growth rates than larger firms. The absolute importance of SMEs to job creation is measured in terms of the proportion of total new jobs that are created by SMEs. New firms generally start out small, falling under the category of SMEs. If successful, the firms may grow rapidly and account for a large share of total job growth in an economy (International Labor Organization, 2013). Thus, it is important to look at two factors: employment growth rate and current employment share. Even though many jobs are destroyed when start-ups go out of business, the net job creation in SMEs is higher than in large firms (IFC, 2010). In the United States, for example, if one subtracts jobs created by start-ups, the net employment growth rate is on average negative (IFC, 2010).

ADVANCING WOMEN'S RIGHTS

SMEs can also help address gender disparities. In Arab regions of the MENA, it has been found that women-owned SMEs tend to hire more female employees than male employees due to various factors including cultural traditions and work environment. Women also feel that there is less potential for harassment in women-owned SMEs than in male-owned SMEs. By increasing the number of female entrepreneurs, the share of women in the workforce may increase (Nasr and Rostom, 2013).

New financing mechanisms are needed to help women start businesses. Land is the most often used form of collateral, but since women are not allowed to own land in many countries capital access is a significant problem. Recognizing the importance of female-owned businesses, several institutions have taken steps to assist women in starting and growing their businesses. Commercial banks in both developing and developed countries have programs aimed toward female entrepreneurs. Microfinance institutions also play a role, with some developing programs that help women access larger loans. Government policies and domestic and international financial institutions can further enhance women's access to finance. In India, for example, the government developed a 14-point action plan for public sector banks to increase women's access to bank finance, though no formal evaluations of the results are available yet (Global Partnership for Financial Inclusion and IFC, 2011).

Innovations in SME Financing in a Developed Market

Despite the importance of SMEs, few countries have sufficiently broad and deep capital markets to meet the financial needs of smaller firms. Indeed, with respect to both low-income and many developed countries, studies frequently cite the lack of financial products and services as a key factor impeding the growth of the SME sector. In many countries, including throughout Europe, the vast majority of business financing comes from the traditional banking sector, which tends to favor lending to large corporations and national champions at the expense of SMEs. Capital markets in the United States are regarded as the exception to this rule given the diversity and depth of non-bank financing options (Milken Institute, 2012).

Since the financial crisis in 2008, however, problems with SME financing—even in the United States—have been exacerbated by the further retreat of banks. In many cases, banks are reacting to shifting market and regulatory dynamics by de-risking lending activity. In Europe and throughout the developing world, this issue has gained new prominence and was formally cited as a significant economic concern at the G20 summit in September 2009 (Association of Chartered Certified Accountants (ACCA), 2014). The crisis has highlighted that conventional banking alone is not sufficient to fulfill the needs of SMEs, and that financial innovation is necessary to ensure that these firms have access to capital needed to grow a business and hire workers.

A lack of viable equity financing options is also problematic—especially for high-growth businesses early in their development that lack consistent cash flows necessary for securing credit. There are only a few private equity firms that specialize in emerging-market SMEs, and equity financing models remain limited (McKinsey and IFC, 2010). Only the largest companies in many emerging economies have access to equity financing by way of national exchanges.

In a 2009 report from the Milken Institute entitled *Stimulating Investment in Emerging-Market SMEs*, the authors argue that if barriers to capital access were removed: "SMEs would impact economic development by providing jobs and income, expanding the middle class, broadening the tax base and ultimately decreasing poverty levels." In order to obtain such growth, several emerging markets have pursued financial innovations to attract capital and expand financing opportunities for local SMEs. The following national examples survey some of these innovations, but begin with developments in the United States given the depth and breadth of its capital markets, and the potential to replicate its innovative capital access models in emerging countries.

CAPITAL MARKET DEVELOPMENTS AND INNOVATION IN THE UNITED STATES

Since the financial crisis of 2008, access to capital for many SMEs in the United States has become increasingly restricted. Structural changes and the relative decline in the number of community and regional banks, coupled with increased risk-aversion, have led to a shortfall in bank lending. Meanwhile, a number of factors, including the real and perceived costs of public market participation, have contributed to a decline in initial public offerings (IPO) activity for small and medium-sized firms—enterprises raising less than $50 million made up nearly 80 percent of the market for most of the 1990s; today they account for less than 20 percent (Gorfine, 2014). Early-stage equity investors have also become increasingly risk averse with respect to certain industries or sectors. Reluctance to lend to or invest in SMEs has forced small and medium-sized companies to look for alternative ways to obtain needed capital in order to finance their operations and grow.

A number of innovative finance models have developed or are being developed in order to help satisfy the capital demands of SMEs. On the lending side federal and state small business programs and initiatives are intended to promote lending to smaller businesses, and Business Development Companies (BDCs) are increasingly serving a range of small and mid-sized companies. On the equity side, the Jumpstart Our Business Startups (JOBS) Act 2012 contains a number of key provisions that have the potential to resurrect the small company IPO, as well as facilitate the emergence of alternative investment and trading platforms. America's SMEs benefit when these various capital access tools operate in harmony and enable a company to meet its capital needs as it grows from a small to more mature entity.

DEBT MODELS

The predominant method of financing SMEs comes in the form of debt. Key structural changes to US markets, however, are shifting where and how SMEs access such capital. From its peak in 2008, the value of small business bank loans declined by 18 percent through 2011 (Cole, 2012). According to one report, bank lending to small businesses contracted by $100 billion between 2008 and 2011 (Cole, 2012).

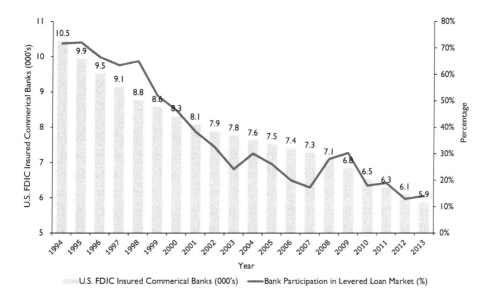

Figure 5.2   Bank consolidation and market share in non-investment grade lending

Source: Significantly adapted from Medley Capital Corporation (2014).

Meanwhile, lending standards have tightened throughout the banking industry in response to heightened domestic and international regulatory requirements. The effect of these rules may result in increased costs to community and regional banks, which could further reduce lending to SMEs. Moreover, bank consolidation and decreasing engagement with smaller borrowers will likely exacerbate the decline in overall SME lending activity.

With this backdrop, government-led and market-driven solutions to improving SME capital access have resulted in a number of innovative credit options for businesses. The following discusses these segments of SME debt markets in the United States and suggests how they might be adapted to serve as a model internationally.

Federal and state initiatives to spur lending

Federal and state-run initiatives seeking to promote lending to SMEs have had mixed results, but remain an important source of financing for many businesses. The Small Business Administration's (SBA) flagship 7a Loan Program offers guarantees on loans issued to SMEs by participating banks, so long as the borrowing SME satisfies certain SBA criteria and the lender complies with stringent SBA loan compliance requirements. Overall, SBA 7a loans totaled $17.9 billion in 2013, and when combined with a sister SBA loan program, made up approximately 4 percent of all small loans to SMEs (US SBA, 2014).

Unfortunately, due to the complexity and cost of participating in the SBA 7a loan program, participation rates amongst small and regional banks is quite low. They simply lack the resources to build internal teams focused on SBA compliance. State-run loan programs have attempted to fill this void with more streamlined and straightforward programs, but are significantly disadvantaged in that, unlike SBA lending programs, states cannot back their own guarantees with their state's taxing power. As a result, the value of a state guarantee program is limited as compared to the SBA program.

It is little wonder, then, that the Treasury Department's $1.5 billion State Small Business Credit Initiative (SSBCI), which is focused on deploying funds to SMEs through state-run programs, has only dispersed half of its funds to date with less than half of that funding being deployed by the states as of December 2013 (Congressional Research Service, 2013).

The SBA's Small Business Investment Company (SBIC) program, however, is frequently considered the model of a successful public–private partnership. Under the SBIC program, the SBA reviews and licenses investment funds focused on SME lending, and then provides the funds with subsidized loans that are ultimately deployed to SMEs. In 2013 SBIC-licensed funds provided more than $3 billion to more than 1,000 small businesses (US SBA, 2012). One of the more common structures for SBIC-licensed funds today is as a registered BDC—an increasingly important funding mechanism for America's SMEs discussed in the next section.

The growth of Business Development Companies (BDCs)

BDCs, a number of which seek licensing through the SBIC program, are a type of publicly registered investment company mandated to serve small and medium-sized business. BDCs are structured as pass-through entities, whereby the company avoids paying corporate income tax so long as more than 90 percent of all income is paid to investors by way of dividends. Many BDCs are publicly traded on national exchanges and permit retail investors access to SME lending markets, which are traditionally the domain of banks and private equity firms.

Given certain regulatory advantages and operational flexibility, BDCs have grown in importance in SME lending as traditional banks retreat from the space. It is estimated that there are currently 43 publicly traded and 11 non-traded BDCs (Segal, 2014), and BDC loan balances have grown from $15 billion just prior to the financial crisis to over $40 billion in 2013 (Deo, 2014). Contrast those numbers with 2003, when there were only three BDCs with combined assets of more than $2 billion (Oberbeck, 2014).

Going forward, the overall volume of BDC loans will likely increase as new participants enter the market. The continued success of the SBIC-licensing program will also play a key role in ensuring that BDCs serve smaller companies within the SME landscape. Given the participation of the general public in investing in BDCs, which then lend these funds out to SMEs, emerging markets should consider replicating this investment structure. It would provide an important alternative model to traditional banks, pool local sources of capital, and democratize the opportunity for the public to lend to their local businesses.

The growth of online lending models

Technology and the internet are also primed to play a growing role in small business lending. Innovative companies are building online platforms that combine elements of social networking, data analytics, and finance in a way that creates an efficient and scalable form of community banking. More specifically, these platforms permit networks of individuals and institutional investors to lend to small businesses at rates that are competitive with traditional banks. Automated analytics allow these platforms to qualify loans quickly and at low cost.

Indeed, so called "big data" analytics are increasingly providing new ways to assess creditworthiness of firms, such as delivering credit scoring based on airtime usage. A company called ZestFinance, for example, uses data from thousands of potential credit variables to offer a "big data underwriting model" (Pearce and Fathallah, 2014). Alternative assessments of creditworthiness that do not rely on traditional credit scores, and instead may look at variables such as online reputation and social media analytics, hold significant promise for SMEs in all countries, including those that lack traditional credit-tracking infrastructure.

To date in the United States, however, online lending platforms have concentrated on consumer loans, and are now facilitating billions of dollars of lending annually. Attention is now turning to small businesses, with industry leader Lending Club recently announcing its entry into the small business lending space (Lending Club, 2014). Yield-starved institutional investors, meanwhile, are lining up to deploy capital through the online lending platforms, thereby hastening the development of this online marketplace.

Services are also needed to appropriately match entrepreneurs with potential investors. The internet creates a possible solution whereby an intermediary platform can effectively serve as a broker between interested parties. The BiD Network, for example, was created in 2008 as this type of matchmaking service, and in the first formal year of operation facilitated 19 matches and total investments of $2.8 million. Matching can also be facilitated through internet information-exchange platforms, which would mirror the model of peer-to-peer lending organizations by allowing investors to access online profiles of small businesses and potentially provide them with microfinance loans (Milken Institute, 2009).

The development of online lending markets will, however, inevitably run up against existing regulatory frameworks that do not contemplate the role of the internet and peer-to-peer models in small business lending. Additionally, innovative credit risk assessment technologies have yet to be tested by a negative turn in the credit cycle, and may raise questions regarding transparency and fairness. Despite the potential for hiccups and hurdles along the way, however, the internet's role in providing capital to small businesses is here to stay, and will inevitably expand to foreign markets.

EQUITY MODELS

Three elements inform recent developments in equity financing in the United States for SMEs. First, following the financial crisis in 2008, traditional equity investors in start-ups and small businesses attempted to de-risk investment by focusing on more mature companies; at the same time, these investors focused on specific high-growth sectors and geographic regions, leaving many companies behind. Second, the internet and modern forms of communication increasingly proved at odds with existing securities laws that restricted how companies seeking to raise capital could communicate with the public. And finally, an effort to democratize investment opportunity gained momentum with specific calls to permit retail investors the chance to invest in a sector that historically was only available to high net worth individuals or private equity investors. The result of these dynamics was the bipartisan JOBS Act 2012, which has resulted in the following notable developments in equity investing.

The birth of crowd investing

The JOBS Act 2012 is perhaps best known for legalizing crowd investing: essentially a model that builds on donation, perk, or pre-order crowdfunding models made popular by sites such as Kickstarter and Indiegogo, except now with the opportunity to buy small equity shares (or debt) in an SME. Though not yet live in the United States until regulators finalize rules, a company will be able to raise up to $1 million within a 12-month period from the general public through a qualified internet platform. In order to limit downside risk, investors are subject to annual investment caps based on their income or wealth. There are also required annual corporate disclosures, investor education requirements, and limits on the nature of general advertising.

The growth of crowdfunding and crowd investing globally, and the ease with which individuals can use the internet to channel funds to promising entrepreneurs and businesses, offers many countries a new channel for funding SMEs. Indeed, given major capital access problems for SMEs in Europe, it is not surprising to see a number of European countries, including Italy and the Netherlands, issuing recent legislation legalizing securities for crowd investing. Going forward, crowd-investing models may also build on existing microfinance internet models, such as Kiva, to facilitate the flow of capital to SMEs in emerging markets. Other international crowdfunding platforms include Cumplo in Chile, ideame in Latin America, and Funding Circle in the UK (Pearce and Fathallah, 2014).

Mass marketing of private offerings

Another portion of the JOBS Act 2012 makes significant changes to how private securities offerings may be marketed. Private securities offerings are exempt from traditional registration with securities regulators in the United States, but historically could only be advertised to select groups of so called accredited investors (which includes wealthy individuals and traditional investment funds). Due to changes in existing law, companies are now permitted to mass market private offerings to the general public as long as the ultimate buyers are verified to be accredited investors. This new tool is permitting companies to use modern forms of communication, including the internet, to access a far broader pool of potential investors. In many respects the opening of the internet to the marketing of private offerings adds transparency to previously opaque markets, and offers to increase the efficiency of matching investors with small businesses.

On a global scale, the opening of private markets to new internet-based platforms could facilitate deeper and more global venture capital and private equity markets. Additionally, the gradual blurring of the line between online investment platforms, alternative trading systems, and exchanges is being hastened by the internet, and may foreshadow a time where exchanging securities in private companies will more readily become an international activity, as opposed to hyper-national. International networks or platforms that facilitate SME investment could help connect SMEs in emerging economies to otherwise inaccessible pools of capital.

Facilitating a mini-IPO

The decline of small company IPOs in the United States is well-documented. While there are many factors contributing to the decline, many point to an overly-burdensome disclosure, compliance, and governance regime that renders the costs too high for small company participation in public markets. The JOBS Act 2012 includes provisions that essentially create a streamlined mini-IPO registration process for offerings of up to $50 million with the aim of right-sizing regulatory costs for the small size of the offering.

Securities sold through this so called Regulation A+ exemption could be marketed to the general public and resold in secondary markets without restriction.

Efforts such as the one included in the JOBS Act 2012 to create a viable framework for small company IPOs could provide important new capital-raising tools to SMEs. Securities sold in this way could also reside and trade on alternative trading systems made available through the internet, and increase public participation in these markets. Some anticipate that large exchanges will develop subsidiary or partnered alternative trading systems for smaller companies that would eventually list on the full exchange once they reach a sufficient size.

Innovations in Emerging Markets

Innovation in SME financing is also taking place in many emerging markets. We provide a few examples below.

SUPPLY CHAIN FINANCE IN MEXICO

Nacional Financiera (NAFIN) in Mexico created a reverse factoring initiative to assist high-risk suppliers through their links to large corporate buyers. Once a buyer agrees to pay on the due date, suppliers' accounts receivable are discounted on a non-recourse basis, thus transferring credit risk to the buyer. Two options are available:

1.   factoring without any collateral or service fees, at variable risk-adjusted rates;

2.   contract financing, which provides financing for up to 50 percent of contract orders from big buyers, again with no fees or collateral, and a fixed rate.

Such arrangements are particularly attractive to SMEs, who often supply to much larger firms and can borrow based on their buyer's credit rating. In developing countries, where financial information structure is weak, these mechanisms provide a good source of funding. Training and assistance are also provided. As of mid-2009, the program had 455 big buyers, more than 80,000 SMEs, and had extended over $60 billion in financing (IFC, 2010).

VENTURE CAPITAL MARKETS IN BRAZIL

The Inovar program created an SME venture capital (VC) market in Brazil, and has since been replicated in Peru and Colombia. It was designed in 2001 by Financiadora de Estudos e Projetos (FINEP) in partnership with the Inter-American Development Bank. Aimed primarily to support new, technology-based SMEs, the program created a platform to share research and information and developed managerial capacity to increase VC investments. The portal has over 2,650 registered entrepreneurs and over 200 investors. FINEP also created a Technology Investment Facility for investors to analyze VC funds, resulting in over five joint due diligences with approximately $165 million committed/approved in 15 VC funds. Finally, the program has created forums for SMEs to interact with potential investors, resulting in 45 SMEs receiving more than $1 billion in funding (IFC, 2010).

ECONOMIC CRISIS SUPPORT IN TURKEY

The Union of Chambers and Commodity Exchanges of Turkey (TOBB) created the TOBB Support Program in 2001. The program brings together 16 Chambers and Commodity Exchanges in Turkey to support SME exporters during crises. Funds from TOBB and its members are used to:

- buy commercial paper issued by Export Credit Bank of Turkey;

- make one-year deposits in Halkbank.

The pools of funds can be used to provide loan packages for SMEs at below-market rates. As of 2010, the program had facilitated $813 million in funding to 33,192 SMEs.

FINANCING WOMEN-OWNED SMES IN NIGERIA

The Enterprise Development Center (EDC), Fate Foundation, and IFC created a program in Nigeria to support African financial institutions and to finance women-owned SMEs. The program has three components:

1.   advisory services to financial institutions;

2.   capacity building for banks to increase growth prospects of women-owned businesses, including training on financial literacy and business planning;

3.   investments by the IFC to support increased lending to women-owned SMEs.

From 2006–2010, the program lent over $35.5 million and trained nearly 700 women (IFC, 2010).

LENDING AND EQUITY FUNDING IN CHINA

Alipay Financial was launched in June 2010 by Chinese e-commerce platform Alibaba. Alipay, a micro-credit company, offers loans from its own cash resources to SME users of its e-commerce service. The company uses transaction and payment data as a proxy for reliable third-party credit information, allowing them to assess risk. Thirty-day working capital advances of up to RMB500,000 were initially provided to fund sales via Taobao, their online marketplace. The company has since expanded and has begun offering a wider range of products. Larger loans are offered to groups of three SMEs acting as guarantors for each other. Later, Alipay Financial began originating loans on behalf of China Construction Bank and the Industrial and Commercial Bank (ICBC) of China to expand its lending capacity. In the first two years, Alipay Financial had made loans worth approximately RMB13bn (ACCA, 2014).

In the United States and Europe, similar alternative financing mechanisms have been started. Reuters reported in September 2012 that e-commerce giant Amazon had begun to offer funding under a program called Amazon Lending. The program is said to offer advances of up to $800,000 per year to some merchants and charging interest rates of 1 percent to 13 percent per year (ACCA, 2014). Meanwhile, the payment company, Square, is now offering customized loans to vendors that use the Square payment system based on individualized credit risk assessments made possible through the payments data (Wagner, 2014). Many of these developments are closely related to the peer-to-peer online lending models discussed in the section on United States innovation above.

LENDING AND MOBILE PAYMENTS IN AFRICA

Efficient access to capital is critical to the growth of SMEs. Traditional loans can take at least six months to be approved, delaying necessary business activities. Services such as M-shwari, a product of M-Pesa, have added loan options by piggybacking off basic mobile payment services. M-shwari has partnered with the Commercial Bank of Africa (CBA) and offers small loans from about $1 up to $235. This service has greatly increased bank account creation at CBA, with 2.15 million bank accounts opened in three months, making it the second largest retail bank in Kenya (ACCA, 2014). Since the service was launched more than 6 million Kenyans now use the service, receiving nearly $90 million in loans, with M-shwari experiencing a default rate of less than 3 percent on the money lent out (Mirani, 2014).

SMEs often have limited infrastructure and need to accept credit card payments on the go. Companies like iZettle, similar to Square, enable customers to accept credit card payments through swipe technology. As smartphones are increasingly being used to accept payments, banks are becoming increasingly distanced from the payment process. Some banks have innovated along with this trend, such as OCBC Bank in Singapore. OCBC created an app for customers to scan barcodes, obtain billing details, and make payments to merchants.

In Africa, the increasing popularity and prevalence of mobile phones has enabled users to send and receive small sums of money on their phones. M-Pesa in East Africa is one such service, which had approximately 20 million users in 2013 (ACCA, 2014). It is now operated by Vodafone and is available in other countries including Afghanistan and India. Similarly, Ecocash enables users to complete simple financial transactions such as sending money to friends or family and paying for goods. Textacash, a service of CABS, allows Zimbabweans to obtain financial services such as balance enquiries, mini-statements, and inter-account transfers through a mobile phone.

General Innovations

In addition to country-specific programs and initiatives, several innovations help SMEs more generally.

RISK-ADJUSTED INVESTMENT RETURNS

Investors frequently complain that SME investment returns are not sufficient on a risk-adjusted basis. In order to solve this problem, funds may be structured more efficiently to cut costs and increase net returns. Smaller funds have high costs relative to overall revenue, while larger funds can reduce costs through economies of scale. Funds could focus on regional application instead of being limited to one country, and multiple funds could consider joining together to drive cost reductions.

A second solution to this issue is to provide technical assistance funds, paid for by grant-based pools, side-by-side with investment funds. Commercial investors would be attracted to these funds due to their higher net return, a result of cost reductions for the fund itself and improved performance of the portfolio business. Technical assistance carries a high cost, but can be one of the best ways to mitigate investment risk. Unfortunately, it can be difficult to sustain funding over time, and so it is important to ensure that funders remain committed.

To encourage banks to supply more capital to SMEs, local governmental institutions could provide guarantees to local banks to cover investment losses, akin to the United States SBA lending programs. Guarantees can also decrease currency risk in the case of default by basing payment in a more stable, foreign currency. Shared Interest is a New York-based nonprofit organization that offers loan guarantees to South African banks. They have found that their guarantees alter bank behavior and risk-appetite, thereby increasing their willingness to lend to SMEs (Milken Institute, 2009).

EXIT MECHANISMS

In emerging markets, exiting investments can be difficult, discouraging investors in the first place. One innovation is to create an exit finance facility. The Overseas Private Investment Corporation (OPIC) is developing a self-sustaining exit vehicle to make capital available to the entrepreneur or a third party to buy out the investor. SMEs contribute some capital to the fund, and OPIC or another financial institution would provide the balance. Standards would need to be established for the type of investments to be funded, and the facility would only fund those entrepreneurs most likely to repay the loan.

A second innovation is to create a permanent capital vehicle (PCV) to facilitate an investor's exit, thereby lowering some of the risk and increasing the willingness of investors to provide capital. In general, a PCV is an investment entity for managing capital for an unlimited time horizon, such as pension funds or social security funds.[4] In the case of SMEs, one type of PCV could structure funds more efficiently and provide a more sustainable source of capital, similar to the format of a BDC in the United States. Shares of the fund would be liquid and could be readily traded, facilitating investor exit. It would decrease investment costs by reducing start-up and other administrative expenses, preventing the need to create a new fund. Furthermore, a PCV reduces the pressure on fund managers to exit and pay off investors, keeping investments in place longer. These benefits would offer SMEs the possibility of achieving risk-adjusted returns.

The second type of PCV would be similar to a mezzanine buyout fund. Once their investment companies are somewhat stable, investors could sell their equity interests into this structure, largely a bond fund with 30 or more holdings. The fund would produce income and returns for the investors. It would not take any venture risk, but would incentivize early risk-takers.

Finally, deals could involve royalties, allowing investors to share in the profits of a company. Since the investor does not hold an ownership stake, downsides are minimized. Business Partners Ltd.[5] has pioneered the use of such royalties, obtaining revenue from the investee without taking equity (Milken Institute, 2009). They have a set minimum in royalty payments, so that even when the company experiences a loss, Business Partners Ltd. receives a smaller payment.

Conclusion

It is widely recognized that SMEs play a critical role in sustainable development of a country's economy. They are the driver of economic growth, job creation, and innovation. A major challenge faced by SMEs is access to financing, and this barrier impedes the growth of the SME sector. As discussed in this paper, both developed and emerging markets have pursued innovative approaches to make debt and equity financing more readily available to SMEs. Several of these programs have been initiated by the private sector while others are administered by governments. Reviewing the global landscape of capital access tools can hopefully spread ideas and best practices that can be tailored for the needs of each country's SME sector.

---

4   www.investopedia.com.
5   Business Partners Ltd. is a South African SME investment company.

References and Bibliography

ACCA. (2014). *Innovations in Access to Finance for SMEs.* London: Association of Chartered Certified Accountants.

Ayyagari, M., Demirgüç-Kunt, A., and Beck, T. (2003). *Small and Medium Enterprises across the Globe: A New Database.* Policy Research Working Paper 3127. The World Bank Group.

Cole, Rebel A. (2012). *How Did the Financial Crisis Affect Small Business Lending in the United States?* U.S. Small Business Administration.

Dilger, R., (2013). *State Small Business Credit Initiative: Implementation and Funding Issues.* Congressional Research Service.

Deo, L.P. (2014). *RLPC: FSIC Readies NYSE Listing.* www.reuters.com, April 1.

Frequently Asked Questions. (2012). U.S. Small Business Administration.

FY 2015 Congressional Budget Justification and FY 2013 Annual Performance Report. (2014). US Small Business Administration.

Gorfine, D. (2014). *How the Feds Can Save the IPO Market.* www.marketwatch. com, May 9.

GPFI and IFC. (2011). *Strengthening Access to Finance for Women-Owned SMEs in Developing Countries.* October.

IFC. (2010). *Scaling-Up SME Access to Financial Services in the Developing World.* October.

IFC Advisory Services. (2010). *The SME Banking Knowledge Guide.*

Deijl, C., Kok, J., and Veldhuis-Van-Esssen, C., (2013). *Is Small Still Beautiful?* International Labor Organization. April 16.

Kushnir, K., Mirmulstein, M.L., and Ramalho, R. (2010). *Micro, Small, and Medium Enterprises Around the World: How Many Are There, and What Affects the Count?* World Bank/IFC.

Lending Club. (2014). *Lending Club Launches Business Loans.* March 20.

Stein, P., Goland, T., and Schiff, R. (2010). *Two Trillion and Counting: Assessing the Credit Gap for Micro, Small, and Medium-Size Enterprises in the Developing World*. McKinsey and IFC. October.

Mirani, L. (2014). *How to Manage All your Financial Affairs from a $20 Mobile Phone*. www.qz.com, June 19.

Nasr, S., and Rostom, A. (2013). *SME Contributions to Employment, Job Creation, and Growth in the Arab World*. Policy Research Working Paper 6682. The World Bank Group, October.

Oberbeck, C. (2014). *BDCs Provide Capital*. www.themiddlemarket.com, April 3.

Pearce, D., and Fathallah, S. (2014). *Rethinking SME Finance Policy – Harnessing Technology and Innovation*. blogs.worldbank.org, March 10.

The Milken Institute. (2012). *Size and Composition of Financial Systems Differ Widely Among G-20 Member Countries*. www.globalbanking.org.

Scherer, J., Yago, G., and Zeidman, B., (2009). *Stimulating Investment in Emerging-Market SMEs*. The Milken Institute, October.

US Small Business Administration. (2012). *The SBIC Program FY 2012 Annual Report*.

Segal, J. (2014). *BDCs Take Off as Mainstream Investors Seek Credit Alternatives*. www.institutionalinvestor.com, January 28.

Wagner, K. (2014). *Square's New Business Strategy: Lend Money to Small Businesses*. www.mashable.com, May 28.

http://www.forbes.com/best-small-companies. Last accessed May 2014.

http://www.investopedia.com. Last accessed May 2014.

http://www.medleycapitalcorp.com. Last accessed May 2014.

http://www.sbecouncil.org/about-us/facts-and-data. Last accessed May 2014.

Chapter 6

The Governance Mindset: Is Sustainability a Board Issue?

CORAL INGLEY

Introduction

This chapter is presented in two parts and draws initially on the findings from two studies conducted within the last decade among directors across a wide range of large New Zealand corporate entities in relation to their perceptions and understandings of the concept and practice of governance. The two separate studies sampled a closely similar director population and were conducted approximately six years apart in 2003 and 2009. Both studies examined directors' attitudes and perceptions regarding various aspects of their governance role and board tasks. The two studies are thus suitable for comparison with regard to boards' priorities for sustainability, and any shifts in these priorities that might have occurred among boards in the interim between the earlier and later studies.

From the earlier study, conducted in 2003, it was apparent that the concepts relating to sustainability and corporate social responsibility had yet to move from the margins to the mainstream in corporate thinking and be taken seriously as a strategic issue. The later study, conducted in 2009, revealed that because the discourse of conformance (compliance) overwhelmingly dominates other principal modes of governance discourse, such as strategy and innovation, and notions of sustainability, ethical behavior, and risk management, these modes are unintentionally suppressed. Despite an interval of more than half a decade between the two studies, boards in New Zealand companies did not appear to have become significantly more externally oriented in their focus and remained fixated on the compliance dimension of their governance role. These two studies suggest that stakeholder relationships and corporate sustainability have not been part of the stream-of-consciousness among directors when it comes to governance—that is until a recent event which brought corporate social responsibility and the strategic significance of sustainability into sharp focus. Not only did the issues surrounding this event impact profoundly on the corporation concerned and bring into question its governance competence at the top of the company, there were also serious flow-on implications for the entire New Zealand economy.

The first part of this chapter considers conceptual aspects of corporate governance and sustainability as a theoretical background, and then summarizes the two studies conducted among corporate boards and senior executives. The second part of the chapter presents a short case study which lends support to the findings from the two studies with regard to the corporate mindset that prevailed up to the events described in the case study. The wider implications are that for corporations and indeed governments, sustainability is not just a fancy concept with little if any day to day real business relevance.

Theoretical Background

Corporate governance is topical in the public domain and the concept of corporate sustainability has gained increasing importance in recent years as organizations face pressures to be socially and environmentally responsible corporate citizens. Many companies now publish reports on their triple bottom line performance and on sustainability themes. However, there is little general agreement over what constitutes corporate sustainability and how it can best be achieved. Current approaches vary, ranging from adaptations of products and processes for resource efficiency and pollution reduction, to stakeholder and community engagement initiatives. Some organizations have sought to change their values and beliefs as part of a culture change aligned with adopting a corporate-wide philosophy of social responsibility.

Given that a top-down approach is often used to introduce sustainability initiatives (Harris and Crane, 2002), a key question concerns the attitudes and perceptions of the organization's leadership and, in particular, the board of directors, toward their governance and leadership role in supporting or driving sustainability. Linnenluecke et al. (2007) suggested from their study that organizational leaders may have a different understanding of corporate sustainability than employees at other levels in the organization, and questioned the assumption made by researchers that sustainability values are disseminated in a top-down manner.

Conceptual Understandings of Corporate Sustainability

Corporate sustainability has different meanings to different people and there are many definitions of the concept in the literature. Russell et al. (2007) identified four distinct categories of conceptual understanding, noting that these understandings of corporate sustainability vary by organization type according to differences in the arrangement of their governance structures. These authors defined the concept as pertaining to a corporation that is working toward long-term performance and positive outcomes for the natural environment, as well as supporting people and social outcomes, and is adopting a holistic approach to sustainability across the business.

The Global Reporting Initiative's (GRI) *Sustainability Reporting Guidelines* (2013) state that:

- Environmental impact refers to an organization's impact on living and nonliving natural systems, including eco-systems, land, air and water. Examples include energy use and greenhouse gas emissions.

- Economic impact means an organization's impact both direct and indirect on the economic resources of its stakeholders and on economic systems at the local, national and global levels.

- Social impact relates to an organization's impact on the social system within which it operates. This includes labor practices, human rights and other social issues.

In *Business for Social Responsibility* White, (2006) defines corporate sustainability as: "achieving commercial success in ways that honour ethical values and respect people, communities and the natural environment." According to Schacter (2005), corporations that espouse sustainability must address social, environmental, and economic demands from stakeholders, and not just financial demands from shareholders. For companies, irrespective of where they are located or operating, this understanding obliges them to be responsive to the legal, ethical, commercial, and other expectations society has for business, and to make decisions that address fairly the interests and claims of all key stakeholders (Cramer and Hirschland, 2006; Schacter, 2005).

In addition to a multiplicity of definitions, the rapidly developing interest in corporate sustainability has led to a variety of terms in the literature. The terms used, sometimes interchangeably, to describe the concept include business ethics, corporate citizenship, corporate accountability, and corporate social responsibility. Interpretations of the concept range from a basic level of engagement to the most demanding degree of system-wide commitment (Clarke, 2007; Russell et al., 2007; Schacter, 2005).

The attention being paid to social sustainability has emerged from trends such as globalization and privatization, requiring businesses to assume wider responsibilities in relation to various stakeholder groups and the social environment in which they operate (Carroll, 1999; Dunphy et al., 2003; Freeman, 1984). Numerous studies have published results concerning business-related social issues, including occupational health and safety, discrimination, business ethics, fraud, corporate philanthropy, minority concerns, community welfare, and stakeholder demands (Carroll, 1979; Preston, 1986; Shrivastava, 1995). More recent to emerge are concepts such as "socially sustainable businesses" (Gladwin et al., 1995) and "corporate social sustainability" (Dyllick and Hockerts, 2002).

In the traditional strategy and management literature the term corporate sustainability is used to refer to economic performance, growth, and long-term profitability of organizations (Peteraf, 1993; Porter, 1985). Behind this understanding of sustainability is the key assumption that the firm operates in the interests of its owners (in other words, shareholders) to maximize their wealth. Accordingly, it is thus essential for management to expand consumption of the firm's products and services so as to increase its profits. In this view investments that may be socially or ecologically desirable, but that do not benefit directly the firm's shareholders, should not be undertaken because they result in inferior returns to shareholders relative to other firms (Friedman, 1970; Levitt, 1958; White, 1995. Conversely, studies have suggested that economic returns alone are insufficient for overall corporate sustainability. Such studies have found that improved firm performance and greater competitive advantage can result when firms adopt a social sustainability orientation. A broadening of the understanding of corporate sustainability in this way represents the most significant departure of the concept from orthodox management and governance theory, which is focused on profit maximization for the benefit of shareholders.

Boards, Governance and Corporate Sustainability

It is notable that while corporate sustainability has progressed from being a marginal concept to being accepted as part of the mainstream business agenda, the concept has only recently begun to emerge in relation to corporate governance and the fiduciary role of the board. Corporate sustainability is most closely aligned conceptually with the stakeholder perspective in corporate governance, and is only beginning to emerge as a focus for discourse and study in this literature.

The dominant view in corporate governance is that of the agency perspective, which focuses on management and shareholders/owners as the sole constituents and the alignment of their potentially conflicting interests for better governance practice. It is agency theory that underlies the shareholder model of capitalism. In contrast, stakeholder theory—which incorporates aspects of three theories: agency theory, stewardship theory, and the resource-based view—is a more inclusive approach because it takes into account multiple constituents in the corporate social context and the obligation by corporations to act as socially responsible citizens (Ingley and van der Walt, 2004). While agency theory underpins the shareholder model of capitalism, the stakeholder perspective has led to the emergence of a stakeholder model of capitalism.

Kiel and Nicholson (2003) contended that, like agency and stewardship theories, stakeholder theory seeks to explain corporate performance. However, it differs from both perspectives over who should have ultimate control in managing corporate entities. While agency and stewardship theories differ as to whether control should be the province of directors or owners, both perspectives are based on the central premise of shareholder wealth maximization (Kiel and Nicholson, 2003). Stakeholder theory, in contrast, places ultimate control in the social domain with equitably shared benefits as the outcome of wealth generation, although this is a contested view since the firm then assumes the nature of a public good rather than the rights of property ownership (Charron, 2007). The view that directors owe a fiduciary duty to corporate stakeholders other than shareholders has also been criticized on the basis of a conflict over serving two masters, but is countered by company law,[1] which states that directors owe their fiduciary duty not to shareholders but to corporate entities (Kiel and Nicholson, 2003; Kostant, 1999). According to the stakeholder perspective, directors must serve as stewards of communication, or mediators, among corporate stakeholders, a role which is considered essential for efficiency and co-operation in today's global economy (Healy, 2003; Perrini, 2006).

---

1   At least in Anglo Saxon jurisdictions, for example, in OECD and Commonwealth countries, such as the United States and New Zealand.

Kiel and Nicholson (2003) highlighted the different emphases placed by the shareholder and stakeholder models of corporate governance, respectively, on different aspects of corporate behavior. Accountability is emphasized in the shareholder model, while long-term stability to develop competitive advantage is central to the stakeholder model. The shareholder model is argued to have the advantage of allowing the market to control the system, and thus tending to make corporations more publicly accountable while allowing rapid decision-making for greater responsiveness by companies to changes in strategic direction (Kiel and Nicholson, 2003). Despite stakeholder theory's claims for the importance of stakeholder engagement in creating sustainable organizations, this perspective is limited when seeking to address issues relating to risk (Benn and Dunphy, 2007). The problem concerns the operationalization of a system of governance that integrates the concerns of both human and non-human stakeholders, and addresses simultaneously both economic and environmental goals.

Concurrent with the mainstreaming of corporate sustainability, what constitutes the board's fiduciary duty has also expanded requiring new structures for considering social and environmental issues that have not been part of the board's oversight role in the past and for which they may not have the skills to address (Cramer and Hirschland, 2006). As highlighted by Clarke (2007) board members until recently have tended to view the notion of corporate sustainability as grandiloquence aimed at mollifying environmentalists and human rights campaigners. With the increase in public attention on social and environmental issues, boards are beginning to realize that sustainability issues have a direct impact not only on financial performance but also on corporate reputation and other intangible assets (Schacter, 2005). According to Clarke (2007) leading edge companies are now regarding corporate sustainability as part of a normal business agenda. Moreover, they are also considering ways of developing internal structures and processes to give it greater emphasis. By being instrumental in shaping and overseeing corporate sustainability strategies and actively engaged in being a responsible and responsive enterprise, boards can strengthen their potential as a strategic influence on long-term value creation (Cramer and Hirschland, 2006; Davies, 1999; Healy, 2003; Kiel and Nicholson, 2003; Schacter, 2005). Predictions are that companies which are not focusing on corporate sustainability may, in the near future, be regarded as outliers (Clarke, 2007; Massie, 2003), while evidence suggests that there is a marked difference between the financial performance of environmental leaders and laggards.[2]

---

2   Corporate environmental governance: A study into the influence of environmental governance and financial performance http://www.environment-agency.gov.uk/business/444255/887223/1251983/?lang=_e.

The growing complexity in the global marketplace together with increasing demands from stakeholders for greater regulatory control of boards, more transparency in governance reporting, and higher standards of board performance mean that directors are under increasing pressure to govern their organizations effectively (Garratt, 2003; Ingley and van der Walt, 2001). Boards are consequently required to be more accountable not only to shareholders but also to other stakeholders, and to be more professional in their directorship (Bosch, 1995; Davies, 1999; Hawkins, 1997).

The Earlier Study

The earlier study conducted in 2003 (Ingley, 2008) examined the responses by 418 board executive and non-executive directors to survey questions, which included socially-related aspects of their governance role and reported on their external orientation and receptiveness toward wider social obligations. The key question concerned the extent to which these companies aligned more closely with the shareholder orientation advocated by Friedman (1970), or with the wider sustainability perspective promoted by Massie (2003) and the GRI (2002) as reflected in the boards' view of their governance role with regard to their external (community) relationships and social responsibilities.

Key indicators in the study, with regard to the board's task focus, included reviewing social responsibilities, developing corporate vision, leading strategic change, and taking responsibility for the ethical conduct of the organization's activities. Rated on a five-point scale, and ranked in order of importance, the majority of respondents (94.7 percent) regarded the board's involvement in strategy as important or very important, followed closely by evaluating CEO performance (93.7 percent), determining risk exposure (92.8 percent), and responsibility for ethical conduct (88.7 percent). All of these board tasks are conventional responsibilities for directors and present no surprises with regard to the relative importance assigned to each indicator. However, the task of reviewing social responsibilities was rated as important or very important by significantly fewer respondents (54.0 percent) and ranked low overall among other board tasks.

The relatively weak competence of boards was particularly notable from the study regarding their effectiveness in representing shareholder interests and the external focus by boards on stakeholder issues. While close to 40 percent of respondents reported a strong influence in their company's relationship with shareholders, only 20 percent rated their board's influence as strong regarding relationships with key stakeholder groups. Moreover, fewer than 10 percent of respondents rated non-executive directors on their boards as highly effective in representing shareholders' interests and understanding stakeholders' issues. These results suggest that the boards in these companies were neither fully cognizant of the importance of engaging with their external stakeholders nor of the need to develop the competences to do so. This result was consistent with the relatively lower emphasis placed by many of these boards on reviewing social responsibilities and linking with external networks.

When considered in conjunction with aspects relating to risk and ability to conceptualize issues facing the organization, a considerable proportion of the boards represented in the study appeared to be supremely complacent at best, and at worst dubiously competent in fulfilling key obligations in their directorial role. Considerably less than 20 percent (16.6 percent) of respondents believed their board was strongly able to influence the company's risk exposure, and less than 6 percent felt they could strongly influence media perceptions of the organization. With an almost exclusively internal orientation these boards put their organizations at risk from ignoring the interests, concerns, and claims of their key stakeholders to whom they are ultimately accountable. These organizations were thus not only vulnerable to risk generally but by not fully appreciating their role in risk management as a strategic governance requirement (Ingley and van der Walt, 2008) they were also putting their reputational assets at risk through ignoring the power of stakeholders to affect the welfare of the firm (Jensen, 2000).

In the New Zealand context it was apparent from the study that the concept of corporate sustainability had yet to move into boardroom thinking and be taken seriously by directors as a strategic issue. The findings suggested that these boards held a narrow view of their fiduciary duty and highlighted the extent of influence that Friedman's (1970) shareholder-oriented view exerted among New Zealand boards regarding the responsibility of business. Insofar as these boards were indicative of the level of commitment to corporate sustainability as part of their governance role, New Zealand companies (with notable exceptions[3]) clearly were not aligned with leading thought and best practice.

---

3   As demonstrated by such companies as those rated in the GRI and the Dow Jones Sustainability Group Index (DJSGI). Such exceptions include New Zealand retailer, The Warehouse, which has designed a software program that controls its energy use so effectively that its power consumption has been halved, and Snowy Peaks, whose subsidiary company, Untouched World, is an international success story based on a foundation of environmental sustainability

In corporate governance, both in scholarship and practice, attention has focused on accountability, the regulatory environment of governance, the assurance of compliance with regulations, and control over the organization's management, as well as the search for universal principles of conduct. It is therefore not surprising to find such an emphasis among the New Zealand directors, especially given the wave of corporate governance reforms that captured attention around the time the study was conducted, notably the US Sarbanes Oxley Act 2002, the UK Combined Code 1998 (updated regularly), as well as the New Zealand Securities Commission's Principles of Corporate Governance 2004 together with updating of the New Zealand Stock Exchange's rulings for publicly listed companies.

Against this preoccupation with rules, regulations, and compliance, board members' everyday experience has tended to be ignored. Gabrielsson and Huse (2004) concluded from their review of 127 empirical articles[4] that the vast majority of researchers considered boards to be a black box, so that while aiming to gain a better understanding of how to improve corporate governance practice, they: "neglect board processes, such as interactions among groups of actors, board leadership, the development of rules and norms within boards, and the board decision-making culture." A more recent study (Carroll et al., 2012), also conducted among boards of large New Zealand entities but with a different sample from that in the earlier study, sought to reveal directors' governance-related mindsets and examine the possible consequences for governance processes and outcomes.

The Recent Study

Directors' mindsets are defined in the more recent study (Carroll et al., 2012) as frames of beliefs, assumptions, and images (Rhinesmith, 1992) that may affect perceptions and resulting behaviors, and thereby have a strong influence on social processes. By uncovering the beliefs, assumptions, and images that comprise these mental models, the study examined the meanings of governance for those involved in executing it. The study also sought to investigate how those meanings both reflect and respond to challenges and contradictions in governance practice. Key questions concerned the conceptualizations that

---

and renewal, with its range of natural, ecologically friendly, knitted designer apparel (Grayson and Hodges, 2004).

4   The paper by Gabrielsson and Huse presents a review of empirical studies on boards of directors and governance published in six leading international academic journals in general management.

directors internalize, the board roles they see themselves playing, the dynamics between these roles, and the inherent paradoxes between them, as well as how they might be resolved.

In this study interviews were conducted with 36 CEOs and 25 Chairs[5] of participating organizations which, as with the 2003 study, ranged across public, private, state-owned, multinational, and not-for-profit sectors in New Zealand. Interviews focused on the areas of leadership, governance, strategy and ethics. As stimuli, these four words were printed on cue-cards (one word per card) and used by interviewers to elicit participants' stream-of-consciousness responses. Participants were invited to move and juxtapose the cards as they discussed relationships between concepts. Interviewers shaped questions which probed and helped participants to elaborate their thinking. Nine interviewers collected 84 hours of recorded material, which was transcribed and then analyzed paying attention to the participants' syntax, imagery, word choice, and text structure for indications of how governance is formed in directors' mindsets, with consequent structuring effects on their actions (Alvesson and Kärreman, 2000, p.1138). The intention in this discourse analysis process was to move beyond analyzing "pure talk" (Alvesson and Kärreman, 2000, p.1138) to discerning how such talk may shape governance thought and practice. Participants discussed not only the legal parameters of corporate governance but—often using narrative and metaphor—also their live governance experiences.

Themes in the discourses captured from the interviews dealt primarily with the pursuit of compliance and control, and were expressed through metaphoric images of watchdog, border control, and inspectorate, which evoke the board's distance from management and reflect an agency perspective of governance. The watchdog image comprised expressions of constraint such as checks and balances, doing the right things, power, and references to decision-making and authority. The idea of governance as a surveillance mechanism was conveyed by verbs such as "observe", "look", "be aware of", "probe down" to "ensure that management knows that there are others"—"who are watching", where governance is a "discipline" and a "responsibility". The border control image spoke of "boundaries", "lines", "rails" and "safety nets", emphasizing control, correction, moderation of "unbridled drive", and imperatives: "what you can do and cannot do", where governance is perceived as guarding the organization. The inspectorate theme concerned the enactment of conformance

---

5   The difference in CEO and Chair figures reflects multiple appointments of Chairs across participating organizations, and internationally-based Chairs not available for interview.

through policing policy, rules, regulations, and requirements, by "monitoring" and "audit", reflecting a shareholder orientation that is aligned with the agency perspective.

A further theme related to discourses of deliberation, comprising the images of mentoring service, select committee, and debating forum. This theme involved intentionality, weightiness, thoughtfulness, timeliness, and presented a construction of governance that seemed to act *for* management, rather than *over* it. This construction conveyed a more positive view, as expressed by the mentoring image through words such as: "effective", "inspiring" offering "support", "wisdom", "guidance", and such phrases as "not one-on-one but corporate mentoring to the whole organization", as well as a sense of value from "guidance", "judgment" and experience" which are consistent with a stewardship role of the board. The select committee image centered on board activities that were "querying", "testing", and that "challenge", thereby applying a "wider view" in decision making. There was a delicate balance in these discourses between having "an overview" and the less constructive extremes expressed in "crash test", and "destruct"—activities which seemed pervasive: "it is their God-given role in life to actually stress-test everything"—where the focus is on management who are the "crash test dummies". The debating forum theme conveyed some of the elements of the select committee image, such as "testing", although more dynamic, with conversation "around the table" that encourages constructive "debate" and the ability "to talk openly and frankly", where "disparate views" and "different points of view" are sought, and where different viewpoints were encouraged and respected. This image was characterized by language that expressed collaboration among board members, where the discussion and debate in the boardroom is ongoing, thinking is distilled, and where there is consensus and a sense of working together, resulting in a good understanding and where a decision point is reached.

Images also emerged from discourses relating to creative capacity, or the ability to be productive, involving reflection and frame-breaking, as well as the pursuit of innovative and strategic thinking and practice. A strategy image conveyed a sense of directors wanting involvement with the strategy process: "making sure management is thinking about sensitivities, the risks about the strategic plan … so it is not just rubber stamping." However, in practice, strategizing is said by participants to be constrained—it is difficult thinking at a higher level and so hard it gets done … poorly, where the reality is frustratingly less than desired because: "… some of the boards [that I'm on or have been on] … spend more time on some of those governance [compliance] issues than they do thinking about the strategic direction," and instead default to: "stuff they are more comfortable with, which is management." Strategizing was seen in this image as a deferred governance role because the demands of conformity claim the board's time and attention, because it is a complex and time-consuming task, and because defaulting to management and control is prevalent.

The nature and extent of boards' contribution to strategy is widely debated from a range of perspectives (Daily et al., 2003), with variability regarding the advocated and actual level of engagement by boards in the strategy process. While empirical evidence indicates that a large majority of board problems are strategic in nature (for example, Brooks, 2009), data for the discourses in the recent study reported above showed that strategy and innovation do not feature strongly in directors' mindsets. Where traditionally boards may have limited their involvement to ratifying management's strategic plans, regulatory requirements, global financial interdependencies, and other contextual complexities increasingly point to a greater strategic role for boards. When confronted with strategic or creative challenges the reality appears to be, however, that whereas managers default from leadership to management, directors default from strategy to compliance (Carroll, et al., 2012).

Images that comprised the main discourses in the recent study appear to be broadly reflective of directors' mindsets, with inevitable consequences for the way governance is practiced. Mental constructions such as those expressed in the discourses have material implications (Morgan and Ramirez, 1984), influencing decisions about who is to govern, for example, as well as how agendas are set and what is on them, how directors are acculturated, and what is the nature of the interpersonal interactions that occur among them around the board table. While representing distinct themes that highlight priorities with regard to what captures board attention, the discourses are also mutually interactive surfacing conflicts and tensions within and between the themes that raise new questions about how governance is conceptualized and practiced.

The main discourses in the study are broadly consistent with the board's control, service, and strategy roles (Zahra and Pearce, 1989). The compliance theme within the conformance discourses dominated the data, preoccupying participants and almost engulfing them in what seemed to be regarded as a routinized box-ticking chore. The compliance theme also pervaded other discourses, evident for example in the select committee image within the discourses of deliberation with reference to ensuring conformance through a crash test. As the dominant discourse the compliance theme parallels the dominance of the agency perspective apparent, for example, in the implied distinction between the roles of governing and managing and the sense that the board controls and acts *over* management. At the same time this dominant discourse seems paradoxically misaligned with the board's service role in acting *for* management: providing counsel, challenging assumptions, engaging in debate, and leading, or at least contributing to, strategy making and innovation.

The dominant discourse in this study may also reflect institutionalization and groupthink in governance (Demb and Neubauer, 1992) where boards interpret narrowly their fiduciary obligation as being centered on management control and shareholder primacy. An unintended consequence is a potentially stifling influence on board strategy and service tasks (Buchanan and Donahoe, 2003), where risk aversion predominates (Montgomery, 2008). In particular, attention to external considerations was striking by its absence—there was no mention of stakeholders, and no apparent consciousness of social responsibilities or references to corporate sustainability. While the study did not explicitly set out to examine attitudes toward sustainability, it is all the more pertinent that such reference did not feature in thinking and discourse when directors were asked about governance. The following case study shows how these consequences can play out in reality, with far-reaching implications beyond the case company itself.

Fonterra

Fonterra is New Zealand's largest company with annual revenue around NZ $20 billion, and is the world's biggest dairy exporter accounting for approximately 30 percent of world dairy trade. In 2012 Fonterra exported around 2.6 million metric tonnes of product, representing around 21 percent of all global dairy exports, including 46 percent of global exports of whole milk powder. Fonterra also collects and processes milk from outside New Zealand, including Chile and Australia. From these two countries approximately 2.3 billion liters of milk were collected and manufactured by the company in 2012. Headquartered in Auckland, New Zealand, Fonterra also has farms in China, and employs around 10,000 people around the world.

The company's dairy products account for about a quarter of New Zealand's export earnings, and China is its biggest buyer of milk powder. Other key markets for Fonterra include Asia, India, Russia, Africa, and the Middle East. The New Zealand dairy industry is worth NZ $14 billion a year to the country's economy, and Fonterra sends 95 percent of the production from its 10,500 New Zealand farmer suppliers offshore. The company, which is a farmer-owned co-operative with public units listed on the NZX and ASX stock exchanges, was formed in 2001 with statutory support from a giant merger of most of the New Zealand dairy industry. Fonterra makes up 89 percent of the New Zealand industry today, and operates under the Dairy Industry Restructuring Act 2001. In 2009 the company published on its website its sustainability strategy for the first time, with the intention of reporting annually on progress on its key sustainability indicators.

The following case study has been sourced from the company's website, as well as other publicly available media including TVNZ, *The New Zealand Herald*, *Waikato Times*, and Reuters Press. The company's website prominently displays the caption: "Dairy for life" and states that food safety is Fonterra's number one priority—and that the company always acts with this in mind.[6] These promises were made by the company and by its brand long before the events that overtook it in August 2013.

On August 2, 2013 botulism fears were raised after Fonterra identified a potential quality issue in whey concentrate from one of the company's New Zealand processing plants. After a period of extensive testing Fonterra concluded that the company had a potential food safety risk with three batches, or 38 tonnes, of a particular type of whey protein concentrate called WPC80. The tests showed that this risk was extremely small, but that it was a risk nonetheless. In view of the company's claim to put food safety before all else, Fonterra immediately advised New Zealand's Ministry for Primary Industries (MPI), as well as eight commercial customers who had received the potentially affected product, and publicly announced a precautionary recall just after midnight that night.

Fonterra's commercial customers use whey protein concentrate in a range of products including infant formula and beverages. This means that while the potentially affected 38 tonnes of WPC80 was a Fonterra ingredient, the final products containing the whey protein were those of the eight customers and were sold under their brand names. When Fonterra alerted its eight commercial customers, they immediately began to investigate where in their supply chains products containing the affected WPC80 were, and whether any of this product was on retail shelves. However, most of the products were found in Fonterra's customers' own warehouses which meant that they were able to put them aside

---

6   http://www.fonterra.com/nz/en.

and ensure that they would not reach retail outlets. Where some products were already available in retail stores, these were immediately recalled. Fonterra's Chief Executive, Theo Spierings, apologized for the anxiety caused, stating that: "We are moving quickly and establishing key facts about what has happened and, as they emerge, we are taking appropriate action." Spierings assured the public that even though Fonterra did not have all the information about product location on hand at that point, the company's priority was to alert people to the potential risk as they continued to gather facts and, along with their customers, identify and contain affected products. He further stated that the company was: "taking appropriate action" and placed two senior managers on leave, pending the inquiries. Earlier that week the managing director of the company's New Zealand milk products business, Gary Romano, resigned with immediate effect after the discovery of the bacteria in the milk product which had been shipped to the eight customers in nine countries, including China.

The botulism scare was Fonterra's third problem in six years. China is particularly sensitive to milk powder contamination warnings after a string of infant formula food safety scandals in recent years, two of which have involved Fonterra. In July 2008 Fonterra's partner in China, the Sanlu dairy processing company, was at the center of a baby milk poisoning scandal. On July 16, 2008 Gansu Province reported to China's Ministry of Health that there was an increase in the incidence of kidney ailments among babies, and that these babies had consumed Sanlu's milk powder. As a consequence of drinking Sanlu infant formula, which was contaminated with melamine, an industrial chemical, six babies died, hundreds of thousands fell ill, and hundreds more suffered kidney problems.

In early September 2008 Fonterra, which owned 43 percent of Sanlu, notified the New Zealand Government of the problem, which in turn notified Beijing officials, and made the crisis public. The World Health Organisation was also notified. Sanlu then admitted that its milk powder had been contaminated and halted production. Nineteen arrests were made, but a product recall was issued only after the New Zealand Government intervened. Sanlu was subsequently found by a Chinese Government investigation to have known about the contaminated milk eight months earlier, according to China's official Daily News, but had lied about it. By mid-September two babies were confirmed to have died. A few days later products were recalled in Hong Kong after testing positive for melamine. By this stage the number of babies who were ill after having consumed the milk rose to 54,000 and 4 more babies were confirmed to have died. Taiwan then banned Chinese milk products, and other countries around the world began testing the products. In early October parents of the affected babies filed a lawsuit against Sanlu and six more people were detained over the melamine scandal. The lawsuit, however, was subsequently put on hold by officials. At that time Fonterra donated more than 8,000,000 dollars to a Chinese charity, but stated that it wanted to retain its stake in Sanlu saying that it had a long-term commitment to China.

One month later, China's Ministry of Health revised the number of victims to more than 290,000 and more than 22 million infants were examined for kidney problems. That same month Fonterra was named in Swiss firm RepRisk's top ten world list of companies among those most criticized for their impacts on the environment, health, and communities. At the top of RepRisk's list was Sanlu Group. By the end of that month a court in Shijiazhuang, China, issued a bankruptcy order against Sanlu in response to a petition from a creditor.

In late January 2009 two men were sentenced to death in China for their part in the contaminated milk scandal. Sanlu's chairwoman, Tian Wenhua, claimed that a Fonterra-appointed director gave her a document showing the levels of the industrial chemical melamine permitted by the European Union. Fonterra denied the claims. The company's chairman, Henry van der Heyden, said that there was nothing to warrant dismissing any Fonterra executives and that no action would be taken against its management who had: "acted absolutely appropriately" over the scandal. The poisoned baby milk scandal was estimated to have cost Fonterra a NZ $139 million impairment charge which the company said reflected the cost of the product recall and the company's loss of Sanlu brand value.

Other markets in Asia are also very sensitive to infant food and dairy product food safety warnings. Early in 2013 Fonterra was at the center of another product contamination scare involving dicyandiamide, a nitrate-leaching inhibitor known as DCD, residues of which were found in New Zealand dairy products for export. Traces of DCD were found in product test samples, prompting the Wall Street Journal to ask: "is New Zealand milk safe?" Fonterra's chief executive, Theo Spierings, held a crisis team meeting as Chinese consumers panicked about infant formula. Fonterra had halted 42 tonnes of China-bound milk powder in May 2013, because of high nitrite levels.

The issue of high nitrite levels was first raised by the official China Daily in late July 2013, dealing another blow to Fonterra before the company announced in August that it had found the botulism bacteria that could cause food poisoning in some products. Fonterra had to apologize for the DCD milk powder contamination scare in China after contaminated whey protein concentrate had been sold there, as well as to Malaysia, Vietnam, Thailand, and Saudi Arabia, and used in products including infant milk powder and sports drinks. The company said that the shipment of powder had been halted at the Chinese border in May after tests showed nitrite levels higher than allowed in China, although it had been approved for export after testing in New Zealand. Nitrites occur naturally in water, soil, and food and can be used as fertilizers and preservatives. Excessively high levels, however, can be toxic.

Fonterra's group director of food safety and quality, Ian Palliser, said that the milk powder showed nitrite levels of between 1.4 parts per million (ppm) and 1.8 ppm when it was shipped from New Zealand, but showed higher levels in Chinese tests. According to Palliser: "The limit is 2 parts per million in China and the product tested at somewhere between 2.4 ppm and 2.8 ppm." He added that China had a much lower threshold for nitrite levels than New Zealand, where levels of up to five ppm are considered safe for domestic consumption, and argued that the levels were: "not a food safety issue whatsoever." Because the levels were below the New Zealand standards, he claimed, the product could have been sold safely in New Zealand. Fonterra said that it had been in full control of the affected product, and none of it had reached the retail supply chain.

In mid-August 2013 the company had two internal inquiries being undertaken into how whey protein concentrate came to be contaminated with bacteria that can cause botulism and then sold to customers earlier in March. The New Zealand Primary Industry's Minister publicly announced plans for an official enquiry into how ingredients made by Fonterra became contaminated by botulism-causing bacteria, as the country tried to salvage its reputation as an exporter of safe agricultural products. The inquiry, held alongside the company's two internal investigations and another by the country's agricultural regulator, examined how the potentially contaminated products entered the international market, and whether adequate regulatory practices were in place to deal with the issue. It hoped to provide answers to questions that were raised about the incident, both domestically and internationally, and was seen as an important step in reassuring the country's trading partners that such issues were taken seriously. Fonterra had come under attack at home and abroad for dragging its feet in disclosing the discovery of the bacteria, and Chief Executive, Theo Spierings, welcomed the inquiry saying in the statement that the company would provide all necessary information. The New Zealand Foreign Affairs Minister, Murray McCully, also visited Beijing to smooth relations, and the Prime Minister visited China later in the year to discuss the contamination issue after completion of the inquiry. The New Zealand Government had voiced frustrations over Fonterra's perceived feet dragging in disclosing the contamination issue, and during his visit to China, Foreign Minister Murray McCully sought to distance the country from Fonterra's woes. "Fonterra has some work ahead of it in rebuilding Chinese consumer confidence," he told reporters in Beijing after meetings with State Councilor Yang Jiechi and Foreign Minister Wang Yi. "We expect from our exporters that there should not be any mistakes," he said. "When Fonterra disappoints customers, they also disappoint New Zealand." In meetings with McCully, Yang was reported by Chinese state media, Xinhua, to have urged New Zealand to improve food safety, saying that: "We hope the New Zealand side will appropriately handle food safety issues, including the safety of dairy products exported to China, and substantially ensure Chinese consumers' interests."

In late August 2013 MPI said it had received further test results confirming that the bacteria found in the whey protein concentrate manufactured by Fonterra was not the botulism-causing clostridium botulinum. As it turned out, the organism was confirmed by the ministry as clostridium sporogenes which is not capable of producing botulism-causing toxins. The ministry stated that no known food safety issues are associated with the clostridium sporogenes bacteria, although at elevated levels certain strains may be associated with food spoilage. A failure of hygiene during processing remained a concern for customers incorporating whey protein concentrate into their products. However, the concern primarily related to quality and the potential for spoilage when used in foods that support growth of clostridium sporogenes from spores. The research involved a total of 195 tests carried out in both the United States and New Zealand. Fonterra had originally commissioned independent testing from AgResearch, as one of only two research facilities in New Zealand capable of carrying out testing for the bacteria. At the same time, MPI commissioned a further array of tests to validate the initial results. The new results did not affect the various reviews and inquiries underway.

On the back of the global botulin bacteria scare, a Sri Lankan Court in Colombo issued a summons on September 21, 2013 to four top officials of Fonterra's local company, Brands Lanka, to face contempt charges for not adhering to an earlier ruling that banned sales and advertising of all Fonterra milk products for two weeks. The ban followed a complaint by a health sector trade union that the company's marketing was misleading. The trade union obtained the court ban because Fonterra products suspected of being contaminated with DCD were still on the market despite an order from the Sri Lankan health ministry to recall them after tests by its Industrial Technology Institute (ITI) found DCD in some Fonterra milk powders. Fonterra recalled two of its batches of branded product, but disputed the accuracy of the testing and, despite the court ban, continued to distribute its milk powder products to retailers along with leaflets saying its products were still fit for human consumption. Fresh ITI tests of milk powder subsequently returned a negative result.

Despite the negative findings from these tests, there were still unanswered questions about the contamination scare and how it was handled which was why MPI was continuing with its compliance review and the Government would proceed with its ministerial inquiry. The New Zealand Government's major opposition party called the false test results: "a complete systems failure by the Ministry for Primary Industries," saying that: "our failure to ensure the highest standards of testing, monitoring and auditing means the damage has been done to New Zealand's international reputation'" and that: "This fiasco continues to be a disaster for our clean, green brand. The inability of the ministry's systems means our reputation is always at risk."

Criticism was also levelled at both the Government and Fonterra by the New Zealand Infant Formula Exporters Association which had been dismayed and disturbed with the way the botulism scare was handled initially, with its members losing millions of dollars over the scandal. The Association said that New Zealand needed a more coordinated and coherent approach to food scares. "Anything that can bring New Zealand's brand into disrepute must be managed very carefully. Anything that can bring New Zealand's brand of feeding infants worldwide into disrepute must be handled with the utmost care and responsibility," the Association urged. Danone, the parent company of Nutricia Australia New Zealand, which produces Karicare infant formula—one of the affected and recalled products—was understood to be suing Fonterra for $320 million for reputational damage.

New Zealand investors, likewise, were highly critical of Fonterra, its board and the company's handling of the botulism scare and believed that a shake-up was needed in the boardroom with a far wider range of skills required as befits a major global group. Fonterra's website boldly states that: "Our board of directors is responsible for the leadership and direction of Fonterra," (Fonterra website) but this leadership was criticized as sadly lacking, with no public sighting of the chairman until the fifth day after the crisis broke. The company's board is seen to lack directors with experience in crisis management and its composition is regarded by investor groups as a major issue. The dairy co-operative has 13 directors, 9 of whom are elected by supplier shareholders and the remaining 4 are appointed by the board and approved by shareholders at the annual meeting. The elected directors must have a milk supply relationship with Fonterra while the appointed independent directors: "are selected to ensure our board has the appropriate skills and competencies to lead our organization effectively." One of the board's major roles, according to its Board Charter (p.2), is to: "determine the company's risk profile and ensure that management has appropriate policies and internal controls in place in respect of risk management, regulatory compliance, health and safety and environmental sustainability." Earlier in the week of the crisis in August 2013, Gary Romano, the company's main New Zealand-based spokesman (who subsequently resigned), was casually dressed in an open-necked shirt but later in the week all of the company's spokesmen, including Romano, were formally dressed in suits and ties. The belated move to formal attire was just one of the indicators that Fonterra did not have a clear predetermined crisis management plan. This raised the question as to why the board had not appointed independent directors with hands-on experience of crisis management, manufacturing, and food safety issues. At the time only one director had this background, with ten years of downstream dairy industry experience with Danone as a senior vice-president and a member of Danone's group executive committee. The complete dominance of the board by dairy suppliers and independent directors with limited crisis management, manufacturing, and food safety experience was seen by investor critics to be a major risk, making another crisis more likely without a larger proportion of independent directors with wider experience and a greater range of skills on the board.

At the end of October 2013 the independent inquiry team released a report with 33 recommendations for preventing and mitigating another crisis. The inquiry team found that Fonterra had failed to recognize the: "explosive reputational risk" involved in the scare. A list of things that went wrong included the: "belated recognition (and delayed escalation to senior management and the board) of the explosive reputational risk involved." Fonterra had failed to join the dots between botulism, infant food products, consumer sensitivities, and Fonterra's global reputation, the report said. A number of factors, including a lack of senior oversight of crucial decisions, and problems with tracing potentially affected product, had contributed to the event. The report further stated that Fonterra's crisis management planning, including the external communications aspects, was inadequate for a crisis of this kind and scale: "Fonterra's management of the crisis in the critical early period, including the external communications aspects, was not well executed." According to the report there was: "some lack of alignment" between the Government and Fonterra during the first critical fortnight of the scare. The report suggested more robust testing and cleaning regimes that align with international best practice, improving engagement with stakeholders to shift a Fortress Fonterra perception, establish specialized risk and crisis management plans, and develop a strong communications team with local knowledge of key markets.

Fonterra's chief executive, Theo Spierings, said that the company had learned lessons from what had been: "a difficult experience, subsequently found to be a false alarm. Fonterra is emerging from this experience with a culture of developing more transparency, accountability and retaining utmost focus on food safety and quality." He further stated that the company is eight to ten years behind other dairy players overseas when it comes to sustainability, and was disappointed that Fonterra was so far behind adding that if New Zealand wanted to grow its dairy industry it cannot do so in the way it had been done in the last ten years: "because we will hit the wall in terms of the environment and sustainability. We have got to get our act together." Spierings said that while Fonterra had numerous sustainability projects, none was connected with the company's strategy and in a 2011 annual sustainability report there was almost nothing in it on sustainability. The 2013 annual report was the first from the company to have an extensive section on sustainability. That the dairy sector was so far behind was attributed to a rapid transition in the first few years of the twenty-first century from predominantly livestock farming to dairy, resulting in a dairy boom which got ahead of where the environmental responsibility should have been, but the sector was working hard to get things back to a more sustainable long-term balance.

Conclusion

In the wider global context corporate sustainability is becoming established by leading companies as a critical element of strategic direction and potentially as a key driver of business development, as well as an essential component of risk management. Among such companies there is also a growing recognition of a clear, direct relationship between corporate governance, corporate responsibility, and sustainable development (Clarke, 2007, p.219). Grayson and Hodges (2004) and Cramer and Hirschland (2006) have observed that mainstream investors are showing increased interest in socially responsible business. They contend that with many of the largest companies elevating corporate sustainability issues to board level, clearly there is perceived value in adopting such an approach in doing business. The agenda for boards and company directors is also changing, and enlightened directors are beginning to acknowledge that corporate sustainability is a strategic corporate issue that requires board oversight. Such corporations are recognizing that there is an increasing overlap between the sustainability and corporate governance agendas, requiring high performance boards and transformative thinking around corporate sustainability (Elkington, 2007). The implication for corporate decision-making is that sustainability is a governance issue which therefore belongs on the board's agenda (Schacter, 2005).

At the time of the 2003 study, New Zealand companies were not alone in lagging behind in thought and practice regarding their responsibility to stakeholders, as indicated by Dulewicz's and Herbert's (2003) UK research. Other commentators also noted that efforts elsewhere by companies to improve their social and environmental performance were less successful than was hoped for (Elkington, 2007). Yet it would appear that despite an interval of six years between the two studies, boards in New Zealand companies have not become significantly more externally oriented in their focus, and remain fixated on the compliance dimension of their governance role. Whether this is a characteristic of a country that lags behind in leading edge thinking and is fixated on a shareholder-oriented view of corporate governance, or whether directors lack understanding of, and imperatives for, their role regarding sustainability—perhaps due to generational factors (in other words, the age of board members), or whether it is an unintended consequence of governance reforms, it is apparent that stakeholder relationships and corporate sustainability have not become part of directors' stream of consciousness when it comes to governance.

The challenge for directors is to guide the corporation along the best possible path among competing claims of shareholders and stakeholders. For this task boards will require a greater appreciation of the relationships—societal as well as financial—that sustain the corporation. They will also need to develop their capacity to oversee the corporation's response to demands for greater rigor in managing and disclosing information about their social impact (Schacter, 2005). By engaging with stakeholders on corporate sustainability matters boards are also well positioned to help their corporations to secure major opportunities for building competitive advantage (Grayson and Hodges, 2004). In adopting an outward orientation such boards create a process for checking and balancing company direction outside the limited inward preoccupations that may have prevailed in the boardroom (Cramer and Hirschland, 2006; Elkington, 2007; Grayson and Hodges, 2004).

Boards that recognize the value of asking new questions and seeking new perspectives are better able to fulfil their core governance duties.

Those that ignore stakeholder perspectives and sustainability issues will likely also find themselves presiding over diminishing shareholder value (Clarke, 2007; Cramer and Hirschland, 2006). As emphasized by Porter and Kramer (2006) these emerging priorities need to be integrated into the center of corporate governance and operational management because: "Without a careful process for identifying evolving social effects of tomorrow, firms may risk their very survival."

White (2006, p.17) asserted that:

> Rethinking corporate governance is part of a larger unfolding story of how to address the governance deficit in a dynamic, globalizing world where traditional boundaries and behaviors are rendered increasingly obsolete. It is against this backdrop that boards must emerge from the shadows to the forefront of stakeholder governance to assert their unique role as trustees—indeed, creators—of the socially responsible corporation of the future.

Progressive companies that are forward-thinking about corporate sustainability have begun to transform their boards' engagement on environmental, social, and governance issues. Dexterous boards that change their thinking and approach to these issues recognize the importance of minimizing major surprises and mitigating risks to their business, and in this way help to avoid the kinds of strategic errors that have beleaguered companies in the past (White, 2006).

References and Bibliography

Adair, J. (2007). *Leadership for Innovation: How to Organize Team Creativity and Harvest Ideas*. London: Kogan Page.

Alvesson, M., and Kärreman, D. (2000). Varieties of Discourse: On the study of organizations through discourse. *Human Relations*, Vol. 53(9), 1125–49.

Benn, S., and Dunphy, D. (2007). *Corporate Sustainability: Challenges for Theory and Practice*. London: Routledge.

Bosch, H. (1995). *The Director at Risk: Accountability in the Boardroom*. Sydney: Pitman Publishing.

Brooks, L. (2009). *Business and Professional Ethics for Directors, Executives and Accountants* (5th ed.). Mason, Ohio: Thomson South-Western.

Buchanan, R., and Donahoe, J. (2003). Boards Will be Frozen by Caution's Icy Hand. *Financial Times*, Section 11. 30 July.

Carroll, A.B. (1999). Corporate Social Responsibility. *Business and Society*, Vol. 38(3), 268–95.

Carroll, A.B. (1979). A Three-dimensional Conceptual Model of Corporate Social Performance. *Academy of Management Review*, Vol. 4(4), 497–505.

Carroll, A.B., Ingley, C., Levy, L., and Inkson, K. (2012). *Discourses of Governance: Paradox, Paralysis and Generativity*. Proceedings of the 8th European Conference on Management, Leadership and Governance. Pafos, Cyprus, 8–9 November.

Chait, R. (2006). *Governance as Leadership*. Independent Schools Council of Australia National Conference, Hobart.

Chait, R., Ryan, W., and Taylor, B. (2004). *Governance as Leadership: Reframing the Work of Nonprofit Boards*. New Jersey: Wiley.

Charron, D.C. (2007). *Stockholders and Stakeholders: the Battle for Control of the Corporation*. Cato Journal, Vol. 27(1), 1–22.

Clarke, T. (2007). The Materiality of Sustainability: Corporate Social and Environmental Responsibility as Instruments of Strategic Change? In Benn, S. and Dunphy, D., *Corporate Sustainability: Challenges for Theory and Practice*. London: Routledge, 219–51.

Cramer, A., and Hirschland, M. (2006). The Socially Responsible Board. *The Corporate Board*, Vol. 161, 20–24.

Daily, C., Dalton, D., and Cannella, A. (2003). Corporate Governance: Decades of Dialogue and data. *Academy of Management Review*, Vol. 28(3), 371–82.

Davies, A. (1999). *A Strategic Approach to Corporate Governance*. Aldershot: Gower Publishing Limited.

Demb, A., and Neubauer, F.F. (1992). *The Corporate Board: Confronting the Paradoxes*. New York: Oxford University Press.

Dulewicz, V., and Herbert, P. (2003). *Does the Composition and Practice of UK Boards Bear any Relationship to the Performance of Listed Companies*? Paper presented at 6th International Conference on Corporate Governance and Board Leadership, Henley Management College, UK, 6–8 October.

Dunphy, D.C., Griffiths, A., and Benn, S. (2003). *Organizational Change for Corporate Sustainability: A Guide for Leaders and Change Agents of the Future*. New York: Routledge.

Dyllick, T., and Hockerts, K. (2002). Beyond the Business Case for Corporate Sustainability. *Business Strategy and the Environment*, Vol. 11(2), 130–41.

Elkington, J. (2007). The Power of Disruption. *Director*, Vol. 60(7), 24 February.

Elkington, J. (1997). *Cannibals with Forks: The Triple Bottom Line of 21st Century Business*. Oxford: Capstone Publishing.

Fama, E., and Jensen, M. (1983). Separation of Ownership and Control: Corporations and Private Property. *Journal of Law and Economics*, Vol. 26, 301–25.

Fonterra website:
http://www.fonterra.com/nz/en/about/our+governance/board+of+directors/board+of+directors
http://www.fonterra.com/nz/en/About/Our+Governance/Corporate+Governance

Freeman, R.E. (1984). *Strategic Management: A Stakeholder Approach*. Boston: Pitman.

Friedman M. (1970). The Social Responsibility of Business is to Increase its Profits. *The New York Times Magazine*, 13 September, 32–3, 122, 124, 126.

Gabrielsson, J., and Huse, M. (2004). Context, Behavior, and Evolution: Challenges in Research on Boards and Governance. *International Studies of Management and Organization*, Vol. 34(2), 11–36.

Garratt, B. (2003). *Thin on Top: How to Measure and Improve Board Performance*. London: Nicholas Brealey Publishing.

Gladwin, T.N., Krause, T., and Kennelly, J.J. (1995). Beyond Eco-efficiency: Toward Socially Sustainable Business. *Sustainable Development*, Vol. 3(1), 35–43.

Global Reporting Initiative (GRI) (2013). *G4 Sustainability Reporting Guidelines*, Amsterdam: GRI. http://www.globalreporting.org.

Grayson, D., and Hodges, A. (2004). *Corporate Social Opportunity: 7 Steps to Make Corporate Social Responsibility Work for Your Business*. Sheffield: Greenleaf Publishing.

Harris, I., and Shimizu, K. (2004). Too Busy to Serve? An Examination of the Influence of Overboarded Directors. *Journal of Management Studies*, Vol. 41(5), 775–98.

Harris, L.C., and Crane, A. (2002). The Greening of Organizational Culture. *Journal of Organizational Change Management*, Vol. 15(3), 214–34.

Hawkins, J.A. (1997). Why Investors Push for Strong Corporate Boards. *The McKinsey Quarterly*, Vol. 3, 144–8.

Healy, J. (2003). *Corporate Governance and Wealth Creation in New Zealand*. Palmerston North, NZ: Dunmore Press Limited.

Ingley, C.B. (2008). Company Growth and Board Attitudes to Corporate Social Responsibility. *International Journal of Business Governance and Ethics*, Vol. 4(1), 17–39.

Ingley, C.B., and van der Walt, N.T. (2008). Risk Management and Board Effectiveness. *International Studies of Management and Organization*, Vol. 38(3), 43–70.

Ingley, C.B., and van der Walt, N.T, (2004). Corporate Governance, Institutional Investors and Conflicts of Interest. *Corporate Governance: An International Review*, Vol. 12(4), 534–51.

Ingley, C.B., and van der Walt, N.T. (2001). The Strategic Board: The Changing Role of Directors in Developing and Maintaining Corporate Capability. *Corporate Governance: An International Review*, Vol. 9(3), 174–85.

Jensen, M. (2000). Value Maximization, Stakeholder Theory, and the Corporate Objective Function. *Harvard Business School*, Working Paper 00–058.

Jensen, M. (1989). Eclipse of the Public Corporation. *Harvard Business Review*, Vol. 67, 61–73.

Kiel, G., and Nicholson, G. (2003). *Boards That Work: A New Guide for Directors*. Sydney: McGraw-Hill Australia Pty Ltd.

Knoepfel, I. (2001). Dow Jones Sustainability Group Index: A Global Benchmark for Corporate Sustainability. *Corporate Environmental Strategy*, Vol. 8(1), 6–14.

Kostant, P.C. (1999). Exit, Voice and Loyalty in the Course of Corporate Governance and Counsel's Changing Role. *Journal of Socio-Economics*, Vol. 28(3), 203–46.

Levitt, T. (1958). The Dangers of Social Responsibility. *Harvard Business Review*, (Sep/Oct), 41–50.

Linnenluecke, M.K., Russell, S.V., and Griffiths, A. (2007). Subcultures and Sustainability Practices: The Impact on Understanding Corporate Sustainability. *Business Strategy and the Environment*, Vol. 18(7), 432–52.

Massie, R. (2003). Address, *Global Agenda*, World Economic Forum, Annual Meeting, Davos, Switzerland.

Montgomery, C. (2008). Putting Leadership Back into Strategy. *Harvard Business Review*, Vol. 86, 54–60.

Morgan, G., and Ramirez, R. (1984). Action Learning: A Holographic Metaphor for Guiding Social Change. *Human Relations*, Vol. 37(1), 1–27.

Perrini F. (2006). The Practitioner's Perspective on Non-Financial Reporting. *California Management Review*, Vol. 48(2), 73–103.

Peteraf, M. (1993). The Cornerstones of Competitive Advantage: A Resource-Based View. *Strategic Management Journal*, Vol. 14(3), 179–91.

Porter, M.E. (1985). *Competitive Advantage*. New York: Free Press.

Porter, M.E., and Kramer M.R. (2006). Strategy and Society: The Link Between Competitive Advantage and Corporate Social Responsibility. *Harvard Business Review*, Vol. 84(12), 78–92.

Preston, L.E. (1986). Business and Public Policy. *Journal of Management*, July 30, Vol. 12(2), 261–75.

Rhinesmith, S. (1992). Global Mindsets for Global Managers. *Training and Development*, Vol. 46(10), 63–8.

Russell, S., Haigh, N., and Griffiths, A. (2007) Understanding Corporate Sustainability: Recognizing the Impact of Corporate Governance Systems. In Benn S. and Dunphy D. (2007) *Corporate Sustainability: Challenges for Theory and Practice*. London: Routledge, 36–56.

Schacter, M. (2005). Boards Face New Social Responsibility. *CA Magazine*, May 2005, 12.

Shrivastava, P. (1995). Creating Sustainable Corporations. *Business Strategy and The Environment*, Vol. 4, 154–65.

White A.L. (2006). The Stakeholder Fiduciary: CSR, Governance and the Future of Boards. *Business for Social Responsibility*, April. White Paper: AW Corporate Boards 4–24–06 J BA. Online. Available at http://www.bsr.org. Last accessed September 28, 2012.

White, A.L. (1995). The Performance of Environmental Mutual Funds in the United States and Germany: Is there Economic Hope for Green Investors? *Research in Corporate Social Performance and Policy Supplement* 1, 323–44.

Zahra, S.A., and Pearce, J.A. II. (1989). Board of Directors and Corporate Financial Performance: A Review and Integrative Model. *Journal of Management*, Vol. 15(2), 291–334.

Chapter 7

Sustainability Issues in Corporate Social Responsibility and Strategy: Sustainable or Temporary Competitive Advantage in Today's Dynamic Environment?

GÜLER ARAS AND NABYLA DAIDJ

Introduction

One of the most used words relating to corporate activity and strategy at present is "sustainability". Indeed it can be argued that it has been so heavily overused, and with so many different meanings applied to it, that it is effectively meaningless. The term sustainability currently has a high profile within the lexicon of corporate endeavor. Therefore it is frequently mentioned as central to corporate activity without any attempt to define exactly what sustainable activity entails. This is understandable as the concept is problematic and subject to many varying definitions—ranging from platitudes concerning sustainable development, to the deep green concept of returning to the "golden era" before industrialization—although often it is used by corporations merely to signify that they intend to continue their existence into the future.

The ubiquity of the concept and the vagueness of its use mean that it is necessary to re-examine the concept, and to consider how it applies to corporate activity. Many people talk about the triple bottom line as if this is the panacea of CSR and, therefore, inevitably concerned with sustainability. We regard it as self-evident that corporations need to be concerned with the three aspects of CSR and equally self-evident that all corporations are so concerned. This is not new and is not really what CSR is all about. Instead we focus our concern differently and re-use the going concern principle of accounting to argue that what really matters for a corporation's continued existence is the notion of sustainability. For us this is the cornerstone of both CSR and corporate activity.

The broadest definition of CSR is concerned with what is—or should be—the relationship between the global corporation, governments of countries, and individual citizens. More locally the definition is concerned with the relationship between a corporation and the local society in which it resides or operates. Another definition is concerned with the relationship between a corporation and its stakeholders. For us, all of these definitions are pertinent and represent dimensions of the issue. At the same time, of course, a similar debate is taking place in the arena of ethics concerning whether corporations should be subject to increased regulation, or whether the ethical base of citizenship has been lost and needs replacing before socially responsible behavior will ensue—the perennial debate.[1] However this debate is represented, it seems that it is concerned with some sort of social contract between corporations and society (Aras and Crowther, 2009c).

In strategy, sustainable competitive advantage has traditionally been the key concept used by strategic management to explain a firm's success (Porter, 1980; Kay, 1993). CSR contributes to develop a sustainable advantage. But despite its importance in the field of strategy and competitive advantage, sustainability has not been clearly defined and different theoretical positions persist.

Sustainability

Sustainability implies that society must use no more of a resource than can be regenerated. This can be defined in terms of the carrying capacity of the eco-system (Hawken, 1993) and described with input–output models of resource consumption. Viewing an organization as part of a wider social and economic system implies that these effects must be taken into account not just for the measurement of costs and value created in the present but also for the future of the business itself. This approach to sustainability is based upon the Gaia hypothesis (Lovelock, 1979), a model in which the whole of the eco-sphere, and all living matter therein, is codependant upon its various facets and forms a complete system. According to this hypothesis, this complete system, and all components of the system, is interdependent and equally necessary for maintaining the Earth as a planet capable of sustaining life (Aras and Crowther, 2009c).

---

1   The ethics versus regulation debate has been a feature of CSR since its inception. Of course, neither satisfactorily answers all the issues which is why the debate continues.

Such concerns are pertinent at a macro level of society as a whole, or at the level of the nation state, but are equally relevant at the micro level of the corporation, the aspect of sustainability that concerns us in this work. At this level, measures of sustainability would consider the rate at which resources are consumed by the organization in relation to the rate at which resources can be regenerated. Unsustainable operations can be accommodated for either by developing sustainable operations, or by planning for a future lacking in resources currently required. In practice, organizations mostly tend to aim toward less unsustainability by increasing efficiency in the way in which resources are utilized. An example would be an energy efficiency program.

Sustainability is a controversial topic because it means different things to different people. Nevertheless, there is a growing awareness (or diminishing naïvety) that one is, indeed, involved in a battle about what sustainability means and, crucially, the extent (if at all) it can be delivered by corporations in the easy manner they promise (United Nations Commission on Environment and Development (Schmidheiny, 1992)).

There is a further confusion surrounding the concept of sustainability: for the purist sustainability implies nothing more than stasis—the ability to continue in an unchanged manner—but often it is taken to imply development in a sustainable manner (Marsden, 2000; Hart and Milstein, 2003) and the terms sustainability and sustainable development are for many viewed as synonymous.

As far as corporate sustainability is concerned then the confusion is exacerbated by the fact that the term sustainable has been used in management literature over the last 30 years (see, for example, Reed and DeFillippi, 1990) to merely imply continuity. Thus Zwetsloot (2003) is able to conflate CSR with the techniques of continuous improvement and innovation to imply that sustainability is thereby ensured. An almost unquestioned assumption is that growth remains possible (Elliott, 2005), and therefore sustainability and sustainable development are synonymous. Indeed the economic perspective of post-Cartesian ontologies predominates and growth is considered to be not just possible but also desirable (see, for example, Spangenberg, 2004). So it is possible therefore for Daly (1992) to argue that the economics of development is all that needs to be addressed, and that this can be dealt with through the market by the clear separation of the three basic economic goals of efficient allocation, equitable distribution, and sustainable scale. Hart (1997) goes further and regards the concept of sustainable development merely as a business opportunity, arguing that once a company identifies its environmental strategy then opportunities for new products and services become apparent (Aras and Crowther, 2013).

There seem, therefore, to be two commonly held assumptions which permeate the discourse of corporate sustainability. The first is that sustainability is synonymous with sustainable development. The second is that a sustainable company will exist merely by recognizing environmental and social issues and incorporating them into its strategic planning. We reject both of these assumptions — both are based upon an unquestioning acceptance of market economics predicated in the need for growth. While we do not necessarily reject such market economics, we argue that its acceptance has led to the assumptions about sustainability which have confused the debate. Thus we consider it imperative at this point to reiterate the basic tenet of sustainability: that sustainable activity is activity in which decisions made in the present do not restrict the choices available in the future. If this tenet of sustainability is accepted, then it follows that development is neither a necessary nor desirable aspect of sustainability. Sustainable development may well be possible, and even desirable in some circumstances, but it is not an integral aspect of sustainability.

Our second point is that corporate sustainability is not necessarily continuing into the future with little change except to incorporate environmental and social issues — all firms are doing this in some way. Neither is corporate sustainability a term which is interchangeable with the term CSR. And environmental sustainability — the context in which the term is generally used — is not the same as corporate sustainability.

Corporate Sustainability

Sustainability is a fashionable concept for corporations and their reporting previously described it as environmental reporting. CSR reporting is now often described as sustainability reporting (Aras and Crowther, 2007a). Corporate websites also tend to discuss sustainability. But it is apparent that sustainability and sustainable development are used as interchangeable terms. It is apparent, therefore, that a very powerful semiotic (Guiraud, 1975; Kim, 1996) of sustainable activity has been created — conveniently as Fish (1980) shows that truth and belief are synonymous for all practical purposes. It has been argued elsewhere (Aras and Crowther, 2008a) that this is a deliberate ploy, because one of the effects of persuading people that corporate activity is sustainable is that the cost of capital for the firm is reduced as investors are misled into thinking that the level of risk involved in their investment is lower than it actually is.

Developing Standards of Sustainability

The features of sustainability in terms of the factors involved have been discussed before by Aras and Crowther (2007b, 2007c, 2008c). Here we wish to focus upon its operationalization in terms of the development of standards. Our argument has been that sustainability must involve greater efficiency in the use of resources, and greater equity in the distribution of the effects of corporate activity. For standards to be developed then, of course, the effects must be measurable and the combination must, of course, be manageable. This can be depicted as the model of sustainability shown as Figure 7.1.

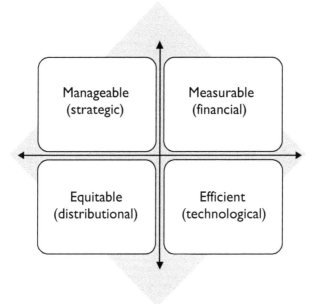

Figure 7.1   The facets of sustainability
Source: Aras and Crowther, 2009c.

This acts as a form of balanced scorecard to provide a form of evaluation for the operation of sustainability within an organization. It concentrates upon the four key aspects, namely:

1.   strategy

2.   finance

3.   distribution

4.   technological development.

Moreover, it recognizes that it is the balance between these factors which is the most significant aspect of sustainability. From this, a plan of action is possible for an organization which will recognize priorities and provide a basis for performance evaluation.

Furthermore Aras and Crowther (2009c) argue that any approach to sustainability must be:

- manageable

- measurable

- equitable

- efficient.

Traditional approaches do not satisfactorily address these issues and are, therefore, unlikely to be successful for the development of strategies for sustainability. Sustainability requires a radical rethink and a move away from the cozy security of the Brundtland definition. Aras and Crowther therefore revised the accepted terms of sustainability and sustainable development, preferring instead to use the term "durability" to emphasize the change in focus.

The essential features of durability can be described as follows:

- Efficiency is concerned with the best use of scarce resources. This requires a re-definition of inputs to the transformational process and a focus upon environmental resources as the scarce resource.

- Efficiency is concerned with optimizing the use of the scarce resources (in other words, environmental resources) rather than with cost reduction.

- Value is added through technology and innovation rather than through expropriation.

- Outputs are redefined to include distributional effects for all stakeholders.

Sustainability Issues in Strategy and Competitive Advantage

Sustainability is a complex issue with many ramifications affecting all aspects of corporate activity, society, environment, and stakeholders (Aras and Crowther, 2009a). This section provides a theoretical overview of the concept of sustainability with a special focus on the strategic perspectives concerning competitive advantage. Sustainability is a key issue in strategic management. Companies try to improve their performance thanks to a strengthened competitive advantage based on cost and/or differentiation.

STRATEGY AND SUSTAINABILITY

Johnson et al. (2012) mention the acronym SAF related to three criteria for evaluating strategic options: suitability (S), acceptability (A), and feasibility (F). Suitability deals with the rationale of the strategy. Acceptability is evaluated by stakeholders. Feasibility relies on the optimal use of tangible resources and intangible assets. "Suitability is concerned with assessing which proposed strategic address the key opportunities and constraints an organization faces (…). Acceptability is concerned with whether the expected performance outcomes of a proposal strategy meet the expectations of stakeholders (…). Feasibility is concerned with whether a strategy could work in practice" (Johnson et al., 2012, pp.261–5). We could add to this list sustainability. "Sustainability has the potential to affect all aspects of a company's operations, from development and manufacturing to sales and support functions (…). The solutions to the challenges of sustainability are interdisciplinary, making effective collaboration with stakeholders particularly critical" (Berns et al., 2009, p.24).

The main purpose of strategy is to enable an organization to a sustainable competitive advantage. There are several categories of advantage: comparative advantage (country level), competitive advantage (firm level), keystone advantage developed by Iansiti and Levien (2004), cooperative advantage, network advantage, and so on. For example, Hatani and McGaughey (2013) have analyzed how interfirm networks build and sustain competitive advantage across borders from an evolutionary perspective: "Competitive advantage does not reside in a single firm's capabilities or resources, but in interfirm networks that compete with other networks" (ibid., p.455).

A firm's potential for competitive advantage is determined not just by internal factors such as its own resources and competencies (distinctive resources and core competencies) but also by the conditions of the national and international environments (current market conditions and macro-economic fundamentals) in which it operates.

Generally, the adoption of CSR practices by firms aims to improve the societal, social, and environmental impact of their activities:

- The societal dimension is related to relationships with various stakeholders (employees, clients, suppliers, competitors, and so on).

- The social level includes best management practices, knowledge sharing (based on trust), better employment conditions, promotion of a workplace culture, and fair working environment.

- The environmental challenges take into consideration scarce resources, climate changes, land degradation, pollution of rivers and oceans, and so on.

The CSR practices that gradually emerge involve a higher degree of implicit forms of rules and policies. Firms have to combine two different approaches: the maximization of short-term profitability demanded by shareholders and the need to take into account the growth over the longer term (stakeholders). CSR has an impact on value creation in the short and long term.

In order to combine financial efficiency and social progress, Porter and Kramer (2011) proposed a new concept of shared value defined as follows: "The solution lies in the principle of shared value, which involves creating economic value in a way that also creates value for society by addressing its needs and challenges. Businesses must reconnect company success with social progress. Shared value is not social responsibility, philanthropy, or even sustainability, but a new way to achieve economic success. It is not on the margin of what companies do but at the center. We believe that it can give rise to the next major transformation of business thinking" (ibid., p.4). They suggested using creating shared value (CSV) rather than CSR (see Table 7.1).

Table 7.1   CSR versus CSV?

CSR	CSV
Value: doing good	Value: economic and societal benefits relative to cost
Citizenship, philanthropy, sustainability	Joint company and community value creation
Discretionary or in response to external pressure	Integral to competing
Separate from profit maximization	Integral to profit maximization
Agenda is determined by external reporting and personal preferences	Agenda is company specific and internally generated
Impact limited by corporate footprint and CSR budget	Realigns the entire company budget

Source: Adapted from Porter and Kramer (2011, p.16).

CSR: A Contribution to Competitive Advantage

What are the links between CSR and competitive advantage? CSR is more and more considered as an opportunity and a way to develop a competitive advantage rather than a cost (Grayson and Hodges, 2004). Berns et al. (2009) conducted the first annual business of Sustainability Global Survey of more than 1,500 corporate executives and managers about their perspectives on the intersection of sustainability and business strategy. Several benefits in addressing sustainability issues have been quoted—new sources of revenue or cash flow, cost savings, employee satisfaction, and competitive advantage.

There are two basic types of competitive advantage. Lower cost is the ability of a firm to design, produce, and market a comparable product more efficiently than its competitors. At prices at or near competitors, lower cost translates into superior returns; and differentiation is the ability to provide unique and superior value to the buyer in terms of product quality, special features, or after-sale service. Differentiation allows a firm to command a premium price which leads to superior profitability provided costs are comparable with those of competitors. Porter (1980) argued that a business can develop a sustainable competitive advantage based on cost, differentiation, or both: "Competitive advantage cannot be understood by looking at a firm as a whole. It stems from the many discrete activities a firm performs in designing, producing, marketing, delivering and supporting its product. Each of these activities can contribute to a firm's relative cost position and create a basis for differentiation" (Porter, 1985, p.33). CSR can create a differentiation advantage by improving brand image and/or company reputation.

In strategy, companies have to achieve a sustainable advantage in order to survive. The idea emerged in 1984 when Day explained that there are two types of strategies that may help to "sustain the competitive advantage" (Day, 1984, p.32). Other authors (Hall, 1980; Henderson, 1983) insisted on the need for firms to possess unique advantages in relation to competitors in order to survive.

From Sustainable to Temporary Advantage: The Resource-Based View (RBV) Approach

The idea of considering firms as a large set of resources goes back to the seminal work of Penrose (1959). But this concept received renewed attention in the 1980s in particular by Wernerfelt (1984, 1989). RBV has become an influential framework for analyzing corporate strategy (Barney, 1991; Peteraf, 1993; Hoopes et al., 2003). This approach considers the firm as a collection of resources which are tied to the firm's management—firms are heterogeneous with respect to their resources and capabilities.

RBV has become an influential approach for analyzing corporate strategy. The aim is not to focus on the external environment of the company but instead to thoroughly analyze the company's resources.

The resources are of various kinds: physical (machines, manufacturing facilities); human (qualifications, degree of adaptability of employees); and financial (the various sources of liquid assets). They may also be intangible and may be based on goodwill (existence of intangible assets such as a patent, brand, or knowhow). "Resources and capabilities can be viewed as bundles of tangible and intangible assets, including a firm's management skills, its organizational processes and routines, and the information and knowledge it controls" (Barney, 2001, p.625). Intangible assets are particularly important in that they are hard to access and imitate. They often constitute strategic resources, in other words unique resources from which the company's competitive advantage stems.

The most competitive company is the one which possesses the most advantageous resources and the competencies necessary for the implementation and combination of these resources (Barney, 1991; Peteraf, 1993; Wernerfelt, 1984). Peteraf (1993) analyzed links between the resource-based model and sustainable competitive advantage. Barney (1991) contributed to the discussion by considering that firms can achieve sustainable competitive advantage thanks to resources that must possess four attributes: rareness, value, inability to be imitated, and inability to be substituted (see Table 7.2).

Table 7.2   From competitive disadvantage to sustainable disadvantage: the RBV conceptual framework

Is resource			Supported by organization	Competitive Implications	Performance
Valuable?	Rare?	Difficult to Imitate?			
No	–	–		Competitive disadvantage	Below normal
Yes	No			Competitive parity	Normal
Yes	Yes	No		Temporary competitive advantage	Above normal
Yes	Yes	Yes		Sustained competitive advantage	Above normal

Source: Adapted from Barney and Wright (1997), p.11.

Can CSR be considered as a resource, competence, or capability? The analysis of the strategic capacity of a company depends on several factors. To describe a general overview of a firm, the RBV analysis must be combined with the competence-based view (CBV) representing the second level of analysis. The concept of resources is thus often associated with the concept of organizational competencies, in other words the routines, knowhow, and processes that are specific to the company and to its collective learning process. They must be difficult to imitate in order to create a sustainable advantage. They form part of the: "core competencies that are the collective learning in the organization, especially how to coordinate diverse production skills and integrate multiple streams of technologies" (Prahalad and Hamel, 1990, p.82). Moreover, these competencies: "enable the organization to outperform its competitors or to offer a level of value that is clearly superior" (Johnson and Scholes, 2001, p.178). With strong core competencies in its existing business, a company can seek new customers by developing new value chains. Core competencies have to be analyzed in relation to resources and distinctive capabilities. Both of them provide sustainable competitive advantage.

When companies adopt CSR practices, they have to develop new competencies related to encourage intra-collaboration between employees and strong social interaction ties, to create trust culture, to promote share common values and norms, to adopt vision and long-term thinking, to focus on management quality, to develop skills in engaging and communicating with external stakeholders... Most of these actions are based on shared information and knowledge (explicit and tacit). These competencies rely on a dynamic process (see Table 7.3) and they could evolve.

Table 7.3   From distinctive capabilities to dynamic capabilities

Grant (1991)	Grant makes distinctions between resources and capabilities. Resources are inputs into the production process. These could be financial resources, physical resources, human resources, technological resources, reputation, and organizational resources. But resources are not productive in themselves. A capability, according to Grant, is the capacity for a team of resources to perform some task or activity. Thus, resources are the source of a firm's capabilities and these in turn are the main source of its competitive advantage.
Amit and Schoemaker (1993)	They make a distinction between resources and capabilities. They define resources as: "stocks of available factors that are owned or controlled by the firm. Resources are converted into final products or services by using a wide range of other firm assets and bonding mechanisms such as technology, management information systems, incentive systems, trust between labor, and more" (1993, p.35). Capability refers to the capacity of a firm to deploy resources using organizational processes to affect a desired end. Capabilities are "information-based, tangible or intangible processes that are firm-specific and are developed over time through complex interactions among the firm's resources" (1993, p.35).
Pavlou and El Sawy (2005)	Functional competencies have to be distinguished from dynamic capabilities, the first being: "the purposive combinations of resources that enable accomplishing a given task – perform operational activities (for example, ability to identify valuable alliance opportunities)," and the latter being: "the ability to renew functional competencies by reconfiguring the existing combinations of resources" (2005, p.7).
Di Guardo and Galvagno (2006)	"The ability to build new capabilities that lie in higher levels in the relevant hierarchy of competencies is referred to as dynamic capabilities (Teece, Pisano and Schuen, 1997), integrative capabilities (Verona, 1999), combinative capabilities (Kogut and Zander, 1992) or absorptive capacity (Cohen and Levinthal, 1990). What is actually involved in the ability, that we will simply call dynamic capabilities, is, in essence, the creation and the integration of new competencies out of the already existing stocks of prior competencies held by the organization. This is perhaps the most critical ability of a firm, which is the ability to feel the need to reconfigure its existing structure of competencies and to accomplish successfully the necessary transformations" (Amit and Schoemaker, 1993; see also Collis (1994, p.3) for a critique on this premise).
Helfat and Peteraf (2003); Helfat et al. (2007)	Dynamic capabilities can transform functional competencies into several directions to match environmental needs.

Source: Developed by the authors, based on analysis of the articles cited.

The Development of the Temporary (or Transient) Advantage Concept

As we have shown in the two previous tables, other kinds of competitive advantage have emerged in the strategy literature (Daidj, 2015). The debate on what actually constitutes competitive advantage ensued in both strategic management and economics (Rumelt et al., 1991; Waring, 1996). Numerous researchers (D'Aveni, 1994; Ferrier, 2001; Wiggins and Ruefli, 2002) have proposed the term of temporary competitive advantage, also known as transient, fleeting, or short-term advantage.

Afuah (2009) explained that according to the strategy a firm pursues, the firm may have a sustainable competitive advantage, temporary competitive advantage, competitive parity, or competitive disadvantage (Table 7.4). The author defined six categories of strategies (Afuah, 2009, pp.18–19):

1. In strategy 1 the set of activities that the firm performs creates value that customers perceive as unique, and the firm is able to appropriate the value so created. This strategy is not so common.

2. In strategy 2 the firm conducts activities that enable it to create value that customers perceive as unique, and put it in a position to appropriate the value. It also has what it takes to perform the activities, but the strategy is such that the firm cannot take advantage of change. During the period before the change, the firm has a temporary competitive advantage.

3. In strategy 3 the firm creates value and takes advantage of change, but can appropriate the value created only for the short period that it takes competitors to imitate it. It has the resources and capabilities to perform the value creating activities. Thus the firm also has a temporary competitive advantage.

4. In strategy 4 the firm can neither appropriate the value created nor take advantage of change, even though it creates value and has what it takes to perform the activities. Such a strategy is also said to give the firm competitive parity. Most producers of commodity products have comparative parity.

Table 7.4 Competitive consequences of new game strategy

First-mover advantage	Activities: Is the firm performing the right activities? Does it have what it takes (resources and capabilities) to perform the activities?	Value: Is the value created by the strategy unique, as perceived by customers, compared to that of competitors?	Appropriability: Does the firm make money from the value created?	Change: Does the strategy take advantage of change (present or future) to create unique value and/or position itself to appropriate the value?	Competitive consequence
Strategy 1	Yes	Yes	Yes	Yes	Sustainable competitive advantage
Strategy 2	Yes	Yes	Yes	No	Temporary competitive advantage
Strategy 3	Yes	Yes	Yes/no	Yes	Temporary competitive advantage
Strategy 4	Yes	Yes	No	No	Competitive parity
Strategy 5	No/yes	No	Yes	No	Competitive parity
Strategy 6	No	No	No	No	Competitive disadvantage

Source: Adapted from Afuah (2009, p.19).

5.   In strategy 5 the firm has what it takes to perform some activities, but not others. It can appropriate some of the value created, even though the value is not unique. It is vulnerable to change. A firm that pursues such a strategy also has competitive parity with competitors.

6.   In strategy 6 the set of activities that a firm performs neither creates unique value nor puts the firm in a position to appropriate value created by others, nor does the firm have what it takes to perform the activities. The firm is said to have a competitive disadvantage.

In his groundbreaking book published in 1994, D'Aveni introduced the concept of hypercompetition. He explains that competitive advantage is, by definition, destined to disappear in such a context, and that it is futile to attempt to defend a sustainable competitive advantage. The only sustainable position is that of movement, and long-term, or sustained, above-average profitability is not feasible. D'Aveni et al. (2010) thus propose "the age of temporary advantage" as an alternative concept. A competitive firm should constantly be able to reposition itself in terms of its value proposition, its *savoir-faire*, and its financial capacity in light of the changing entry barriers and time frames of evolving competitive dynamics. Hypercompetitivity thus presupposes permanent transformation of competitive advantages. Other authors (Brown and Eisenhardt, 1998; MacMillan, 1989; Hamel, 2000) have also highlighted that firms in competitive industries are almost systematically seeking the same temporary advantages, rather than focusing on more sustainable long-term strategies.

More recently, Rita Gunther McGrath (2013) asserts that sustainable competitive advantage is obsolete for competing in today's dynamic world. She proposes referring to another concept known as "transient competitive advantage" because markets change in a radical way. "Stability, not change, is the state that is most dangerous in highly dynamic competitive environments" (McGrath, 2013, p.7). "The end of competitive advantage means that the assumptions that underpin much of what we used to believe about running organizations are deeply flawed" (McGrath, 2013, p.18). She gives several examples of companies which were not able to see change coming such as Kodak, Sony, Research in Motion (RIM), Blockbuster, and so on. According to the author, the new playbook is based on six assumptions of competing in arenas (not industries alone) and exploiting temporary competitive advantages:

- continuous reconfiguration

- healthy disengagement

- using resource allocation to promote deftness

- building an innovation proficiency

- leadership and mindset

- personal meaning of transient advantage.

Debating Notions of Duration and Sustainability of Competitive Advantage

Despite its importance in the field of strategy and competitive advantage, sustainability has not been clearly defined and different theoretical positions persist. Coyne (1986) explains: "perhaps it is because the meaning of 'sustainable competitive advantage' is superficially self-evident that virtually no effort has been made to define it explicitly" (Coyne, 1986, p.54). Two approaches can be distinguished in relation to the interpretation of competitive advantage:

1. Sustainable competitive advantage is linked to a time continuum. Porter (1985), for example, illustrates this logic by describing competitive advantage as: "the fundamental basis of above-average performance in the long run" (Porter, 1985, p.12). Hill and Jones (2004) also do so when they consider that an organization: "has a sustained competitive advantage when it is able to maintain above-average profitability over a number of years" (Hill and Jones, 2004, p.76). What "long run" involves is not specified, neither is the exact number of years.

2. Sustainable competitive advantage is not directly linked to time but to the possibility of duplication by competitors (Lippman and Rumelt, 1982; Rumelt, 1984; Barney, 1991). "A firm is said to have a sustained competitive advantage when it is implementing a value creating strategy not simultaneously being implemented by any current or potential competitors and when these other firms are unable to duplicate the benefits of this strategy" (Barney, 1991, p.102).

The definition of success for an organization is often multiple and involves much more than profit maximization. Indeed profit maximization in a long-term perspective can involve very different behavior to that of a short-term perspective. Often the approach taken is that of satisfying—the balancing of the long term with the short term, and the balancing of the expectations of all stakeholders. These, in combination with a desire for growth—now often called sustainable development—and survival form the objectives of an organization, and a mix of these in the form of a balanced scorecard will be the objectives of an organization and its definition of success will be dependent upon meeting these objectives (Aras and Crowther, 2009a).

Thus, by the start of the twentieth century it had been accepted that firms had a corporate identity which was distinct from that of their owners and that such firms embodied a presumption of immortality (Hein, 1978). In legal terms a company therefore is a person with the power to contract like any other individual[2] although the reality is that this power is vested in the managers of the company. The effect of this is that managers can enter into transactions for which they have no liability for non-fulfillment. Effectively, with the introduction of this concept of limited liability, risk was transferred away from the legal owners of a business and onto those with whom that business was transacted. Equally, the ability of managers to engage in those transactions on behalf of the business without any necessary evidence of ownership—merely delegated responsibility—meant that most risk was thereby transferred away from the business. The potential rewards from owning a business became divorced from any commensurate risk—effectively separating the risk–reward relationship upon which finance theory is based. Still these changes have not been sufficient and so recent concern has been with the free market as a mediating mechanism. The argument, of course, is that unregulated transacting will benefit everyone, but this is only true in a situation of perfect competition.[3] With the sort of power inequalities which exist in the present this philosophy only justifies exploitation by the powerful of the corporate world. This then creates an environment in which CSR is needed (see Aras and Crowther, 2009a).

---

2   Wenlock (Baroness) v River Dee Co, 1887.
3   One of the first assumptions of economics is that of perfect competition—readily acknowledged to be an unrealistic set of assumptions which are quickly relaxed in theory. This of course never gets a mention by the free marketers—or even their critics!

Conclusion

Strategic management is concerned with developing the tools and techniques to analyze industries and competitors, and developing strategies to gain competitive advantage. The external models stress the fact that the company must adapt to its environment and find attractive and profitable sectors. The internal diagnosis focuses on identifying distinctive resources and core competencies which secure competitive advantage. To meet market current challenges and future changes, firms need the right tools to compete in global markets and build new business models.

CSR practices are closely related to strategic planning focusing on managing interaction with environmental forces which include competitors, government, suppliers, customers, various interest groups, and other stakeholders. Long-range planning could aid in the anticipation of major strategic issues and in the recognition of environmental (industry, technology) changes. But as it is more and more difficult to plan beyond the one- to five-year time horizon typical of most investments, companies have developed several responses to the planning challenges in order to have a more agile strategic planning process. CSR could allow these firms to achieve sustainable advantage even if the environment is unstable (technology and customer preferences changes, new markets entrants, and so on) and turbulent.

The discourses of sustainability all adopt a viewpoint of the acceptability, or otherwise, of sustainable development. Equally, these discourses accept that sustainability is possible but disagree about the circumstances in which it is possible and about the resultant level of economic activity.

References and Bibliography

Afuah, A. (2009). *Strategic Innovation. New Game Strategies for Competitive Advantage.* New York: Routledge.

Amit, R., and Schoemaker, P. (1993). Strategic Assets and Organizational Rent. *Strategic Management Journal,* Vol. 14(1), 32–46.

Aras. G., and Crowther, D. (2013). Sustainable Practice: The Real Triple Bottom Line. *The Governance of Risk,* Emerald Book Series: Developments in Corporate Governance and Responsibility.

Aras. G., Kutlu O., and Aybars, A. (2011). The Interaction Between Corporate Social Responsibility and Value Added Intellectual Capital: Empirical Evidence from Turkey. *Social Responsibility Journal*, Vol. 7(4), 622–37.

Aras. G., Kutlu O., and Aybars, A. (2010). Managing Corporate Performance: Investigating the Relationship between Corporate Social Responsibility and Financial Performance in Emerging Markets. *International Journal of Productivity and Performance Management*, Vol. 59(3), 229–54.

Aras. G., and Crowther, D. (2009a). Corporate Sustainability Reporting: A Study in Disingenuity? *Journal of Business Ethics*, Vol. 27, 279–88.

Aras. G., and Crowther, D. (2009b). Making Sustainable Development Sustainable. *Management Decision*, Vol. 47(6), 975–88.

Aras. G., and Crowther, D. (2009c). The Durable Corporation in a Time of Financial and Economic Crisis. *Economics and Management*, Vol. 14, 211–17.

Aras. G., and Crowther, D. (2009d). Introduction: Corporate Governance and Corporate Social Responsibility in context. In G. Aras and D. Crowther (eds), *Global Perspectives on Corporate Governance and Corporate Social Responsibility*. Aldershot: Gower.

Aras, G. (2008). Corporate Governance and the Agency Problem in Financial Markets. In D. Crowther and N. Capaldi (eds), *Ashgate Research Companion to Corporate Social Responsibility*. Aldershot: Ashgate.

Aras, G., and Crowther, D. (2008a). Evaluating Sustainability: A Need for Standards. *Issues in Social and Environmental Accounting*, Vol. 2(1), 19–35.

Aras. G., and Crowther, D. (2008b). Developing Sustainable Reporting Standards. *Journal of Applied Accounting Research*, Vol. 9(1), 4–16.

Aras. G., and Crowther, D. (2008c). Governance and Sustainability: An Investigation into The Relationship between Corporate Governance and Corporate Sustainability. *Management Decision*, Vol. 46(3), 433–48.

Aras. G., and Crowther, D. (2008d). The Social Obligation of Corporations. *Journal of Knowledge Globalisation*, Vol. 1(1), 43–59.

Aras, G., and Crowther, D. (2007a). Is Globalization Sustainable? In S. Barber (ed), *The Geopolitics of the City*, 165–94. London: Forum Press.

Aras, G., and Crowther, D. (2007b). Sustainable Corporate Social Responsibility and the Value Chain. In D. Crowther and M.M. Zain (eds), *New Perspectives on Corporate Social Responsibility*, 119–40. Shah Alam, Malaysia: MARA University Press.

Aras, G., and Crowther, D. (2007c). What Level of Trust is Needed for Sustainability? *Social Responsibility Journal*, Vol. 3(3), 60–68.

Barney, J.B. (2001). Resource-based Theories of Competitive Advantage: A Ten-year Retrospective on the Resource-Based View. *Journal of Management*, Vol. 27, 643–50.

Barney, J.B. (1991). Firm Resources and Sustained Competitive Advantage. *Journal of Management*, Vol. 17(1), 99–120.

Berns, M., Townend, A., Khayat, Z., Balagopal, B., Reeves, M., Hopkins, M.S., and Kruschwitz, N. (2009). Sustainability and Competitive Advantage. *MIT Sloan Management Review*, Vol. 51(1), 19–26.

Brown, S.L., and Eisenhardt, K.M. (1998). *Competing on the Edge: Strategy as Structured Chaos*. Boston, MA: Harvard Business School Press.

Cohen, W.M., and Levinthal, D.A. (1990). Absorptive Capacity: A New Perspective on Learning and Innovation. *Administrative Science Quarterly* Vol. 35(1), 128–52.

Collis, D.J. (1994). How Valuable are Organisational Capabilities? *Strategic Management Journal*, Vol. 15, 143–52.

Coyne, K.P. (1986). Sustainable Competitive Advantage: What It Is, What It Isn't. *Business Horizons*, Vol. 29(1), 54–61.

Daidj, N. (2015). *Developing Strategic Business Models and Competitive Advantage in the Digital Sector*. Hershey, PA: IGI Global.

D'Aveni, R.A. (1994). *Hypercompetition*. New York: The Free Press.

D'Aveni, R.A., Dagnino G.B., and Smith, K.G. (2010). The Age of Temporary Advantage. *Strategic Management Journal*, Vol. 31(13), 1371–85.

Daly, H.E. (1996), *Beyond Growth*. Boston, MA: Beacon Press.

Daly, H.E. (1992). Allocation, Distribution, and Scale: Toward an Economics that is Efficient, Just, and Sustainable. *Ecological Economics*, Vol. 6(3), 185–93.

Day, G.S. (1984). *Strategic Market Planning: The Pursuit of Competitive Advantage*. St. Paul, MN: West Publishing Company.

Di Guardo, C.M., and Galvagno, M. (2006). *The Dynamic Capabilities View of Coopetition: The Case of Intel, Apple and Microsoft*. Presented at the 2nd EIASM Workshop on Coopetition, Bocconi University.

Elliott, S.R. (2005). Sustainability: An Economic Perspective. *Resources Conservations & Recycling*, Vol. 44, 263–77.

Ferrier, W. (2001). Navigating the Competitive Landscape: The Drivers and Consequences of Competitive Aggressiveness. *Academy of Management Journal*, Vol. 44, 858–77.

Fish, S. (1980). *Is There a Text in this Class? The Authority to Interpret Communities*. Cambridge, MA: Harvard University Press.

Grant, R. (1991). The Resource-Based Theory of Competitive Advantage: Implications for Strategy Formulation. *California Management Review*, Vol. 33(3), 114–35.

Grayson, D., and Hodges, A. (2004). *Corporate Social Opportunity*. Sheffield: Greenleaf.

Guiraud, P. (1975). *Semiology*. London: Routledge and Kegan Paul.

Hall, W.K. (1980). Survival Strategies in a Hostile Environment. *Harvard Business Review* Vol. 58(5), 75–85.

Hamel, G. (2000). *Leading the Revolution*. Boston, MA: Harvard Business School Press.

Hatani, F., and McGaughey, S.L. (2013). Network Cohesion in Global Expansion: An Evolutionary View. *Journal of World Business* Vol. 48(4), 455–65.

Hart, S.L. (1997). Beyond Greening: Strategies for a Sustainable World. *Harvard Business Review*, Jan/Feb 1997, Vol. 75(1), 66–76.

Hart, S.L., and Milstein, M. B. (2003). Creating Sustainable Value. *Academy of Management Executive*, Vol. 17(2), 56–67.

Hawken, P. (1993). *The Ecology of Commerce*. London: Weidenfeld & Nicholson.

Hein, L.W. (1978). *The British Companies Acts and the Practice of Accountancy 1844–1962*. New York: Arno Press.

Helfat, C., Finkelstein, S., Mitchell, W., Peteraf, M.A., Singh, H., Teece, D.J., and Winter, S.G. (2007). *Dynamic Capabilities: Understanding Strategic Change in Organizations*. Oxford, UK: Blackwell.

Helfat, C., and Peteraf, M. (2003). The Dynamic Resource-based View: Capability Lifecycles. *Strategic Management Journal*, Vol. 24, 997–1010.

Henderson, B. (1983). The Anatomy of Competition. *Journal of Marketing*, Vol. 47(1), 7–11.

Hill, C.W. and Jones, G.R. (2004). *Strategic Management: An Integrated Approach*. Houghton, Boston, MA: Mifflin Company.

Hoopes, D.G., Madsen, T.L., and Walker, G. (2003). Guest Editors' Introduction to the Special Issue: Why is there a Resource-Based View? Toward a Theory of Competitive Heterogeneity. *Strategic Management Journal*, Vol. 24, 889–902.

Iansiti, M., and Levien, R. (2004). *The Keystone Advantage: What the New Dynamics of Business Ecosystems Mean for Strategy, Innovation, and Sustainability*. Harvard: Harvard Business School Press.

Johnson, G., and Scholes, K. (2001). *Exploring Public Sector Strategy*. Harlow: FT Prentice Hall.

Johnson, G., Whittington, R., and Scholes, K. (2012). *Fundamentals of Strategy* (Second Edition). Essex: Pearson Education.

Kay, J. (1993). The Structure of Strategy. *Business Strategy Review*, Vol. 4(2), 17–37.

Kim, K.L. (1996). *Caged in Our Own Signs: A Book about Semiotics*. Norwood, NJ: Ablex Publishing.

Kogut, B., and Zander, U. (1992). Knowledge of the Firm, Combinative Capabilities, and the Replication of Technology. *Organization Science*, Vol. 3, 383–97.

Lippman, S., and Rumelt, R. (1982). Uncertain Imitability: An Analysis of Interfirm Differences in Efficiency under Competition. *Bell Journal of Economics*, Vol. 13, 418–38.

Lovelock, J. (2006). *The Revenge of Gaia*. Harmondsworth: Penguin.

Lovelock, J. (1979). *Gaia*. Oxford: Oxford University Press.

MacMillan, I.C. (1989). How Long can you Sustain a Competitive Advantage? In L. Fahey (ed.), *The Strategy Planning Management Reader*. Englewood Cliffs, NJ: Prentice Hall.

McGrath, R.G. (2013). *The End of Competitive Advantage: How To Keep Your Strategy Moving as Fast as Your Business*. Boston, MA: Harvard Business Review Press.

Marsden, C. (2000). The New Corporate Citizenship of Big Business: Part of the Solution to Sustainability. *Business & Society Review*, Vol. 105(1), 9–25.

Millstein, I.M., and MacAvoy, P.W. (2003). The Active Board of Directors and Performance of the Large Publicly Traded Corporation. *Columbia Law Review*, Vol. 8(5), 1998, 1283–322.

Pavlou, A.P., and El Sawy O.A. (2005). *Understanding the 'Black Box' of Dynamic Capabilities: A Missing Link to the Strategic Role of IT in Turbulent Environments?* Working paper.

Penrose, E.T. (1959). *The Theory of the Growth of the Firm*. New York: John Wiley & Sons.

Peteraf, M.A. (1993). The Cornerstones of Competitive Advantage: A Resource-Based View. *Strategic Management Journal*, Vol. 14(3), 179–91.

Porter, M.E. (1985). *Competitive Advantage*. New York: The Free Press.

Porter, M.E. (1980). *Competitive Strategy: Techniques for Analyzing Industries and Competitors*. New York: The Free Press.

Porter, M.E., and Kramer, M.R. (2011). The Big Idea. Created Shared Value. *Harvard Business Review*, Vol. 89(1), 1–17.

Prahalad, C.K., and Hamel, G. (1990). The Core Competence of the Corporation. *Harvard Business Review*, Vol. 68(3), 79–91.

Reed, R. and DeFillippi, R.J. (1990). Causal Ambiguity, Barriers to Imitation, and Sustainable Competitive Advantage. *Academy of Management Review*, Vol. 15(1), 88–102.

Rumelt, R. (1984). Towards a Strategic Theory of the Firm. In R. Lamb (ed.), *Competitive Strategic Management*, 556–70. Englewood Cliffs, NJ: Prentice Hall.

Rumelt, R.P., Schendel, D., and Teece, D.J. (1991). Strategic Management and Economics. *Strategic Management Journal*, Vol. 12, 5–29.

Schmidheiny, S. (1992). *Changing Course.* New York: MIT Press.

Spangenberg, J.H. (2004). Reconciling Sustainability and Growth: Criteria, Indicators, Policies. *Sustainable Development*, Vol. 12, 76–84.

Teece, D.J., Pisano, G., and Shuen, A. (1997). Dynamic Capabilities and Strategic Management. *Strategic Management Journal*, Vol. 18(7), 509–33.

Verona, G. (1999). A Resource-based View of Product Development. *Academy of Management Review*, Vol. 24(1), 132–42.

Waring, G.F. (1996). Industry Differences in the Persistence of Firm-Specific Returns. *American Economic Review*, Vol. 8(5), 1253–65.

Wernerfelt, B. (1989). From Critical Resources to Corporate Strategy. *Journal of General Management*, Vol. 14(3), 4–12.

Wernerfelt, B. (1984). The Resource-based View of the Firm. *Strategic Management Journal*, Vol. 5(2), 171–80.

Wiggins, R.R., and Ruefli, T.W. (2002). Sustained Competitive Advantage: Temporal Dynamics and the Incidence and Persistence of Superior Economic Performance. *Organization Science*, Vol. 13(1), 81–105.

Zwetsloot, G.I.J.M. (2003). From Management Systems to Corporate Social Responsibility. *Journal of Business Ethics*, Vol. 44(2–3), 201–7.

PART III
Future Perspectives and Solutions

Chapter 8

Systemic Crises in Global Markets: In Search of Regulatory and Sustainable Solutions

THOMAS CLARKE

Introduction

The global financial crisis in 2008 and its aftermath consisted of multiple and compounding failures in financial markets, institutions, regulation, and governance. The "animal spirits" unleashed in unfettered securities markets, massive incentivization of risk-taking and leverage, and the abandonment of effective governance and ethical commitments occurred in a regulatory vacuum. Governments were convinced that lightening the burden of regulation was the means to promote more dynamic financial markets and business development. The realization of the consequences of unchecked systemic risks for global markets has prompted national governments and international agencies into a major series of regulatory reforms and interventions in financial markets and institutions, the effect of which remains to be discerned.

The global financial crisis was a multidimensional, interconnected, and systemic crisis. Among the causes of the crisis were international macro-economic imbalances, institutional and risk management failure, corporate governance failure, and regulatory, supervisory and crisis management failure. Understanding the compounding impact of these interconnected series of failures is the key to understanding the scale and intensity of the crisis. The G20 (Financial Stability Board (FSB)), IMF, OECD, EU (De Larosière Report[1]), US (Dodd–Frank Act 2010), UK, Australia, and other countries' analysis and prescriptions recognize this was a systemic crisis requiring systemic solutions.

---

1   The de Larosière report, issued by a panel led by the former French central banker, Jacques de Larosière, calls for an overhaul of Europe's financial regulation system.

Without profound changes in financial systems, structures, cultures, processes, and behavior further global financial crises may be anticipated, and the consequences could be disastrous for global economic stability and security. The question is will the ongoing global effort at regulatory reform achieve significant change, or be marginalized by the exigencies of dealing with immediate problems such as sovereign debt, or ignored in the next dash for economic growth (Coffee, 2012)?

The Global Financial Crisis and the Inevitability of Recurrent Crises

The prolonged systemic crisis in international financial markets commencing in 2007/2008 was also a crisis in corporate governance and regulation, exposing the dangers of unregulated markets, nominal corporate governance, and neglected risk management. As a World Bank report concluded:

> *If there is one lesson from the current crisis—a lesson consistent with the Asian financial crisis—it is that corporate governance matters. The central irony of the governance failures in this crisis is that many took place in some of the most sophisticated banks operating in some of the most developed governance environments in the world. (Ard and Berg, 2010)*

The ascendancy of Anglo-American markets and governance institutions was based on the apparent sophistication and efficiency of this system in the management of finance and risk. However, risk was not hedged; it was deeply interconnected, international, and unknown. The market capitalization of the stock markets of the world had peaked at $62 trillion at the end of 2007, but was by October 2008 in free fall, having lost $33 trillion dollars, over half of the total value in 12 months of unrelenting financial and corporate failures.

A debate has continued for some time about the costs and benefits of the financialization of advanced industrial economies. The long progression of financial crises around the world serves as a reminder that the system is neither self-regulating nor robust. The explanation of why investment banks and other financial institutions took such spectacular risks with extremely leveraged positions on many securities and derivatives, and the risk management, governance, and ethical environment that allowed such conduct to take place demands detailed analysis.

Firstly, there is a sense of the instability of the international financial economy and the inevitability of recurrent crises:

> *Systemic crises, which are ubiquitous throughout financial history, are inevitable notwithstanding good faith regulatory efforts to avoid them. The recurrence of financial crises can be explained in at least four different but non-exclusive ways. The first is the inherent fragility of banks (including their non-bank substitutes), given the liquidity promise to bank capital suppliers and the illiquid nature of bank assets. The second is the inherent instability of a capitalist financial system, which has a strongly pro-cyclical bias that tends towards asset bubbles and increased leverage. The third is the risk that in the process of financial innovation, the systemic risks of an innovation will flip from the minor to the major with unforeseen consequences. Cutting across all of these accounts is a fourth explanation: the constrained capacity of regulators, in light of cognitive gaps and pro-cyclical political economy pressures, to foresee systemic risks and cabin them. Paradoxically, successful control of systemic risk is also risk-creating, as parties come to rely on a benign financial environment. Thus, systemic breaks in the financial sector will inevitably occur on a potentially violent scale. (Gordon and Muller, 2010, p.4)*

As the financialization of the global economy has progressed in recent decades, it has been punctuated by a series of financial crises of growing significance. These crises included the early 1980s third world debt crisis; the 1987 Black Tuesday market crash when global markets fell 20 percent in one day; the late 1980s unwinding of the junk bond fuelled merger and acquisitions boom in the US; the bursting of the Japanese bubble economy; the early 1990s crash of banks in three Nordic countries; the Savings and Loans crash in the US; the 2001 NASDAQ crash leading to the collapse of Enron and WorldCom and a string of other major US corporations; and the 2007/2008 global financial crisis.

Yet it is important to realize that the most recent crisis proved qualitatively different from earlier episodes. This was the first truly global financial crisis impacting on all regions and countries, involving the collapse or near collapse of many major financial institutions across the Western world, demonstrating the ineffectiveness of all forms of existing regulatory apparatus, and necessitating the intervention of internationally coordinated state action to salvage financial markets on a scale unprecedented (and unimaginable) in earlier times.

International Financial Contagion

The US Treasury and the Federal Reserve, who were the regulators with responsibility to supervise markets, were ill-prepared for the events of 2007 and 2008 according to the US National Commission (2011) into the financial crisis:

> They were hampered because they did not have a clear grasp of the financial system they were charged with overseeing, particularly as it had evolved in the years leading up to the crisis. This was in no small measure due to the lack of transparency in key markets. They thought risk had been diversified when, in fact, it had been concentrated. Time and again, from the spring of 2007 on, policy makers and regulators were caught off guard as the contagion spread, responding on an ad hoc basis with specific programs to put fingers in the dike. There was no comprehensive and strategic plan for containment, because they lacked a full understanding of the risks and interconnections in the financial markets. Some regulators have conceded this error. We had allowed the system to race ahead of our ability to protect it ... Just a month before Lehman's collapse, the Federal Reserve Bank of New York was still seeking information on the exposures created by Lehman's more than 900,000 derivatives contracts. (2011, xxi)

In a second authoritative report by the US Congress, the Financial Crisis Inquiry Commission (2011) revealed that the global financial crisis had brought a tumultuous end to six years of galloping inflation in both financial institutions' profitability, and in the inflation of the market capitalization of the S & P 500 index. The scale of the disaster one sage commented demonstrated the unerring capacity of Wall Street to have a once in a life time catastrophe approximately every six years.

The abolition of the Glass–Steagall Act (1933) in 1999 paved the way for a regulatory loosening of the US financial system, enhanced in 2004 by a new Securities and Exchange Commission (SEC) rule intended to reduce regulatory costs for broker–dealers that were part of consolidated supervised entities. Essentially, this involved large broker–dealers using their own risk management practices for regulatory purposes enabling a lowering of their capital requirements—the core capital a bank is required to hold to support its risk-taking activities which normally includes share capital, share premium, and retained earnings. In addition the SEC amended the definition of net capital to include securities for which there was no ready market, and to include hybrid capital instruments and certain deferred tax assets, reducing the amount of capital required to engage in high risk activities. Finally, the rule eased the calculations of counterparty risk, maximum potential exposures, margin lending, and allowed broker–dealers to assign their own credit ratings to unrated companies. Einhorn comments on this regulatory capitulation of the SEC:

> *Large broker–dealers convinced the regulators that the dealers could better measure their own risks, and with fancy math, they attempted to show that they could support more risk with less capital. I suspect that the SEC took the point of view that these were all large, well-capitalized institutions, with smart, sophisticated risk managers who had no incentive to try to fail. Consequently, they gave the industry the benefit of the doubt. (Einhorn, 2008a, p.16)*

The verdict of the US National Commission (2011, p.xviii) was that 30 years of deregulation and reliance on self-regulation by financial institutions had stripped away the safeguards that might have helped avert the catastrophe:

> *…There was pervasive permissiveness; little meaningful action was taken to quell the threats in a timely manner. The prime example is the Federal Reserve's pivotal failure to stem the flow of toxic mortgages, which it could have done by setting prudent mortgage-lending standards. The Federal Reserve was the one entity empowered to do so and it did not. The record of our examination is replete with evidence of other failures: financial institutions made, bought, and sold mortgage securities they never examined, did not care to examine, or knew to be defective; firms depended on tens of billions of dollars of borrowing that had to be renewed each and every night, secured by subprime mortgage securities; and major firms and investors blindly relied on credit rating agencies as their arbiters of risk. (2011, p.xvii)*

The US National Commission (2011, p.xviii) was convinced the dramatic failures of corporate governance and risk management at many systemically important financial institutions were a key cause of the financial crisis. The assumptions at the time were that the instincts for self-preservation within financial firms would shield them from excessive risk-taking without a need for regulatory restraint that might stifle innovation—the reality was very different:

> *Too many of these institutions acted recklessly, taking on too much risk, with too little capital, and with too much dependence on short-term funding. In many respects, this reflected a fundamental change*

in these institutions, particularly the large investment banks and bank holding companies, which focused their activities increasingly on risky trading activities that produced hefty profits. They took on enormous exposures in acquiring and supporting subprime lenders and creating, packaging, repackaging, and selling trillions of dollars in mortgage-related securities, including synthetic financial products ... Financial institutions and credit rating agencies embraced mathematical models as reliable predictors of risks, replacing judgement in too many instances. Too often, risk management became risk justification. (2011, p.xviii)

The same recklessness regarding compensation practices pervaded Wall Street, as the US National Commission commented:

Compensation systems—designed in an environment of cheap money, intense competition, and light regulation—too often rewarded the quick deal, the short-term gain—without proper consideration of long-term consequences. Often, those systems encouraged the big bet—where the payoff on the upside could be huge and the downside limited. This was the case up and down the line—from the corporate boardroom to the mortgage broker on the street. (2011, p.xix)

Advancing Global Regulatory Governance

In recent years following the global financial crisis there has been an immense attempt at developing effective regulatory policy to guide intervention in financial markets, including a coordinated effort to find regulatory solutions to recurrent financial crises with the international regulatory guidance of the G20, the application of the key standards of the FSB, together with the work of the IMF, Basel Committee, IOSCO, and OECD. It must be acknowledged that at the supra-national level sustained efforts have been made to achieve better alignment of governance institutions and practices, risk management, and remuneration with market discipline, supervision, regulation, and transparency in the international financial sector. The question is how resilient will this new regulatory architecture prove as new forms of systemic risk emerge, and to what extent over the years will it be effectively enforced by national regulators, and implemented by financial institutions?

In principle this panoply of international regulatory initiatives will serve to strengthen the robust interaction of governance oversight, risk management, and remuneration at board level in financial institutions. However, the first analysis of bank self-assessment reports by the Basel-based FSB—established in April 2009 to coordinate at the international level the work of national financial authorities and international standard setting bodies, and to develop and promote the implementation of effective regulatory, supervisory, and other financial sector policies—revealed major financial institutions had significant improvements to make, and it was not evident how much progress had been made with regard to board direction and senior management oversight, risk management, and compensation practices. Many changes that firms had undertaken were organizational and appeared to have been relatively easy to implement. Less clear was whether these organizational changes will—without further effort—improve future governance practices (SSG/FSB, 2009, 22).

It is necessary to continue to survey the strengths and weaknesses of the governance of the global finance sector, examining potential fault lines in the main banking sector with a focus on capital adequacy and on companies' internal risk monitoring and control mechanisms, and the wider corporate finance sector with an emphasis on corporations and market integrity, including disclosure standards, and consumer protection. The objective is to discover the effectiveness of recent reforms aimed at enhancing board oversight, disclosure, risk management, compensation practices, and shareholder engagement, and the success of aligning these more closely with regulation, supervision, and market discipline.

The continuing challenge, and the most evident aspect of the financial crisis, was that it was a multidimensional and interconnected phenomenon— a systemic crisis that required systemic resolution. This challenge begins with vast, international, interconnected financial institutions: "The greater financial and economic impacts associated with problems at larger institutions requires a holistic approach that combines transparency, governance, regulation, supervision, and market discipline" (Lumpkin, 2011, p.1). Lumpkin illustrates how a range of policy alternatives needs to be coordinated in order to achieve an adequate regulatory response to multidimensional financial governance phenomena, including market-based, prudential, structural, and bonding mechanisms.

Effective regulatory governance requires alignment of the different elements of the regulatory and market architecture as Lumpkin convincingly argues in the OECD's *Financial Market Trends*:

> *Measures that rely on market discipline are only as effective as the broader governance framework of which they are a part. Any weaknesses*

in the framework—such as misaligned or improper incentives, weak management information systems, and ineffective or incompetent boards—will mean that firewalls and related control mechanisms cannot be relied upon solely to control or mitigate conflicts of interest or other risks. Rather, as a general rule, internal controls and voluntary mechanisms should be subject to monitoring: authorities should be able to trust these controls and mechanisms, subject to verification, especially when the consequences of a failure could be severe. (Lumpkin, 2011, p.23)

A lack of effective risk governance was widespread in the international finance sector prior to the crisis. Many boards lacked a comprehensive understanding of their institution's risk profile and were unable to judge its appropriateness, in part for the following reasons:

- Incomplete risk information was transmitted to boards, leading to a false sense of security.

- There was a fundamental lack of expertise among non-executive directors.

- Executives used boards as a "group think" function rather than as a forum for vetting strategic risk issues.

- There was an overreliance on regulatory and compliance mechanisms to catch and report new or inappropriate sources of risk. This created a sort of autopilot risk mentality (UK Treasury, 2009).

The Senior Supervisors Group of the FSB highlighted the misalignments that may occur systemically in the governance, risk management, compensation systems, and management information systems:

An overarching observation that relates to many of the areas singled out for improvement is that weaknesses in governance, incentives, and infrastructure undermined the effectiveness of risk controls and contributed to ... systemic vulnerability. In the interviews we conducted for this report, we found that many firms—regardless of whether they required government support—and their supervisors had concluded that the incentives and controls in place throughout the industry had failed. These failures reflected four challenges in governance:

1. *the unwillingness or inability of boards of directors and senior managers to articulate, measure, and adhere to a level of risk acceptable to the firm;*

2. *arrangements that favored risk takers at the expense of independent risk managers and control personnel;*

3. *compensation plans that conflicted with the control objectives of the firm;*

4. *an inadequate and often fragmented infrastructure that hindered effective risk identification and measurement. (SSG/FSB, 2009, p.4)*

Major international financial institutions experienced these weaknesses leading up to the financial crisis, for example, the *Shareholders Report* on UBS, prepared by KPMG, demonstrated in sharp relief the financial consequences of this sustained misalignment of governance, risk management, and compensation as the Swiss Bank careered toward disaster: "UBS's review suggests an asymmetric focus in the investment bank senior management meetings on revenue and profit and loss, especially when compared to discussion of risk issues. Business–peer challenge was not a routine practice in those meetings" (UBS, 2008, p.34).

Enhancing Corporate Governance

In this context the OECD (2010) has reviewed its corporate governance principles and applied them more closely to financial institutions. The Basel Committee on Bank Supervision (BCBS) published its own *Principles for Enhancing Corporate Governance* (2010). Key areas of particular focus include:

- the role of the board;

- the qualifications and composition of the board;

- the importance of an independent risk management function, including a chief risk officer or equivalent;

- the importance of monitoring risks on an ongoing firm-wide and individual entity basis;

- the board's oversight of the compensation systems;

- the board and senior management's understanding of the bank's operational structure and risks.

The principles also emphasize the importance of supervisors regularly evaluating the bank's corporate governance policies and practices as well as its implementation of the Committee's principles.

In a later document on *Core Principles for Banking Supervision* the Basel Committee on Bank Supervision (2011, p.2) maintains:

> *Sound corporate governance underpins effective risk management and public confidence in individual banks and the banking system. Given fundamental deficiencies in banks' corporate governance that were exposed in the last crisis, a new Core Principle on corporate governance has been added in this review by bringing together existing corporate governance criteria in the assessment methodology and giving greater emphasis to sound corporate governance practices. Similarly, the Committee reiterated the key role of robust market discipline in fostering a safe and sound banking system by expanding an existing Core Principle into two new ones dedicated respectively to greater public disclosure and transparency, and enhanced financial reporting and external audit.*

The BCBS Core Principles establish a level of sound supervisory practice that can be used as a benchmark by supervisors to assess the quality of their supervisory systems. They are also used by the IMF and the World Bank, in the context of the Financial Sector Assessment Program (FSAP), to assess the effectiveness of countries' banking supervisory systems and practices (BCBS, 2011, p.7). Finally, the FSB (2011a) published "a peer review on compensation practices" that assesses progress made both by national authorities and by significant financial institutions in implementing the FSB Principles for Sound Compensation Practices and their Implementation Standards.

A small group of countries (Italy, the Netherlands, Singapore, Australia, and the UK) undertook a second round of bank self-assessments against the FSB Principles and Standards in 2010–11. However, recurrent assessments may be required to ensure durable commitments to reform. Also, though instructive, self-assessments do have limitations. There is a need for continuous independent analysis of the progress toward governance, risk management, and remuneration alignment in the international main banking sector and in the wider global corporate finance sector.

Complex Governance of the Conglomerate Structures: Global Systemically Important Financial Institutions (G–SIFIs)

However, it is the level of the scale, complexity, and sophistication of the major international financial institutions that poses the greatest regulatory and governance challenges. Frequently, large financial institutions adopt a conglomerate structure to manage their many businesses. These financial groups face the risks that arise generally in finance, but also face additional risks related to the multiplicity of their components and the complexity of their structure. "Complex, opaque, corporate structures were allowed to flourish, involving poor governance arrangements, less than optimal accounting arrangements, and auditors' judgements being called into question" (Davis, 2011, p.339). Such risks can also be interrelated within or across sectors and across borders (Lumpkin, 2011, p.30).

Complex financial conglomerates give rise to considerable governance problems for boards seeking to monitor conflict of interest, manage risk, and provide appropriate incentives for executives. Financial risks can arise from intergroup or third-party transactions. Reputation may be harmed by these and other activities, including the activity of an unregulated entity. Moral hazard may arise from excessive risk-taking, relying on the support of other members of the group who may not be informed of the level of risk entered into. Governance risks arise out of the complexity of the activities, and the difficulty of reconciling differing interests and responsibilities (Farrar, 2012).

> *These large financial holding companies assembled under one roof a wide array of financial activities, often with different business models and warring operating cultures, and become too complex and unwieldy to be managed well. Mixing different businesses, such as those of commercial banking and investment banking, also allowed firms to exploit differences in rules (governing capital, accounting, and profit/loss recognition and so forth) as applied to different parts of the firm. Such intra-firm arbitrage across business activities naturally leads to risk flowing to where it is least monitored and where capital requirements are lowest. (Hu, 2010, p.32)*

The complexity of a financial conglomerate structure engaged simultaneously in commercial banking, securities, asset management, and insurance is considerable.

The large number of potential risks for financial groups derives from the multi-faceted nature of the issue. Relevant factors to be considered in the analysis include: the size of an institution; the types of constituent entities (i.e. banks, insurance companies, securities firms, asset managers, etc.); the degree of integration along various steps in the value chain; and the structure (holding company, universal bank, parent-subsidiary, etc.) But these same factors can prove to be financially beneficial. It all depends on how well they are managed. (Lumpkin, 2011, p.6)

In Australia the Australian Prudential Regulatory Authority (APRA) has developed a policy on the supervision of conglomerate groups: "History has demonstrated that the failure of one entity (regulated or not) with a conglomerate group may damage or even cause the failure of related entities" (APRA, 2010, p.5).

The FSB identified four firm-wide risk management practices differentiating better performance from worse:

1.   effective firm-wide risk identification and analysis;

2.   consistent application of independent and rigorous valuation practices across the firm;

3.   effective management of funding liquidity, capital, and the balance sheet;

4.   informative and responsive risk measurement and management reporting.

The FSB recognized that implementing these practices comprehensively across large, complex organizations requires considerable resources and expertise, and suggested it was evident that many firms still fell short in these areas (SSG/FSB, 2009, p.2). The FSB has developed a new policy framework to address the systemic and moral hazard risks associated with strategically important financial institutions (SIFIs):

SIFIs are financial institutions whose distress or disorderly failure, because of their size, complexity and systemic interconnectedness, would cause significant disruption to the wider financial system and economic activity. To avoid this outcome, authorities have all too frequently had no choice but to forestall the failure of such institutions through public solvency support. As underscored by this crisis, this has deleterious consequences for private incentives and for public finances. Addressing the "too-big-to-fail" problem requires a multipronged and integrated set of policies. (FSB, 2011b)

The development of the critical policy measures that form the parts of this framework has now been completed. Implementation of these measures will begin from 2012. Full implementation is targeted for 2019. The measures include:

- new international standard to enable authorities to resolve failing financial firms without exposing the taxpayer to the risk of loss (*Key Attributes of Effective Resolution Regimes* (FSB, 2011b));

- requirements for resolvability assessments, and for recovery and resolution planning for global SIFIs);

- requirements for banks determined to be globally systemically important to have additional loss absorption capacity tailored to the impact of their default;

- more intensive and effective supervision of all SIFIs, including through stronger supervisory mandates, resources, and powers, and higher supervisory expectations for risk management functions, data aggregation capabilities, risk governance, and internal controls.

Structural and Behavioral Solutions: Wider Issues of Structure, Ownership, Governance, and Performance

Wrestling with these problems of managing complex financial structures in different jurisdictions has resulted in proposals to adopt structural solutions, for example, in separating universal from investment banking, regulatory and prudential solutions, and efforts to influence behavior.

Certain types of financial business activities are not compatible from a direct risk or moral hazard standpoint and should not be combined. Where that is the case, the obvious policy option is to regulate structure. An alternative view holds that the issue with respect to financial groups is not the formal corporate structure per se, but rather the

> *implications of the corporate structure for proper risk management.*
> *The real question then becomes whether the internal controls and risk*
> *management systems for the group are adequate for the task. Where*
> *such a view holds, policy measures may be directed at regulating*
> *behavior. (Lumpkin, 2011, p.16)*

The President of the Australian Takeover Panel, Kathleen Farrell of Freehills, recently posed the question that while the issue of "too big to fail" was being considered, what if the major financial institutions are becoming too big to manage? Managers may have direct responsibility, but inadequate internal controls reveal wider failure in corporate governance and board understanding. Auditors and shareholders have been complicit in these problems. Hence the regulatory framework needs to align incentives for all participants in a balance of compulsion, supervision and market discipline. If a systemic solution involves better alignment of governance institutions and practices, risk management and remuneration with market discipline, supervision, regulation, and transparency in the international financial sector, then reforms in system, structure, processes, *and* behavior all need to be considered as mutually reinforcing ways of achieving alignment and compliance.

Integrated Solutions to Multidimensional Problems?

It is relevant to briefly examine the extent to which national and reform agendas attempt a holistic and integrated solution to the multidimensional nature of the continuing dilemmas of the international finance sector. The focus will be upon the regulatory responses of the United States as it was at the epicenter of the global financial crisis.

The United States went through the most tumultuous and contested regulatory review and legislative initiative in the Dodd–Frank Wall Street and Consumer Protection Act (2010). This constituted a sweeping legislative reaction to the perceived regulator failures that had allowed the financial crisis to intensify apparently uncontrollably into a global phenomenon. Dodd–Frank included 14 stand-alone statutes, and numerous amendments to the current array of banking, securities, derivatives, and consumer finance laws. The vast majority of the Dodd–Frank provisions did not apply immediately, but required various US regulatory agencies to develop and apply the substantive details of the reforms over a period of several years following the passage of the Act. The centerpiece of the reform is the establishment of a new US framework for monitoring and regulating systemic risk. A Financial Stability Oversight

Council will monitor risk and guide the response of individual financial agencies, and has the power to instruct the Federal Reserve to impose on systemically important financial institutions:

- enhanced capital and leverage requirements

- additional liquidity provisioning

- mandatory contingent capital

- resolution plans (commonly called living wills)

- credit exposure reports

- concentration limits

- supplemental public disclosures

- periodic stress testing

- other risk management protocols.

If systemically important financial institutions get into difficulty a new Liquidation Authority will preempt the bankruptcy process and permit the Federal Deposit Insurance Corporation (FDIC) to seize control of the entity and proceed to liquidate it, rather than allowing the company and its creditors to work out restructuring arrangements as permitted under the US Bankruptcy Code (Weil Gotshal, 2010).

Dodd–Frank did not simplify the complex and fragmented regulatory structure responsible for US financial institutions. However, the Federal Reserve secured new oversight of the subsidiaries of holding companies it regulates, regardless of whether other agencies regulate the subsidiary, making the Federal Reserve the most powerful regulator for the US banking industry. The legislation also places restrictions on the activities of banks, most notably the Volcker Rule which prohibits proprietary trading for its own account rather than customer accounts, and bans certain hedge fund and private equity activities by banks. Recognizing the systemic risk posed by over the counter (OTC) derivatives swaps (that notionally exceeded the Gross National Product of every country in the world combined prior to the crisis), Dodd–Frank required the centralized clearing on exchanges of all swaps suitable for this, enhancing the transparency of the process and allowing monitoring of interest rate swaps, foreign exchange swaps, credit default swaps, commodity swaps, and many other transactions (Weil Gotshal, 2010).

Dodd–Frank requires hedge funds, private equity funds, and venture capital funds to register with the SEC, allowing the agency to collect data from the firms. Ending their existence in the shadows, the legislation subjects hedge funds to new requirements in areas such as record keeping, disclosure, and reporting. The oversight would include assets under management, borrowings, and off balance sheet exposures. In an effort to restrain the irresponsible issue of securities, federal bank regulators and the SEC are jointly to prescribe rules requiring securitizers of asset backed securities (ABS) to retain an economic interest (skin in the game) in the credit risk (generally 5 percent) of any asset transferred, sold, or conveyed to a third party through the issuance of an ABS. This economic interest may not be hedged or transferred to a third party. The SEC is to adopt regulations requiring ABS issuers to disclose—for each tranche or class of security—information regarding the specific assets backing that security. Recognizing the systemic importance of the credit rating agencies, and their role in capital formation and as gatekeepers in the debt markets, the legislation will subject the credit rating industry to heightened oversight, regulation, and expanded liability, and the SEC will establish an Office of Credit Ratings (Weil Gotshal, 2010). In addition the new Bureau of Consumer Financial Protection (BCFP) has been established within the Federal Reserve to regulate consumer financial products and services which will have extensive authority to regulate and enforce substantive standards for any person that engages in the offer or sale of a financial product or service to any consumer. The BCFP is specifically tasked with ensuring transparency and competition in financial services and protecting consumers from discrimination and unfair, deceptive, or abusive acts and practices.

Finally, Dodd–Frank addresses the thorniest regulatory issues of all in the United States: corporate governance and executive compensation. The most controversial governance proposals—majority voting for directors, limits on executive compensation, and mandatory board risk committees for non-financial companies—did not make the final legislation. More modest changes have been included, including proxy access authority, say on pay, further limits on broker discretionary voting, requirements for compensation committee and advisor independence, heightened disclosure of compensation and board leadership, and mandatory clawback policies. Together these proposals shift the balance of governance power a little more toward shareholders:

- proxy access lowers the cost of shareholder nominees for boards;

- say on pay allows a nonbinding shareholder vote on executive compensation;

- brokers prohibited from voting shares without receiving instructions from the beneficial owner.

The insistence on heightened standards of independence for members of compensation committees is intended to enhance their objectivity. The clawback clauses considerably strengthen Sarbanes–Oxley in demanding:

> If a company is required to restate its financial statements due to material non-compliance with relevant reporting requirements, the company must recover from current and former executive officers any excess incentive compensation based on the erroneous data received during the three-year period preceding the date on which the company becomes required to prepare the restatement. (Weil Gotshal, 2010, p.25)

Amounting to 2,600 pages of legislation, Dodd–Frank was certainly a comprehensive and determined effort to rein in the US finance sector; the question is will it succeed in doing so? Gordon and Muller (2010) argue that while the FDIC may provide the means for an orderly liquidation of individual failed banks, it does not offer the possibility of dealing effectively with systemic failure of interconnected financial institutions. They suggest instead a Systemic Emergency Insurance Fund of $1 trillion, funded by risk-adjusted assessments of all major financial firms. This would mutualize systemic risk and provide a major incentive for firms to warn regulators of impending risk. Coffee (2012, p.i) argues that it is only after a catastrophic market collapse that legislators and regulators are able to overcome the resistance of the financial community and adopt comprehensive reform legislation such as Dodd–Frank, but invariably this is followed by: "increasingly equivocal implementation of the new legislation, tepid enforcement, and eventual legislative erosion."

Despite the vast effort of the US legislators who put together the Dodd–Frank Act there are definite indications of lack of traction. Firstly, Dodd–Frank depended more than Sarbanes–Oxley on administrative implementation by a host of regulatory agencies because Congress was not in a position to determine detailed issues such as appropriate regimes for capital adequacy, liquidity ratios, OTC derivatives, and similar complex financial issues. Regulators are confronted by finance executives determined to retain and protect their executive compensation, high leverage, bank profitability, and managerial discretion (Coffee, 2012, p.11). An early indication of the formidable indifference of US finance executives in 2008/2009 to regulation and public scrutiny was the total refusal to give up hugely inflated executive bonuses at companies such as AIG which had failed during the financial crisis and was only rescued with a US government, taxpayer funded, rescue package of support amounting to $180 billion. (In fact, at almost all the financial companies who received assistance under the original $700 billion Troubled Asset Relief Program (TARP), the executives resented so much the constraints that TARP imposed on their compensation packages that they scrambled to repay the money to the US government before the salary restrictions could seriously impact on them.)

Another sharp indicator that little has changed in the US investment banks is recent developments at Goldman Sachs. It must be recognized that Goldman Sachs sailed through the financial crisis adopting the mantle of a white knight though, in fact, it had engaged in almost all of the same doubtful practices as the other Wall Street banks and initiated many of them. Goldman Sachs not only provided the US Treasurer at the time of the crisis, Hank Paulsen, who was primarily responsible for the rescue effort, but earned tens of billions assisting the government in the rescue effort. Then, in April 2010, the SEC announced it was suing Goldman Sachs alleging that they had materially misstated facts regarding a synthetic collateralized debt obligation (CDO) product it had originated in 2007. The SEC alleged that not only had Goldman Sachs allowed the Hedge Fund Paulson & Co to select the underlying mortgage obligations for the CDO but omitted to mention to its clients that Paulson's $200 million invested was in shorting the stock, not a long-term investment: that is rather than Paulson's interests being in alignment with other investors, they were sharply conflicting. The SEC complaint stated that Paulson & Co made $1 billion profit, while other investors lost a similar amount including ABN Amro and IKB Deutsche. In a settlement with the SEC in July 2010, Goldman Sachs agreed to pay $300 million to the US government and $250 million to investors. Lloyd Blankfein, the Goldman Sachs' CEO and Chairman, insisted at a Congressional hearing that in the context of market making, betting against clients was a standard business practice.

The US Senate Permanent Subcommittee on Investigations concluded Goldman Sachs had:

> ... used net short positions to benefit from the downturn in the mortgage
> market, and designed, marketed, and sold CDOs in ways that created

conflicts of interest with the firm's clients and at times led to the bank's profiting from the same products that caused substantial losses for its clients. (PSI, 2011, p.8)

On March 14, 2012 Greg Smith, an executive director of Goldman Sachs, took the unusual step of publishing his letter of resignation in the New York Times in which he stated:

...The environment now is as toxic and destructive as I have ever seen it. To put the problem in its simplest terms, the interests of the client continue to be sidelined in the way the firm operates and thinks about making money ... I attend derivative sales meetings where not one single minute is spent asking questions about how we can help clients. It's purely about how we can make the most possible money off of them.

Yet the first Goldman Sachs Business Principle baldly states: "Our clients' interests always come first. Our experience shows that if we serve our clients well, our own success will follow" (Goldman Sachs, 2011).

Conclusion

The world confronted the most devastating financial crisis since the Great Depression of the 1930s in the global financial crisis. The impact of the global financial crisis continues to reverberate in the sovereign debt crisis. Considerable determination and resolve was demonstrated by the G20 in internationally and collaboratively tackling the crisis in 2008 and 2009. The effort to build a more robust international architecture of regulatory governance is impressive. However, the concern is that the national and institutional commitment to implement regulation will diminish over time. More radical proposals to restructure and reorient financial institutions were considered including in the UK the Vickers (2012) report on the structure of banking which contemplated separating investment from general banking, and the Kay (2012) report on how to resolve short termism. Neither has led to a fundamental restructuring or reorientation of the UK financial system. In Europe the proposals for a tax on financial transactions threatened to constrain high velocity trading while it was under consideration. However, there are grounds to be skeptical about the willingness to face up to the fundamental causes of the financial crisis, and to engage in the institutional and debt restructuring that will be required to achieve a stable international recovery. Essential questions remain to be answered regarding the changes in the structure, regulation, and governance of financial institutions that might be required to fundamentally transform risk-taking incentives and prudent decision-making, with the aim of achieving lasting change in the culture and behavior within financial firms. Finding the answers to these questions will determine whether or when we face another global financial crisis, perhaps even more devastating in its consequences than the last one. What is essential is for international financial markets to be made to work for communities and economies in a sustainable way, rather than the destructive impact finance has wreaked upon the world in its present pursuits.

References and Bibliography

Aglietta, M., and Berrebi, L. (2007). *Désordres Dans Le Capitalisme Mondiale.* Paris: Odile Jacob.

Aglietta, M., and Reberioux, A. (2005). *Corporate Governance Adrift: A Critique of Shareholder Value.* Cheltenham: Edward Elgar.

Amble, B. (2003). *The Diversity of Modern Capitalism.* Oxford: Oxford University Press.

Apra (2010) *Supervision of Conglomerate Groups, Australian Prudential Regulatory Authority,* 18 March http://www.apra.gov.au/CrossIndustry/Documents/ Discussion-paper.

Ard, L., and Berg, A. (2010). *Bank Governance: Lessons from the Financial Crisis.* Crisis Response Public Policy for the Private Sector, Note Number 13. Washington: World Bank Group.

Argitis, G., and Pitelis, C.N. (2008). Global Finance and Systemic Instability. *Contributions to Political Economy,* Vol. 27(1), 1–11.

Argitis, G., and Pitelis, C.N. (2006). Global Finance, Income Distribution and Capital Accumulation. *Contributions to Political Economy,* Vol. 25(1), 63–81.

ASIC. (2009). Submission 378, Parliamentary Joint Committee on Corporations and Financial Services, Canberra: Commonwealth of Australia.

Basel Committee on Bank Supervision (BCBS). (2011). *Core Principles for Banking Supervision Basel Committee on Bank Supervision.* Geneva: BIS.

Basel Committee on Bank Supervision (BCBS). (2010). *Principles for Enhancing Corporate Governance*. Geneva: BIS.

Bebchuk, L.A., and Spamann, H. (2009). Regulating Bankers Pay. *Georgetown Law Journal*, Vol. 98(2), 247–87.

Brown, C., and Davis, K. (2008). *The Sub-Prime Crisis Down Under*. Melbourne University.

Chesnais, F. (2008). *Fin d'un cycle. Sur la portée et le cheminement de la crise financière*. Carré Rouge – La Brèche, 1 (Janvier), 17–31.

City of London. (2008). *The Global Financial Centres Index*. Guildhall. www.cityoflondon.gov.uk/economicresearch.

Clarke, T. (2012). Ethics, Values and Corporate Governance. In *BBVA, Values and Ethics for the 21st Century*, 513–58. Madrid: BBVA. http://www.bbvaopenmind.com/book/en/70/values-and-ethics-for-the-21st-century/.

Clarke, T. (2009). *European Corporate Governance*. London: Routledge.

Clarke, T., and Branson, D. (2012). *Sage Handbook of Corporate Governance*. London: Sage.

Coffee, J. (2006). *Gatekeepers: The Professions and Corporate Governance*. Oxford: Oxford University Press.

Coffee, K. (2012). The Political Economy of Dodd–Frank: Why Financial Reform Tends to be Frustrated and Systemic Risk Perpetuated. Working Paper No. 414. *Columbia Law School Working Paper Series*, 9 January. http://ssrn.com/abstract=1982128.

CTR/CEPS. (2005). *Deep Integration: How Transatlantic Markets are Leading Globalization*. Washington DC: Johns Hopkins University.

Davis, K. (2011). The Australian Financial System in the 2000s: Dodging the Bullet. *RBA Conference Volume*, 301–48.

De Larosière J. (2009) *The High Level Group on Financial Supervision in the EU*, Brussels, February 25. http://ec.europa.eu/internal_market/finances/docs/de_larosiere_report_en.pdf.

Ee, K., and Xiong, K. (2008). Asia: A Perspective on the Subprime Crisis. *International Monetary Fund*, Vol. 45(2), http://www.imf.org/external/pubs/ft/fandd/2008/06/khor.htm. Last accessed November 1, 2008.

Einhorn, D. (2008a). Private Profits and Socialized Risk. *Global Association of Risk Professionals Review*, Vol. 42 (June/July), 10–18.

Einhorn, D. (2008b). *Fooling Some of the People All of the Time: A Long Short Story*. Hoboken, New Jersey: Wiley.

EPI. (2008). *The State of Working America*. Washington: Economic Policy Institute.

Epstein, G.A. (2005). *Financialization and the World Economy*. Northampton, MA: Edward Elgar.

Erturk, I., Froud, J., Johal, S., Leaver, A., and Williams, K. (eds). (2008). *Financialization at Work: Key Texts and Commentary*. London: Routledge.

Esty, B. (1998). The Impact of Contingent Liability on Commercial Bank Risk-Taking. *Journal of Financial Economics*, Vol. 47, 189–212.

European Commission. (2010a). *Green Paper: Corporate Governance in Financial Institutions and Remuneration Policies*. Brussels: European Commission.

European Commission. (2010b). *Directorate General Internal Market and Services*. Feedback Statement Summary of Responses to Commission Green Paper on Corporate Governance in Financial Institutions. Brussels: European Commission.

Farrar, J.H. (2012). The Governance and Regulation of Complex Conglomerates. In Clarke, T. and Branson, D. *The Sage Handbook of Corporate Governance*, 520–29. London: Sage.

Financial Reporting Council (FRC). (2011). *Guidance on Board Effectiveness*. London: FRC.

Financial Stability Board (FSB). (2011a). *Thematic Review on Compensation: Peer Review Report*. Financial Stability Board.

Financial Stability Board (FSB). (2011b). *Key Attributes of Effective Resolution Regimes for Financial Institutions*. Financial Stability Board.

Fleckenstein, F. (2008). *Greenspan's Bubbles: The Age of Ignorance at the Federal Reserve.* New York: McGraw Hill.

Froud, J., and Johal, S. (2008). Questioning Finance, *Competition and Change,* Vol. 12(2), 107–9.

Froud, J., Johal, S., Leaver, A., and Williams, K. (2006). *Financialization and Strategy: Narrative and Numbers.* London: Routledge.

Galbraith, J.K. (1993). *A Short History of Financial Euphoria.* London: Penguin.

Goldman Sachs. (2011). *Report of the Business Standards Committee.* New York: Goldman Sachs.

Goodman, P. (2008). Taking a Hard New Look at the Greenspan Legacy. *New York Times,* October 8.

Gordon, J., and Muller, C. (2010). Confronting Financial Crisis: Dodd–Frank's Dangers and the Case for a Systemic Emergency Insurance Fund. *Columbia Law and Economics,* Working Paper no. 374.

Greenspan, A. (2004). *Risk and Uncertainty in Monetary Policy.* American Economic Association, San Diego, California, 3 January 3. Federal Reserve Board. http://www.federalreserve.gov/BoardDocs/Speeches/2004/20040103/default.htm.

Hilferding, R. (1910). *Finance Capital, A Study of the Latest Phase of Capitalist Development,* Watnick, M. and Gordon, S. (eds) (1981). London: RKP.

Hu, F. (2010). In O. Chittenden (ed.), *The Future of Money.* London: Virgin Books.

IFSL. (2008). International Financial Markets in the UK, International Financial Services London.

IMF. (2008). *Global Financial Stability Report: Financial Stress and Deleveraging.* Washington: International Monetary Fund.

IMF. (2002). The Globalization of Finance, Finance and Development. *International Monetary Fund,* Vol. 39(1). Washington.

IOSCO. (2003). *Report on the Activities of Credit Rating Agencies*. The Technical Committee of the International Organization of Securities Commission, September 2002. http://www.fsa.go.jp/inter/ios/20030930/05.pdf.

IPS. (2008). *A Sensible Plan for Recovery*. Washington: Institute for Policy Studies, October 15.Janszen, E. (2008). The Next Bubble: Priming the Markets for Tomorrow's Big Crash. *Harper's Magazine*, February, 39–45.

Kaletsky, A. (2009). Goodbye, Homo Economicus. *Prospect*, Issue 157, April.

Kay Report. (2012). *The Kay Review of UK Equity Markets and Long-Term Decision Making Report*. UK.

Keynes, J. M. (1936). *The General Theory of Employment, Interest and Money*. London: Macmillan [reprinted 1991, Cambridge: Cambridge University Press].

Kirshner, J. (1999). Keynes, Capital Mobility and the Crisis of Embedded Liberalism. *Review of International Political Economy*, Vol. 6(3), 313–37.

Klettner, A.L., Clarke, T., and Adams, M.A. (2010). Corporate Governance Reform: An Empirical Study of the Changing Roles and Responsibilities of Australian Boards and Directors. *Australian Journal of Corporate Law*, Vol. 24, 148–76.

Klettner, A. (2012). Corporate Governance and the Global Financial Crisis: The Regulatory Response. In T. Clarke and D. Branson, *The Sage Handbook of Corporate Governance*, 556–84. London: Sage.

Krippner, G.R. (forthcoming). *The Fictitious Economy: Financialization, the State, and the Remaking of American Capitalism*.

Krippner, G.R. (2005). The Financialization of the American Economy. *Socio-Economic Review*, Vol. 3(2), 173–208.

Krugman, P. (2008). Cash for Trash. *New York Times*, 21 September.

Laeven, L., and Valencia, F. (2008). Systemic Banking Crises: A New Database. *IMF Working Paper*, WP/08/224. Washington, DC: International Monetary Fund.

Langley, P. (2008). *The Everyday Life of Global Finance: Saving and Borrowing in Anglo-America*. Oxford: Oxford University Press.

Le Roy, P. (2008). *The Subprime Mortgage Crisis: Highlighting the Need for Better Corporate Governance*. Sydney: University of Technology.

Lewis, H. (2007). *'Moral Hazard' Helps Shape Mortgage Mess*. 18 April. http://www.bankrate.com/brm/news/mortgages/20070418_subprime_mortgage_morality_a1.asp?caret=3c. Last accessed November 10, 2008.

Lim, M. (2008). Old Wine in a New Bottle: Subprime Mortgage Crisis—Causes and Consequences. *Working Paper No. 532*. The Levy Economics Institute.

Lockhart, D. (2008). *The Subprime Crisis: Is It Contagious*? Federal Reserve Bank of Atlanta, 29 February. http://www.frbatlanta.org/invoke.cfm?objectid=65C8B587-5056-9F12-125B76D448344BEF&method=display. Last accessed November 10, 2008.

Lumpkin, S. (2011). Risks in Financial Group Structures. *OECD Journal Financial Market Trends*, Vol. 2011(2), 1–32.

Martin, R. (2002). *The Financialization of Daily Life*. Philadelphia, PA: Temple University Press.

McAvoy, P.W., and Millstein, I.M. (2004). *The Recurrent Crisis In Corporate Governance*. Stanford Business Books.

McKinsey and Company. (2008). Mapping Global Capital Markets. *Fourth Annual Report*. San Francisco: McKinsey Global Institute.

Maximus, F. (2008). *Consequences of A Long, Deep Recession – Parts I, II, III*. http://fabiusmaximus.wordpress.com/2008/06/18/consequences, June 18–20.

Mehran, H., Morrison, A., and Shapiro, J. (2011). Corporate Governance and Banks: What Have We Learned from the Financial Crisis? *Staff Report no. 502*. Federal Reserve Bank of New York.

Minsky, H. (1982). *Inflation, Recession and Economic Policy*, New York: Wheatsheaf Books.

Muolo, P., and Padilla, M. (2008). *Chain of Blame: How Wall Street Caused the Mortgage and Credit Crisis*. Hoboken, NJ: Wiley.

Narayanan, M.P. (1985). Managerial Incentives for Short-term Results. *Journal of Finance*, Vol. 40(5), 1469–84.

National Commission (2011). *The Financial Crisis Inquiry Report, Final Report of the National Commission on the Causes of the Financial and Economic Crisis in the United States*, Washington: US Government 0074.

OECD. (2010). *Corporate Governance and the Financial Crisis: Conclusions and Emerging Good Practices to Enhance Implementation of the Principles.* Paris: OECD.

OECD. (2009). *Corporate Governance and the Financial Crisis: Key Findings and Main Messages.* Paris: OECD.Patel, B. (2008). *Credit Crisis and Corporate Governance Implications: Guidance for Proxy Season and Insight into Best Practices.* RiskMetrics Group, April. http://www.riskmetrics.com//system/files/private/CreditCrisisCorporateGovernance20080408.pdf. Last accessed November 1, 2008.

Pettigrew, A., and McNulty, T. (1995). Power and Influence In and Around the Boardroom. *Human Relations*, Vol. 8, 845–73.

Phillips, K. (2008). *Reckless Finance Bad Money: Reckless Finance, Failed Politics, and the Global Crisis of American Capitalism.* New York: Viking Books.

Polanyi, K. (1944). *The Great Transformation: The Political and Economic Origins of Our Time.* Boston, MA: Beacon Press.

PSI. (2011). *Wall Street and the Financial Crisis: Anatomy of a Financial Collapse.* Permanent Subcommittee on Investigations. Washington: United States Senate.

Rosen, R. (2007). *The Role of Securitization in Mortgage Lending.* Chicago Fed, 11 October. http://www.chicagofed.org/publications/fedletter/cflnovember2007_244.pdf. Last accessed November 10, 2008.

Schor, J. (1992). Introduction. In T. Banuri and J. Schor (eds), *Financial Openness and National Autonomy.* Oxford: Clarendon Press.

Scott, W.A. (2008). The Credit Crunch and the Law—A Commentary on Economic and Policy Issues. In R.P. Austin (ed.), *The Credit Crunch and the Law*, Monograph 5, Ross.

Schwarcz, S. (2008). Disclosure's Failure in the Subprime Mortgage Crisis. *Research Paper Series*, Research Paper No. 203, Duke Law School, March.

Senior Supervisors Group (SSG/FSB). (2009). *Senior Supervisors Group Report on Risk Management Lessons from the Global Banking Crisis of 2008*. Financial Stability Board.

Shiller, R. (2008). *The Subprime Solution: How Today's Global Financial Crisis Happened and What to Do About It*. Princeton, NJ: Princeton University Press.

Soros, G. (2008). *The New Paradigm for Financial Markets: The Credit Crisis of 2008 and What it Means*. New York: Public Affairs.

Stiglitz, J. (2010). House Committee on Financial Services Hearing on Compensation in the Financial Industry Testimony, January 22.

Stiglitz, J. (2008a). Realign Wall Street's Interests. *Harper's Magazine*, November, 36–7.

Stiglitz, J. (2008b). Henry Paulson's Shell Game. *The Nation*, 26 September 2008. TARP. (2010). *Troubled Asset Relief Program*, Monthly 105(a) Report—May 2010, US Department of the Treasury, available at: http://www.financialstability. gov/docs/May%202010%20105%28a%29%20Report_final.pdf

UBS. (2008). *Shareholder Report on UBS's Write Downs*. Zurich: UBS AG. www. ubs.com/1/ShowMedia/investors/shareholderreport?contentId=140333&na me=080418ShareholderReport.pdf.

UK Treasury. (2009). *A Review of Corporate Governance in UK Banks and Other Financial Industry Entities: Final Recommendations* (Walker Review), UK Treasury.

US National Commission. (2011). *The Financial Crisis Inquiry Report*. Final Report of the National Commission on the Causes of the Financial and Economic Crisis in the United States. Washington: US Government 0074.

Vickers Report. (2012). *Independent Commission on Banking Report*. UK.

Weil Gotshal. (2010). *An Overview of the Dodd–Frank Wall Street Reform and Consumer Protections Act*. New York: Weil Gotshal.

Whalen, C. (2008). *The Subprime Crisis — Cause, Effect and Consequences*. Networks Financial Institute, Indiana State University, March.

Chapter 9

Disclosure of Corporate Environmental, Social and Governance Data: Toward Effective and Sustainable Systems[1]

STEVE LYDENBERG

Introduction

As we move through the second decade of the twenty-first century governments, investors, and corporations themselves increasingly recognize the valuable role that ESG data can play in corporate management, the assessing of long-term investment risks and rewards, and the alignment of corporate policies and practices with those of society. As these recognitions have grown, calls for the mandating of disclosure of corporate ESG data have increased correspondingly. Globally mandated disclosure may now not be far off.

Exactly what form this disclosure will take, how it will be put to use by corporations, investors, government, and civil society, and how effective and sustainable it will be in aligning corporate policies and practices with public goods, are questions that remain unresolved. Three scenarios are possible:

1.   Corporate disclosure of ESG data will remain quasi-voluntary, with all the problems of inconsistency and irregularity that such systems entail. ESG disclosure becomes little more than a passing fad and eventually fades.

---

1   An earlier version of this essay was published by the International Finance Corporation as its *Private Sector Opinion* series (Issue 32) in January 2014 under the title, "Emerging Trends in Environmental, Social, and Governance Data and Disclosure: Opportunities and Challenges".

2.   ESG disclosure will be mandated in reasonably comparable formats worldwide. Corporate ESG reports continue to be published and evaluated separately from the strategic management of corporations and from the primary considerations of investment decision making.

3.   ESG disclosure will be mandated and integrated systematically into corporations' financial disclosure, merging these two realms and placing them on an equal footing. This integrated disclosure then leads to fundamental changes in corporate management and in investment practice.

Of these three, the third is the most likely to lead to a substantial alignment of corporate policies and practices with the public good. To realize this ambitious goal, however, the ESG disclosure systems must be effective and sustainable.

This essay reviews the evolution of corporate ESG disclosure over the past several decades, argues that fundamental societal factors are driving this evolution toward mandated, comprehensive ESG disclosure worldwide, and speculates on what particulars would be needed for a system of globally mandated ESG disclosure to be effective and sustainable.

Effective and Sustainable Disclosure Systems

In their book, *Full Disclosure: The Perils and Promise of Transparency*, Fung et al. (2007, p.19) argue that, in what they term an "unexpected development in governance," systems of transparency and disclosure: "are gaining strength because conventional forms of government intervention—for example, standards-based regulatory systems or performance-based tax policies—are sometimes ill-suited to the kinds of risks and performance flaws that policymakers now identify for action." This paper explores the applicability of their framework for effectiveness and sustainability to corporate ESG disclosure systems.

As far back as the beginning of the twentieth century, legal and public policy scholars have advocated disclosure and transparency as tools to help align corporate and societal interests. In 1914 Louis Brandeis famously wrote that: "Publicity is justly commended as a remedy for social and industrial diseases. Sunlight is said to be the best of disinfectants; electric light the most efficient policeman" (Brandeis, 1914).

For such data to promote efficient remedies, Fung et al. (2007) argue that government must take the lead by mandating disclosure.

Why is government action needed? There are three reasons according to Fung et al., (2007, p.6):

1.   Only government can compel the disclosure of information from private and public entities.

2.   Only government can legislate permanence in transparency.

3.   Only government can create transparency backed by the legitimacy of democratic processes.

How much disclosure is appropriate and at what level that disclosure should take place have been the subject of ongoing debate. Merritt Fox, for example, has asserted that there is a "socially optimal level of disclosure" for corporate financial data that, although not be subject to empirical calculation, is nevertheless an important guiding principle (Fox, 1999). Others, for example Roberta Romano, have asserted that corporate financial disclosure should be mandated through a decentralized state-based (as opposed to a centralized federal-based) system that would provide corporations a market of disclosure regimes within which they could exercise their free choice (Romano, 1998).

According to Fung et al. (2007), to be effective, the disclosed data must be useful—in other words, prompt response and action by those for whom it is intended. In turn, it can then prompt appropriate actions and reactions by the disclosers—in other words, create changes in their policies or practices in line with the public good.

A policy has effects when the information it produces enters the calculations and they (the users) consequently change their action. Further effects may follow when information disclosers notice and respond to users' actions. A system is effective, however, only when discloser responses significantly advance policy aims (Fung et al., 2007, p.54).

The best designed systems will also produce benefits for disclosers as well for the public at large. They will prompt disclosers to take actions that advance the public good while at the same time pursuing private goals of their own, such as efficiency, profitability, or reputation enhancement.

The three characteristics that are essential for a disclosure system to be effective in practice, according to Fung et al. (2007) are:

1.   The data disclosed must have perceptible *value* to users, and disclosers must see value in any changes in their practices that result from this disclosure.

2.   The data needs to be disclosed in a form that is *compatible* with the ways in which users make their decisions (for example, it is not too difficult or expensive to obtain). Similarly for disclosers, the users' feedback needs to come in a form that is compatible with their decision-making processes (for example, it is timely and actionable).

3.   The data disclosed needs to be *comprehensible* to users (for example, not too complicated) and disclosers need to be able to measure and understand the implications for their policies of the responses to the data by users.

That corporate social responsibility (CSR) disclosure is increasingly perceived by major players in the financial markets as useful and effective can be seen by the assertions of such major players as the Norwegian state-sponsored pension plan which, as of 2014, managed some $700 billion in assets.

The markets value information, and investors also demand information on environmental and social matters. This is an important trend, and we are seeing the increasing adoption of statutory reporting requirements both nationally and internationally. We support this development for one simple reason: companies that are good at providing the market with relevant information will win trust, reduce uncertainty about their operations, and enable investors and other interested parties to assess the risk involved in investing (Folketrygdfondet Ownership Report, 2013, p.7).

To persist over time, however, systems for the mandated disclosure of corporate social and environmental data must be, in the vocabulary of Fung et al., "sustainable". Disclosure systems are often mandated hurriedly in times of crisis and need to be able to be modified to adjust to changing conditions. To make these adjustments, a disclosure system must have the following (Fung et al., 2007, p.109):

•   the ability to expand its *scope* as circumstances change;

- the ability to improve the *quality and accuracy* of its data as the limits of that data or disclosure formats become apparent;

- the flexibility to increase its *usefulness* to consumers, investors, employees, political activists, voters, resident, and/or government officials.

Fung et al. (2007) point to corporate financial disclosure as particularly effective, a conclusion that should encourage advocates of mandated corporate ESG disclosure.[2] Both financial and ESG data disclosure involve comprehensive, complex systems of indicators designed to establish honest markets and to direct corporations to long-term wealth creation in the public interest. However, as these authors stress, the devil is in the detail—and to be as effective and sustainable as financial disclosure, ESG disclosure systems will need to be carefully designed and implemented.

Evolution of ESG Disclosure

Over the past four decades, much progress has been made toward the systematic disclosure of ESG data by corporations. As of 2014 corporations and other organizations worldwide have issued more than 11,000 ESG reports, starting from a negligible base in the 1970s and 1980s. However, because these reports are voluntary and vary substantially, calls for more systematic, mandated disclosure have also accelerated.

In April 2014 the European Parliament passed a directive[3] amending accounting practices for some 6,000 large publicly traded corporations headquartered in the European Union and requiring disclosure of: "policies, risks and results as regards environmental matters, social and employee-related aspects, respect for human rights, anti-corruption and bribery issues, and diversity on boards of directors." More precise guidelines for disclosure were still under development at that time, but they will require: "concise, useful information necessary for an understanding of [corporations'] development, performance, position and impact of their activity, rather than a fully-fledged and detailed report." The European Parliament has taken this step because it

---

2 As an example of a relatively ineffective disclosure system they cite the Worker Adjustment and Retraining Notification system that requires timely notification to workers of plant closures.

3 EU directive, April 15, 2014. Titled: *Improving Corporate Governance: Europe's Largest Companies Will Have to be More Transparent About How They Operate.*

believes that companies that disclose such information: "take a longer-term perspective in their decision-making" and: "ultimately are more successful" (EU press release, 2014).

In addition, in March 2014, a coalition of institutional investors coordinated by the sustainability advocacy group Ceres submitted to the World Federation of Exchanges (WFE) a recommendation that stock exchanges worldwide establish a coordinated set of ESG indicators, disclosure on which would become listing requirements. Simultaneously the WFE launched a Sustainability Working Group to consider their role in promoting sustainability. The proposal would require that companies assess and report on ESG issues material to their operations, report systematically on ten key ESG topics on a comply-or-explain basis—in other words, they can choose not to report on a topic, but must explain their reason for not doing so—and provide a link in their financial filings to an ESG Disclosure Index—in other words, a listing of places on their website or in their sustainability reports where specific ESG data can be found. These two developments indicate the strength of the movement toward globally mandated ESG disclosure and are milestones in the evolution of ESG reporting.

ESG reporting had its origins in reports on corporations' philanthropy and community affairs programs. In the 1970s in the United States, for example, companies that played a major role in the national economy, such as General Motors and Ford, or in local economies such as Cummins Engine in Indiana, were leaders in issuing reports on their philanthropic and community involvement. At that same time, companies in the life insurance industry formed the Clearinghouse on Corporate Social Responsibility through which they invested in, and reported on, their economic development programs in inner cities (Moy et al., 2009). Similarly today in developed and emerging markets corporations establishing CSR programs for the first time frequently focus reporting on charitable giving and local community development initiatives. These CSR initiatives recognize corporations' obligations to local communities, but may not relate to core business strategies.

Starting in the 1970s, various crises and scandals prompted governments, initially in the United States and then elsewhere, to legislate the disclosure of issue-specific ESG data. The 1984 Bhopal disaster, for example, led directly to the passage of the Emergency Planning and Community Right-to-Know Act (1986) in the United States that required relevant companies to report on the storage, recycling, and releases of toxic chemicals at their plant sites. Other countries throughout the world have followed suit with similar toxics-releases legislation, including Mexico where such data became available starting in 2006.[4]

In 1975, in response to concerns about unfair bank lending practices, the United States enacted the Home Mortgage Disclosure Act, which forced banks to disclose the amounts and location of their lending. In 1977, in response to a series of widely publicized bribery scandals, the US Congress passed the Foreign Corrupt Practices Act, which forbids US corporations from making bribes overseas. Regulation and legislation requiring disclosure on a variety of specific issues have similarly been implemented in Europe, Japan and elsewhere in developed markets. In emerging markets corporate governance policies have been the subject of extensive regulatory and disclosure requirements, with countries such as South Africa, the Philippines, Hungary, and Malaysia leading the way (United Nations, 2011). In addition, at various times the US Securities and Exchange Commission has required that specific environmentally and socially related data be disclosed in 10-K and proxy filings (Williams, 1999; Monsma and Olsen, 2007; Smith et al., 2010).

These regulatory actions often take place in response to environmental or social crises or controversies, but typically capture only a random set of ESG data without providing a comprehensive overview of companies' ESG records.

In the late 1990s the need for more systematic ESG disclosure became increasingly clear and prompted the creation of several global initiatives—including the Global Reporting Initiative (GRI) and the United Nations Global Compact—that have made comprehensive disclosure of ESG data worldwide a primary goal. Stressing broad stakeholder engagement and the incorporation of international norms and standards, these initiatives have been remarkably successful in increasing availability of ESG data. For example, as of 2014, the GRI maintained a database of some 14,000 sustainability reports from over 6,000 organizations based to a greater or lesser extent on its reporting framework.[5] A 2013 global survey of corporate responsibility reporting by KPMG found that: "Over half of reporting companies worldwide (51 percent) now include [Corporate Responsibility] information in their annual financial reports." This is a striking rise since 2011 (when only 20 percent did so) and 2008 (only 9 percent) (KPMG, 2013, p.10).

---

4   For a summary of the Mexican legislation see http://www.rtknet.org/files/MexicoPRTR.pdf. Last accessed April 18, 2014.
5   See the GRI database at http://database.globalreporting.org/. Last accessed April 18, 2014.

The best of this new breed of CSR reports represents a quantum leap in comprehensiveness over more limited philanthropic-oriented reports and issue-specific, government-mandated disclosure requirements. Many of these new reports, nevertheless, remain idiosyncratic in their form and content, and sporadic in their publication.

Forces Driving Mandated Disclosure

The need for regular, consistent, and comparable data is not the only compelling factor in the push toward mandated CSR reporting. At least five long-term, fundamental trends are also driving this need.

LACK OF TRUST IN FINANCE

As a result of more than a decade of scandals and crises, the financial services and banking industries are now among the least trusted in our society.[6] Moreover, traditional financial accounting in many regards is no longer seen as adequate or trustworthy. Two pieces of major legislation aimed at reforming accounting standards and banking practices have been passed in the United States since 2000 (Sarbanes–Oxley in 2002 and Dodd–Frank in 2010) without producing an apparent increase in trust in either.

MATERIALITY AND THE LONG-TERM INVESTOR

For institutional investors the potential long-term financial impact of environmental and social issues such as climate change and water scarcity is increasingly apparent (Ceres, 2013). As sovereign wealth funds and national and local pension funds grow in size, their long-term perspective in the marketplace is increasingly driving the demand for data on issues that have long-term financial, as well as sustainability, implications.

DEMOGRAPHICS

As the world rapidly approaches a population of 9,000,000,000, the complexity of problems and the interrelatedness of the parties necessary for their solution increase. To cite just one example, it takes extensive, coordinated efforts by

---

6   See 2013 Trust Barometer Reports Financial Services is Least Trusted Industry Globally. Available at http://www.edelman.com/news/2013-edelman-trust-barometer-reports-financial-services-is-least-trusted-industry-globally. Last accessed April 18, 2014.

governments, nongovernmental organizations, and corporations to assure safe and fair working conditions at suppliers to the apparel and footwear industries. Without substantial monitoring and data, such problems cannot be adequately addressed.

SOCIAL JUSTICE

As hundreds of millions of people around the world are lifted out of extreme poverty they are voicing legitimate demands for access to medicines and healthcare, to telecommunications and information technology, and to financial services on a par with those of their better off peers.[7] Knowing which companies have committed to serving the bottom of the pyramid is essential to progress in satisfying these demands.

NATURAL RESOURCES

Our omnivorous consumer society is posing a dual environmental challenge. The capacity of our ecological systems to absorb the wastes generated by this consumption is in doubt, as witnessed by the increasing concentration of carbon dioxide in our atmosphere and the acidification of our oceans. In addition, the capability of the stocks of certain essential natural resources to feed ongoing consumption is questionable. Various rare earth and precious metals are, for example, already in short supply, and phosphate fertilizers may soon be too (Philpott, 2012).

That these five secular trends are of importance to the mainstream financial community can be seen in the increasing number of signatories to the *Principles for Responsible Investment*[8] to which asset owners and managers with some $35 trillion have committed. In addition, large pension and sovereign wealth funds—such as the Norwegian Pension Fund, the Netherlands-based PGGM (also known as PFZW), and the California Public Employees Retirement System—incorporate the language of sustainability and responsible investment into their policies and practices.[9]

---

7   See the website for the Access to Medicines Index for an example how ESG data is currently being used to assess the performance of the pharmaceutical industry on access to medicines at http://www.accesstomedicineindex.org. Last accessed April 18, 2014.

8   See the brochure for the Principles for Responsible Investments at: http://www.unpi.org/ viewer/?file=wp-content/uploads/PRI_Brochure_2013.pdf. Last accessed October 26, 2014.

9   In 2013 *Responsible Investor* initiated an awards program for the large and small pension funds reporting best on their sustainability and responsible investment practices. For a listing of some of the pension funds with the best reporting on sustainability and responsible investment practices, see http://www.responsible-investor.com/events/events_page/ri_reporting_awards_2013_results. CalPERS and PGGM (aka PFZW) were among those receiving an award.

Who Mandates?

Assuming that the mandating of disclosure of corporate ESG data is, as Fung et al. (2007) would argue, not only desirable but necessary if it is to prove of long-lasting value, the question arises as to which governing bodies can most appropriately and effectively impose such requirements. The two logical, and potentially associated, avenues for the imposing ESG reporting requirements are legislators or regulators, and stock exchanges. In addition it is evident that the accounting profession should play a key role in this process as well.

Government, through legislation or regulation, is unquestionably capable of mandating ESG disclosure. A number of developed governments have already imposed various reporting requirements. Those legislated by France are among the most extensive and specific, with a 2001 law requiring its largest publicly traded companies to report annually on some 40 key ESG indicators along with their financial data. The Toronto Stock Exchange, by contrast, has encouraged ESG disclosure by publishing general guidelines (Toronto Stock Exchange and Chartered Professional Accountants, Canada, 2014).

In the emerging markets, the Indonesian government has required companies listed on its stock exchanges to start reporting on the effects of their activities on society and the environment since 2010. As of 2013, Indian law required major listed companies to implement and report on CSR programs to which 2 percent of earnings must be devoted. Taiwan's financial market regulator mandated CSR disclosure by all listed companies in 2008, and since 2007 Malaysian law compels listed companies to publish CSR information in their annual reports.[10]

The April 2014 decision by the European Parliament to mandate ESG disclosure by large publicly traded corporations represents a major step toward the globalization of such requirements. The mandated disclosure across an economic and financial region of the size and economic scale of the European Union is likely to provide strong momentum to similar initiatives elsewhere around the world.

The listing requirements of stock exchanges are a second avenue through which the worldwide mandating disclosure of ESG data might occur. Frequently viewing ESG disclosure as a means of enhancing the attractiveness

---

10 See the website of the Initiative for Responsible Investment for a listing of such requirements by governments and stock exchanges around the world at http://hausercenter.org/iri/about/global-csr-disclosure-requirements. Last accessed April 18, 2014.

of their companies to investors, emerging market exchanges have taken the lead. The Johannesburg Stock Exchange, for example, launched a socially responsible investment index in 2004, which encouraged CSR disclosure, and then in 2009 required listed companies to integrate their sustainability and financial reporting.

In 2007 the Bursa Malaysia created a framework for CSR reporting and encouraged listed companies to include CSR disclosure in their annual reports. In 2010 the Hong Kong stock exchange launched its Corporate Sustainability Index and the Shanghai Stock Exchange announced the creation of its Environmental Protection Index. From 2012 Brazil's Bovespa Stock Exchange has required listed companies to publish CSR reports or explain why they do not.[11]

The March 2014 petition, sponsored by Ceres, to the WFE and backed by a substantial number of major institutional investors expressing their need for more comprehensive and systematic ESG data, effectively requires stock exchanges around the world to evaluate the desirability of coordinating such requirements.

An additional development likely to drive both government and stock exchanges toward mandating ESG disclosure is the work on the integration of financial and sustainability reporting being headed up by the International Integrated Reporting Council (IIRC), a global effort drawing on expertise from the accounting community. The IIRC is promoting the publication in a single annual report[12] of the sustainability and financial data most material to the long-term success of the firm (Eccles and Krzus, 2010; Eccles et al., 2012). Churet and Eccles have found a positive relationship between integrated reporting and quality of management (Churet and Eccles, forthcoming 2014). In addition, organizations such as the Sustainability Accounting Standards Board (SASB) in the United States have embarked on the development of sets of sustainability

---

11 A number of these stock exchanges are working through the UN-affiliated Sustainable Stock Exchanges Initiative to promote these policies and practices. See the website of this organization for further details at http://www.sseinitiative.org/ Last accessed April 18, 2014. See also, *Carrots and Sticks Promoting Transparency and Sustainability: An Update on Trends in Voluntary and Mandatory Approaches to Sustainability Reporting*, 2009. Available at https://www.globalreporting.org/resourcelibrary/Carrots-And-Sticks-Promoting-Transparency-And-Sustainbability.pdf. Last accessed April 18, 2014.

12 See http://www.sasb.org/wp-content/uploads/2013/07/SASB-Outcome-Review-Report-Healthcare.pdf for an example of SASB's sustainability key performance indicators for the health care industry. Also see http://www.theiirc.org/consultationdraft2013 for its consultation draft of proposed guidelines for the integration of ESG and financial reporting. Last accessed April 18, 2014.

key performance indicators most material to specific industries for inclusion in mandated financial disclosure. Lydenberg (2012) provides an analysis of the relationship between sustainability and financial materiality.

Each of these avenues has its potential advantages: stock exchanges because they have the scope and flexibility to create coordinated, globally mandated ESG disclosure, national or regional legislators because they have the broad legitimacy that the law represents and are protectors of the public interest, and the accounting profession because it has well-established procedures for measuring and monitoring disclosure. In the end, mandated ESG disclosure systems will in all likelihood involve a combination of all three parties.

Why Mandated ESG Disclosure can Drive Fundamental Change

If implemented effectively and sustainably, mandated ESG disclosure has the potential to promote a number of fundamental, long-lasting changes in the corporate and financial worlds.

Currently, even among corporations with the most advanced CSR programs, CSR functions tend to be compartmentalized—with corporate philanthropy, diversity, human resources, ethics, vendor standards, and environment, health and safety operating separately in their different realms. Systematic mandated disclosure would promote a coordinated approach to CSR within the corporate structure, because the systematic nature of this disclosure would clarify the interrelationships between CSR's varied facets. Similarly, senior executives and boards of directors currently tend to consider CSR activities separately from their strategic planning decisions. The integration of CSR data with financial data will highlight the relationship between CSR and long-term strategic planning, and demonstrate the overlap between sustainability initiatives and financial resilience.

ESG disclosure often relates to stakeholders in the corporation (in other words, to consumers, employees, suppliers, communities, and the environment) and, therefore, its mandated disclosure can shift the paradigm within which corporate management views its responsibilities away from a primary focus on the stockowner—the so-called Anglo-American model—toward a more balanced model where investments in, and returns from, key stakeholders are factored into decision-making processes.

The mandating of ESG disclosure can also counteract some of the much lamented short-termism that has crept into corporate management and the financial markets these days. Sustainability issues frequently play themselves over decades and in ways that are highly unpredictable. For this reason, their short-term implications are difficult to quantify or even discern. At the current time these issues include such vital concerns as climate change, water scarcity, diversity, privacy, corruption, equality, and the safety of emerging technologies. The longer-term perspective that sustainability issues impose can provide a counterbalance to the short-term, and often short-sighted, pressure to maximize profitability and returns so prevalent in today's marketplace.

In addition, the systematic disclosure of ESG data will be of use to, and has the potential to broaden the thinking of, fiduciaries. The boards of directors of the world's largest companies and financial institutions have fiduciary duties that, although they differ in certain key respects, place them in a position to profoundly influence the future of society and the environment. This is particularly true of today's fiduciaries with investment responsibilities, who often confine their goals either to beating an asset-based benchmark— for example, the performance of their portfolio versus that of a stock index— or to matching that benchmark at the least possible price—for example, making automated trades in entire stock indexes. The former strategy is known as active management, the latter as passive.

Active managers currently incorporate financial data—but only occasionally ESG data—in projecting the future prospects of their investments. Passive investors tend to ignore the specifics of both financial and ESG data related to specific stocks. Neither involves the comprehensive integration of ESG data.

The comprehensive integration of ESG data into investment decisions implies an approach akin to that advocated by proponents of the universal owner theory. This theory was first propounded by Monks and Minnow (1996), and later elaborated by Hawley and Williams (2000, p.xv). Universal owners are those who have portfolios so large that they represent, and have the potential to affect, the economy—that is to say, the world beyond their portfolios. Individually, as well as collectively, these investors' decisions have substantial implications for how our economy operates, as well as for the preservation or destruction of environmental systems and the creation, preservation, or deterioration of valuable societal assets. The ESG characteristics of particular companies, or of whole industries, help these investors understand the repercussions of their decisions beyond the limited bounds of their portfolios. For these investors, measurement of short-term, or even long-term, stock prices relative to a benchmark has the potential to no longer be the sole relevant investment consideration. Their goals can also include the preservation or enhancement of societal and environmental assets throughout the economy. Only through the comprehensive integration of ESG data can they make investment decisions that achieve these twin goals. Sovereign wealth funds, which globally had assets under management of approximately $6.3 trillion as of 2014,[13] are a primary example of universal investors having the ability to influence entire economies along with long-term interests in assuring that global economies thrive.

Effective and Sustainable Forms of ESG Disclosure

Although the exact form—or forms—of mandated ESG disclosure have yet to be determined, the analyses of Fung et al. (2007) provide a number of basic insights into the frameworks likely to produce the most effective and sustainable regimes.

The company's ESG data will be valuable to its primary users—that is, to investors and other stakeholders in a corporation—when two key requirements are met: the data is both credible for, and applicable to, the primary concerns of these stakeholders. Disclosure requirements will, therefore, need to cover the most material ESG issues for each stakeholder. In addition, the data disclosed for each material ESG issue must go to the heart of the concerns, positive or negative, raised by that issue. The specific data will vary from industry to industry and from issue to issue, but in general this implies that disclosers must address shortcomings and challenges relevant to the most material issues along with their successes. This data must also have value to the disclosers themselves either through its ability to lead to efficiencies in their operations or to enhance their reputation.

The variety of issues of concern to key stakeholders in large, multinational corporations these days means that the number of potentially valuable data points for users and disclosure alike is substantial. In order to be valuable to both, disclosure regimes will need to strike an appropriate balance between comprehensiveness and materiality.

---

13 For estimates of the assets under management of sovereign wealth funds see http://www.swfinstitute.org/fund-rankings. Last accessed April 18, 2014.

For ESG data to be compatible with users' decision making, it needs to be affordable and accessible. Although institutional investors can typically afford to purchase large amounts of data, the same cannot be said of retail investors and many, if not most, other stakeholders. Accordingly, the ESG data will need to be available at no little or no charge to the public, as financial data now is for publicly traded companies. For investors, integrating ESG disclosure into corporations' financial reporting solves the problem of accessibility to data at the point of potential purchase. For other stakeholders, government or civil society organizations supporting stakeholders will need to assure the data disclosed is available at their particular points of decision-making.

To be comprehensible for users, the disclosed ESG data will need to be relatively simple and straightforward. To a certain degree the disclosers may also need to explain or interpret this data, setting it in contexts such as future goals and progress, industry trends, local environmental or social conditions and norms, and the expectations of local or global communities. For companies to understand how investors and stakeholders are using their data, mechanisms for users to provide clear feedback need to be easily available.

To be sustainable, Fung et al. (2007) argue that disclosure systems require scope, quality, accuracy, and usefulness—or what they term "embededness". Flexibility in a mandated ESG disclosure system will be crucial to satisfy the first and third of these three requirements. ESG issues fluctuate over time in their number, nature, and importance and therefore a system that allows for relatively easy adjustments in reporting requirements will help tailor the scope of the reporting appropriately to the needs of the times and locales. The quality and accuracy of the disclosed data, by contrast, can best be assured by third-party monitoring probably modeled on the third-party auditing already in place for financial statements. Finally, it will be important to allow for constant improvements in the usefulness of the data, so that it can become firmly embedded in the daily practices of both users and disclosers.

Other benefits of mandated disclosure will also follow. It will facilitate and expand the scope of much needed academic and practitioner research in the field. Kurtz (2013) provides an overview of research into the relationship between responsible investing and financial performance. To date, most academic research using ESG data has focused on the relationship between a firm's CSR management and its profitability, or on the relationship between investors' use of ESG criteria and their portfolio-level returns. This data will also enable—and indeed call for—research into valuation models that assess the positive and negative ESG externalities created by corporations.

This approach to valuation is particularly challenging because externalities, as economists define them, are factors that markets either have not, or cannot, price. If valuations of ESG externalities are to be expressed in financial terms then, by definition, markets need to be created for them or regulators need to impose costs on them—that is to say, they need to be internalized. The challenge of creating such markets or imposing such costs can be substantial—as can be seen in the ongoing efforts to create markets for the price of carbon emissions or to hold those responsible for greenhouse gas emissions to some level of legal liability. The creation of alternative non-price-related valuation methodologies may sound like a daunting task, but it is not inconceivable given the non-price-related fundamentals implicit in many matters of ESG concern. Bell and Morse (2008) review methodologies for assessing the sustainability of environmental systems in their book *Sustainability Indicators: Measuring the Immeasurable?*

Finally, the existence of comprehensive ESG data should help regulators and legislators make better informed and more nuanced decisions as to when and to what extent regulation and reform are, or are not, necessary. Currently, governments operate with only partial views of the extent and implications of corporate practices in social and environmental matters. They are often driven to action by crises and daily headlines focusing on single issues. More complete ESG data will help these public agents take a longer-term, more comprehensive, view when considering regulation in the public interest.

Conclusion

We appear to be well on our way toward the global mandating of systematic ESG disclosure by corporations. The potential importance of this data to investors, governments and academics, and to corporations themselves, has been too well demonstrated to abandon its pursuit at this time. It can potentially help address systemic challenges such as the achievement of environmental sustainability, the restoring of trust in corporations and the financial markets, the realization of social justice in a world of nine billion people, and the efficient allocation of assets throughout capital markets.

How effectively this comprehensive ESG data will be put to use will depend on the ability of corporate managers and institutional investors to comprehend the long-term benefits that its incorporation into daily practice can have—benefits that can accrue not only to their own profits and returns but to society more generally. These are benefits that must be realized if the challenges of a mid-twenty-first century world are to be met. The hard work of realizing the full potential of this ESG data will only begin, however, after it has been disclosed. The sooner the disclosure of this data is mandated, the sooner that hard work can begin.

References and Bibliography

Bell, S., and Morse, S. (2008). *Sustainability Indicators: Measuring the Immeasurable?* London: Earthscan.

Brandeis, L.D. (1914). *Other People's Money and How Bankers Use It*. New York: Frederick A Stokes Company.

CERES. (2014). *Assessing Water System Revenue Risk: Considerations for Market Analysts* and *Global Investors Survey on Climate Risk 2013*. Available at http://www.ceres.org/resources/reports. Last accessed April 18, 2014.

Churet, C., and Eccles, R. (forthcoming). Integrated Reporting, Quality of Management, and Financial Performance. *Journal of Applied Corporate Finance*, Vol. 26(1).

Eccles, R.G., and Krzus, M.P. (2010). *One Report: Integrated Reporting for a Sustainable Strategy*. Hoboken, NJ: John Wiley & Son, Inc.

Eccles, R.G., Krzus, M., and Rogers, J. (2012). The Need for Sector-Specific Materiality and Sustainability Reporting Standards. *Journal of Applied Corporate Finance*, Vol. 24(2), 65–71.

EU press release. (2014). http://europa.eu/rapid/press-release_STATEMENT-14-124_en.htm. Last accessed April 18, 2014.

Fox, M.B. (1999). Mandatory Securities Disclosure: Why Issuer Choice is not Investor Empowerment. *Virginia Law Review*, Vol. 85(7), 1335–1419.

Folketrygdfondet Ownership Report 2013.

Fung, A., Graham, M., and Weil, D. (2007). *Full Disclosure: The Perils and Promise of Transparency*. Cambridge, UK: Cambridge University Press.

Global Reporting Initiative, et al. (2013). *Carrots and Sticks: Sustainability Reporting Policies Worldwide: Today's Best Practice, Tomorrow's Trend*.

Hawley, J., and Williams, A. (2000). *The Rise of Fiduciary capitalism: How Institutional Investors Can Make Corporate America More Democratic.* Philadelphia, PA: University of Pennsylvania Press.

Hughes, J.A., and Leurig, S. (2013). *Assessing Water System Revenue Risk: Considerations for Market Analysts.* Boston, MA: Ceres.

International Integrated Reporting Council. (2013). *Consultation Draft of the International Integrated Reporting Framework.* London: IIRC.

KPMG. (2013). *KPMG Survey of Corporate Responsibility Reporting 2013.* Available at http://www.kpmg.com/Global/en/IssuesAndInsights/ArticlesPublications/corporate-responsibility/Documents/corporate-responsibility-reporting-survey-2013-exec-summary.pdf. Last accessed May 6, 2014.

Kurtz, L., (2013). *Looking Forward, Looking Back: A Hitchhiker's Guide to Research on Social and Sustainable Investment.* Available at http://fsinsight.org/insights/detail/looking-forward-looking-back-a-hitchhikers-guide-to-research-on-social-and-sustainable-investment. Last accessed April 18, 2014.

Lydenberg, S. (2014). Emerging Trends in Environmental, Social, and Governance Data and Disclosure: Opportunities and Challenges. *Private Sector Opinion.* Vol. 32, 1–15.

Lydenberg, S. (2012). *On Materiality and Sustainability: The Value of Disclosure in the Capital Markets.* Cambridge, MA: Initiative for Responsible Investment.

Monks, R.A.G., and Minnow, N. (1996). *Watching the Watcher: Corporate Governance in the 21st Century.* Cambridge, MA: Blackwell Publishers.

Monsma. D., and Olsen, T. (2007). Muddling Through Counterfactual Materiality and Divergent Disclosure: The Necessary Search for a Duty to Disclose material Non-Financial Information. *Stanford Environmental Law Journal,* Vol. 26, 139. January.

Moy, K., Jensen D., and Murrell, K. (2009). *Community Investment in the Insurance Industry Prepared for Altrushare Securities.* November. http://altrushare.com/pdf/Insurance_Industry_Nov2009.pdf. Last accessed April 18, 2014.

Panwar, J.S., and Blinch, J. (2012). *Sustainable Stock Exchanges: A Progress Report.* United Nations: Sustainable Stock Exchanges Initiative.

Philpott, T. (2012). *Are We Headed toward Peak Fertilizer?* Mother Jones. 28 November.

Romano, R. (1998). A Market Approach to Securities Regulation. *The Yale Law Journal*, Vol. 107(8), 2359–430.

Smith, J.A., Morreale, M., and Drexler, K. (2010). The SEC's Interpretive Release on Climate Change Disclosure. *Carbon & Climate Law Review*, February, 147.

The Corporate Register. http://www.corporateregister.com/. Last accessed April 18, 2014.

Toronto Stock Exchange and Chartered Professional Accountants, Canada, *A Primer for Social and Environmental Disclosure*. March, 2014. Available at http://www.cica.ca/focus-on-practice-areas/sustainability/cica-publications-and-activities/item78049.pdf. Last accessed May 6, 2014.

United Nations Conference on Trade and Development. (2011). *Corporate Governance Disclosure in Emerging Markets: Statistical Analysis of Legal Requirements and Company Practices*. New York and Geneva: United Nations.

Williams, C.A. (1999). The Securities and Exchange Commission and Corporate Social Transparency. *Harvard Law Review*, Vol. 112, 1245.

Chapter 10

What is Sustainable: The Need for Sufficient Reporting and its Accounting Implications

PAUL F. WILLIAMS

Introduction

In June 1969 the faculty of the Yale School of Forestry was invited, for the first time, to participate in the Annual Yale Alumni Seminar. The four lectures given by the forestry faculty are published under the title *Man and his Environment: The Ecological Limits to Optimism* (Mergen, 1970). The lectures dealt with various aspects of the environmental crisis of the day that was most vividly described in the Club of Rome's report (Meadows, et al., 1969). One essay dealt with the pressures of human population growth on a planet of finite resources, and another dealt with the dilemma of reconciling freedom with the responsibility humans have to care for the planet. A third essay discussed the level of existence that might be possible if the population explosion was curtailed and we could learn to live within our means. The fourth essay, and the one from which the title of the collection came, was about values and whether or not the values we humans hold, characterized by boundless optimism in human possibilities, is possible given the environmental difficulties we faced in the 1970s. The optimism inherent in Western capitalism, indicated by popular oxymora like sustainable development and Schumpeter's (1942) cliché "creative destruction," represent rhetorical moves to assure ourselves that tweaking the system is all that is required. Like the parable of the fishes and loaves wherein the multitudes were fed with limited resources, we are reluctant to believe that such miracles might not be forthcoming from the technology in which we have all placed our faith. That we might not be able to have our cake and eat it too, is a prospect that our deeply embedded economic and political values prevent us from giving any serious consideration. The accounting discipline is one totally infused with the optimism bred by faith in technology and the workings of a capitalist system of free markets and unlimited human material aspiration. The development of the accounting discipline since the founding of the accounting profession in the nineteenth century has been shaped to serve this institutionalized optimism.

The awareness of environmental degradation, along with the attitudes in the United States spawned by the New Deal that accepted a greater role for government in ameliorating the social and economic hardships of the average citizen, led to calls for corporations to be more socially responsible (Danley, 1994). Corporate social responsibility (CSR) was the rubric for this movement for business corporations to become promoters of the good society. Accompanying the social responsibility movement was a parallel one calling for corporations to develop systems of reporting upon their social and environmental contributions, that is a system of corporate social reporting (Bauer and Fenn, 1972; Gambling, 1974; American Institute of Certified Public Accountants (AICPA), 1977). Over 40 years have passed since interest in developing systems of measuring and reporting upon corporate social performance began in earnest. The purpose of this chapter is to provide a critique of that effort, and to suggest a rethinking of what CSR and reporting should be about.

CSR = Sustainability

Recently, the old wine of CSR has been put into a new bottle labeled corporate sustainability. As the follow up study to the Club of Rome report (Meadows et al., 2004) has shown the state of environmental degradation has only worsened since the 1970s. Climate change affected by human activity threatens sizeable portions of the human population (Carpenter, 2014). In spite of calls for corporations to behave in more socially and environmentally responsible ways, the circumstances that led to the CSR movement have only gotten worse. Rising temperatures, melting glaciers, accelerating rates of species extinction, colony collapse syndrome for the insect upon which we all depend for fruits and vegetables—the scientific community produces a steady stream of findings pointing to the growing stresses human economic activities are placing on the planet.

The rebranding of CSR as sustainable development or corporate sustainability is a rhetorical shift prompted to some extent by the recognition that what faces humankind is more ominous than what was perceived in the 1970s when corporations were merely being asked to be more socially responsible. "Sustainable" has a connotation of urgency that "responsible" does not. Irresponsibility could persist indefinitely—the free-rider problem of appeals only for CSR is apparent. Sustainability, on the other hand, implies a course that cannot persist. Unsustainable, by definition, cannot persist indefinitely. But talk of sustainability at the level of individual firms retains the optimism that sustainability can be achieved via the same means that, ironically, has brought about concern for sustainability in the first place. Historically, if the economic system that now dominates substantial portions of the world's population had been functioning as the optimistic vision implies, the concern for sustainability would not exist.

Just as CSR was accompanied by corporate social reporting, sustainability has been accompanied by calls for sustainability reporting. An international effort to codify sustainability reporting under the auspices of the Global Reporting Initiative (GRI, 2011a) is well underway. Most very large global corporations voluntarily participate in the initiative by publishing sustainability reports following the GRI recommended guidelines (GRI, 2011b). Like the social reports of the 1970s, the sustainability reports of today have the same basic architecture usually described as the triple bottom line (TBL). The tripartite nature of reporting is reflective of the economic, environmental, and social effects of corporate behavior. The economic line is the traditional financial reporting, highly codified to reflect profitability, liquidity, and solvency. The environmental line is not actually a line, since there is no codified system of measurement that produces any summary metric that can produce a profit measure for environmental performance comparable in meaning to the profit figure reported on the traditional income statement. The social line is even fainter than the environmental one, since social is a rubric that contains every other effect corporations could have that is not economic or environmental. So two of the three lines are mainly descriptions of activities, some accompanied by measures of the effects of those activities, ranging far and wide over the environmental and social landscape.

What these reports convey to their readers is an, as yet, unresolved matter (Bradford et al., 2014). Indeed there seems to be no coherent understanding of what the purpose of such reports is, nor do we understand what actions the reporting of such information will initiate and by whom. If the purpose of such reports is to convey the fact that a company is a responsible company, there is a bit of a paradox. If you are a responsible company, your actions should speak for themselves in the marketplace. If that behavior matters to the marketplace then, since the marketplace is where behavior is allegedly most effectively and efficiently observed, reporting about it seems superfluous. It seems less than virtuous to boast about one's virtue. If being a responsible company is important in its own right, a company should simply be one and spare itself the expense of having to tell people about it.

If sustainability reports are meant to convey information that is actionable by various interested parties, then it would seem those parties' actions should mean something vis-à-vis companies being more responsible. For example, the information to be conveyed by traditional financial statements has long been codified and regulated. As corporations grew in size and became more dependent on external financing, the idea of transparency became more compelling (Previts and Merino, 1998). Transparency was—and still seems to be—the preferred solution to managing financial market risk. If firms are compelled to prepare reports of their financial performance, the content of those reports is regulated, and those reports are subject to independent verification, then financial market participants via their actions in the market place will discipline firms to behave in ways that are conducive to them being responsible economic agents.

By analogy, can sustainability reports be believed to serve the same function as do financial reports? It is doubtful because the analogy does not hold. Financial markets have some degree of leverage to compel firms to do their bidding, because failing to do so means financing will not be forthcoming. If being a good corporate citizen is equally important to financial markets, then sustainability reports can, just as financial reports, activate the leverage that financial markets have to induce companies to be more environmentally and socially responsible. There exists no compelling evidence that this is the case. That it is not the case can be inferred by the invention of stakeholder theory (Freeman, 1984). If financial market participants were all the leverage needed to compel firms to be socially and environmentally responsible, a normative management theory like stakeholder theory would not be necessary.

That management scholars see the necessity to construct a theory obligating management to pay attention to the needs of corporate constituents other than investors, for example, employees, communities, environment, governments, and so on, is an overt recognition that transparency to financial markets alone is not sufficient to ensure responsible corporate behavior. The dilemma for the effectiveness of sustainability reporting then is whether stakeholders are able to exercise the same leverage prompted by information from sustainability reports, as financial markets can from the prompts provided by financial statements. They obviously cannot, because the institutional mechanisms of power afforded shareholders and creditors are not available to stakeholders. What can a stakeholder do? Boycott the products? Seek employment at another firm?

Create a new ecosystem immune from corporate effects? For transparency to work there must be power to act on the information to bring about changes in behavior. The power to leverage the information contained in sustainability reports is not nearly as great as the power to leverage the information contained in traditional financial reports.[1]

Support for this contention comes from the substantial research of social responsibility/sustainability reports that has been conducted over many decades. One of the earliest studies to investigate the information content of CSR reports provided by companies was that of Wiseman (1982). She compared the assessment of environmental performance provided by companies against independent assessments provided by environmental and social responsibility investment organizations, and found that there were significant disparities. Companies' responsibility reports are primarily for the purpose of image management, in other words, to be seen as socially and environmentally responsible rather than to be truthful as to their actual performance. This same characterization of reporting as an image management rhetoric has been observed repeatedly even when the report is relabeled a sustainability report (see, for example, Adams, 2004; Archel et al., 2009; Rodrique, 2014; Tregidga et al., 2014; Milne and Grubnic, 2011; Milne et al., 2009; Deegan et al., 2006). Thus, after five decades of discussion and experimentation with systems of reporting intended to lead companies to be more responsible or sustainable, the evidence thus far does not suggest that much substantive progress has been made. This state of affairs has led some of the most prominent members of the sustainability reporting research community to express grave skepticism about the whole enterprise (Gray and Milne, 2014; Milne and Gray, 2013).

A Simplified "Model" of the Impasse

In order to provide a perspective for understanding the lack of progress in sustainability reporting actually contributing to sustainability, consider a simple accounting model of the problem developed by Williams (2010) and Bayou

---

1   The "balanced scorecard" approach to corporate strategy, which acknowledges the necessity to keep score in ways other than short-term financial outcomes, still is predicated on the supposition that other things for which scores must be kept are to serve ultimately financial performance (Kaplan and Norton, 1996). Only to the extent that other outcomes serve long-run financial performance are those other outcomes to be valued. The balanced scorecard is a variation on the business case argument for sustainability—you make money by being good. Being good is still of only instrumental value.

et al. (2011). The line that represents economic performance for a company, the so-called bottom line, is the familiar accounting identity for net income:

$$Net\ Income = Revenues - Expenses$$

Every accounting tyro is first introduced to this identity along with the balance sheet equation that demands that Assets = Liabilities + Equity. These identities, forming the conceptual foundation of the double-entry system of accounting, always pertain to an entity that is bounded, in other words separated, from the rest of human activity via criteria that are largely legal in nature. What the net income equation conceals about its assumptions, and how those assumptions may prove to be a substantial obstacle to meaningful sustainability reporting, is indicated by expanding the equation with more literal descriptions of its terms. This expansion is provided by Bayou et al. (2011, p.121):

> *Gross income of shareholders = Revenues – Payments to labor*
> *– Payments to suppliers*
> *– Payments to creditors*
> *– Payments to governments*
> *– Net externalities*
> *– Net ambiguities created by standard-setters*

The final term "Net ambiguities created by standard-setters" is not of any particular interest for the purposes of this paper other than to illustrate that, even in the absence of externalities that are unaccounted for, accounting is unable to precisely account for what it presumes to account for, in other words, net income. Net income is not a natural kind, but a human invention—an interpretive concept à la Dworkin (2011).

As Bayou et al. (2011) describe the translated equation, net income of the company is actually the gross income that accrues to its owners—shareholders in the case of a corporation. Revenues are the resources that the company is able to capture preferably by legal means and as monetary resources whose liquidity allows for the distribution of those resources—this, of course, would be much more difficult if we lived in a world that did not have the institutional wherewithal to have money. Expenses, which are distributions of a company's resources to third parties other than owners, are actually payments made to acquire the means to capture revenues. Payments to labor are the gross incomes of people who provide labor, payments to suppliers are the gross incomes of other companies that provide goods and services, payments to creditors are the gross incomes of creditors who provide debt financing, payments to governments—usually in the form of taxes—are payments for a system to enforce contracts, protect property, educate workforces, and so on.

Net externalities are the costs and benefits that companies visit upon others for which they receive no economic benefit in the case of positive externalities, or for which they pay nothing in the case of negative externalities. What is immediately apparent from this more literal enunciation of the net income equation is the extent to which net income is not something attributable solely to an individual firm. Externalities are pervasive, both positive and negative, and without them no firm could produce the income it allegedly produces using current accounting conventions. For example, automobile manufacturers report net incomes which we take for granted are attributable to those firms since their income statements always have headings that contain their names. But it is quite obvious that an auto company's net income is not solely attributable to the company. Sales of automobiles are greatly influenced by the availability, or lack thereof, of highways upon which to drive them. Indeed the utility and design of automobiles is intimately related to the quality of the highways upon which they may be driven. If sole responsibility for building the highways upon which their autos can be used were that of auto manufacturers, there would be no profitable auto companies—nor likely any auto companies at all. Yet the investment to build the system of highways upon which automobiles attain their service potential, and the cost of maintaining those highways is not charged against the accounts of the companies.

What we see from the analysis of the income equation is that attributions of economic success to individual economic actors, is an intellectually careless thing to do. For an argument about the carelessness of not recognizing this joint revenue problem in the area of social justice and taxation, see Murphy and Nagel (2002). In the parlance of attribution theory it is to commit the fundamental attribution error which is to attribute success to one's own efforts and failure to outside forces. The current system of economic performance reporting is based, therefore, on an error, which is that we can sensibly isolate the economic success of individual firms even while neglecting to account for the significant costs and benefits that arise from the fact that any firm is merely a component of a huge, complex system of interdependencies and relationships. We can clearly see that a firm's alleged economic performance— its net income as reported by accountants—is a function of that firm's relationships with employees, suppliers, creditors, governments, and with the social and physical environment. And to the extent that the firm has the ability to shift costs away from it and impose them on its relationships, the more misleading is its net income performance represented by traditional accounting methods.

To develop a system of sustainability reporting it would seem to be necessary to recognize this systemic, relational system that current systems of accounting are inadequate to reveal. Sustainability reporting cannot simply be adding two more legs to the stool to make up a TBL system; this simply adds two legs even weaker than the one leg the stool has been supported with in the past. The failure to develop a system of sustainability reporting that provides information that has action implications meaningful to actual sustainability, stems from a false premise that underlies the current system of financial reporting whose consequences were illustrated above. This false premise has been described by Corning (2011, p.10):

> The claim that a society is merely a facultative arrangement – a marketplace or perhaps a vehicle for material and moral improvement – downplays or even denies its true nature. Our fundamental collective purpose is to provide for the basic survival and reproductive needs of our people – past, present, and future.
>   In other words,
>   ... an organized, interdependent society is quintessentially a "collective survival enterprise". To borrow a term from sociobiology, it's a "superorganism". (Ibid)

The Ecological Limits to Markets

This false premise guiding traditional accounting systems is evident in the claim enunciated in the concepts statements of both the Financial Accounting Standards Board (FASB) and the International Accounting Standards Board (IASB) (2010) that the purpose of financial reporting is to provide decision useful information, specifically information for making investment and credit decisions by individuals about individual firms. But if, as we have argued above, a society is a system of relationships—a superorganism—how is it justified for a regulatory function like accounting to rationally defend a focus on abetting individuals to make rational, in other words, economically self-interested, decisions? Williams and Ravenscroft (2014) argued that decision usefulness as a basis for justifying accounting standards is incoherent, because the ability to demonstrate that any accounting datum is somehow more decision useful than another is an insuperable empirical problem because decision usefulness is not an inherent property of any accounting datum. What might make an accounting datum decision useful is some other property beside decision usefulness, and it is this property that should guide accounting policy choices. The justification comes from a belief that markets are an effective mechanism for coordinating the actions of individual members of society into an *efficient* solution for all members of society. If maximum, veritable information is provided to individuals acting in markets, then some kind of social optimum is achieved. This belief is evident in talk about making capital markets more efficient allocators of capital. It is also apparent as the rationale for sustainability reporting—if firms provide information about their social and environmental performance to individuals (stakeholders) acting in markets, firms that are responsible will allegedly reap some reward through the market mechanism.

The problem is that markets do not actually work this way.[2] In standard neoclassical economic theory reference is made to market forces, and laws, like that of supply and demand, but as McCloskey (1985) has argued these are rhetorical flourishes and not descriptions of nature. Market is a metaphor and not an actual thing that exists as a natural kind. Economics over time has managed through sophisticated mathematics to create the illusion that economic propositions have scientific status equivalent to those of physics. But that is false (Rosenberg, 1992). The fallacy starts with the very concept of market. As Chang (2010) has pointed out a market is subject to constant changes brought about by cultural and political actions. The example he provides is that of the so-called labor market. At one time, that market included slaves and children. That market no longer includes those categories as freely available for trading. So obviously, unlike the force of gravity or electromagnetic forces of nature, market forces are subject to amendment by moral and legal considerations. The implication of this for people's faith in pronouncements of economic scientists is quite profound. Chang states: "Free market economists may want you to believe that the correct boundaries of the market can be scientifically determined, but this is incorrect. If the boundaries of what you are studying cannot be scientifically determined, what you are doing is not a science" (Chang, 2010, p.10). What nature binds us to as constraints on our choices, is not how we are bound by so-called market forces. Markets themselves are trumped by moral and political considerations. There is never a market solution in itself, because any solution a market provides is determined by the nature of the market and that is always subject to human design. Paradoxically that design

---

2   It is beyond the capacity of this chapter to go into extensive demonstration of why this is so. Sources that provide elaborate critiques, by economists themselves, of the extreme failures of conventional economic theory include Keen, 2001; Ormerod, 1994; Marglin, 2008; Nelson, 2001; Cassidy, 2009; Medema, 2009; Basu, 2011.

is not the result of market forces—markets do not design themselves. Markets work only if conscious human design enables them to work.

Proponents of market logic for shaping societies base their confidence in such logic on an article of faith. Adam Smith (1937) famously referred to an "invisible hand" that guided the affairs of society in optimal directions without any need for government planning or intervention. The invisible hand is obviously a metaphor alluding to the divine guidance in human affairs provided by "the Hand of God"—also invisible. Dogmatic faith in the working of markets is a theological position, not one based on any substantive evidence that markets actually operate as the Hand of Providence does to provide for every need.[3] Of course this is a misplaced faith. Even Adam Smith set little store in the invisible hand metaphor, and certainly did not intend for it to be interpreted to endorse the use of market logic to every aspect of human existence (Wolfe, 1989).

Foley (2006) describes the misplaced faith in markets as Adam's Fallacy. More specifically:

> *The moral fallacy of Smith's position is that it urges us to accept direct and concrete evil in order that indirect and abstract good may come of it. The logical fallacy is that neither Smith nor any of his successors has been able to demonstrate rigorously and robustly how private selfishness turns into public altruism. The psychological failing of Smith's rationalization is that it requires a strategy of wholesale denial of the real consequences of capitalist development, particularly the systemic imposition of costs on those least able to bear them, and the implacable reproduction of inequalities that divide one from another in society. (Foley, 2006, p.3)*

As Foley notes Adam's Fallacy is a moral one, so any position vis-à-vis the role of markets in society is a moral one. The question is not what that role is, but what should that role be. The title of this collection *Sustainable Markets for Sustainable Business* begs an important question, which is whether any market should be sustained. For example, should the market for coal be sustained? That is not a question that can be answered by markets, because it is a political and moral decision whether that should be the case. The owners of coal would

---

3   From the King James translation of the Bible, Matthew 6:26: "Look at the birds of the air, for they neither sow nor reap nor gather into barns; yet your heavenly Father feeds them. Are you not of more value than they?"

want to sustain the market for coal until all of the coal that could be extracted for a price exceeding its cost of extraction was burned up. But that would be extremely imprudent for all of humankind given the extent to which the burning of coal is contributing to climate change. This is just as the owners of slaves in the United States fought the bloodiest war in American history to sustain the market in slaves. Markets are surely part of the solution to the problem of sustainability, but not before we recognize that faith in markets is a fundamental part of the problem.

Accounting for Sustainability: Back to the Future

The implications for accounting for sustainability that devolve from the argument provided above, are the focus of the final section of this chapter. CSR and its successor sustainability reporting have been in the developmental stage for nearly half a century, with little to show in the way of progress. Lack of progress is attributable to a lack of commitment on the part of accountants to consider what the implications of a genuinely sustainable economy are, and what that would involve in terms of accounting's current premises. As the simplified model presented earlier illustrated, an economy is a system of relationships and not merely the sum of actions by individual economic actors. Even the current model of accounting focused exclusively on measuring income and financial position is woefully incomplete, because it ignores the spaces representing the relationships among individuals, organizations, institutions, societies, and the physical environment.

A useful perspective to take on these spaces is what John McCumber (2005) has described as the "edge of ethics." According to McCumber:

> The edge of ethics is the place where nature, society and community guide me, even as I seek to transform them. It is the place where I have to respect things and people instead of act on or with them — i.e., where I must situate myself with respect to them. At the edge of ethics, individual actions are channeled by relationships, which can harden into institutions.
>
> My basic claim is that in order to act ethically, we must have defined the situation we are in: we must have satisfied ourselves that we know what sort of thing is happening and what sort of thing needs to happen. (Ibid., p.164)

An implication of this view is that before we can know what to do in the way of ethical action we must know where we are, in other words, where we are situated. Bayou et al. (2011) provide an analysis of current accounting policy that leads them to conclude that accounting's critical function in democratic societies is to assist in the key necessity of situating businesses, vis-à-vis the relationships of business, at the edges of community, society, and the environment.

If accounting is to contribute in a positive way to the very real problem of sustainability, its stated goal of providing information useful for economic decision-making needs to be rethought. From the very origins of accounting as a social function, going back at least six millennia, its primary purpose has been to facilitate civic administration (Schmant-Besserat, 1992; Soll, 2014). The organizing principle that gave accounting's function coherence has always been accountability (Ijiri, 1975). Accounting has undergone a radical shift in purpose, initiated by the financial reporting revolution (Beaver, 1981) when the discipline substituted the values of serving markets for those of holding someone to account. If there is to be anything that qualifies as sustainability accounting then the accounting discipline needs to return to a principle of accountability as its core metaphor, because what the problem of sustainability requires is a system of monitoring that situates corporate action vis-à-vis the relationships it has with community, society, and the environment. A truly sustainable corporation is one that has internalized its negative externalities, a likely unattainable goal but something about which society needs information. Some corporations are likely to be successful in a profitability sense only because they are able to externalize costs by imposing them on employees, communities, society, and the natural environment. If that is the case, we need to know this. Sustainability is not about doing good deeds, it is about accountability. A system of sustainability reporting must contain at its core the understanding that corporate sustainability actions are those for which a firm is actually accountable. They are actions that are required not merely to be seen as a socially responsible corporation but required out of moral necessity.

Earlier in this chapter the economy in which we all live was referred to as a superorganism, that is, a collective survival enterprise. According to Corning (2011) this superorganism involves an implied biosocial contract and this contract is:

> ... *focused on our relationships—the social interactions that occur*
> *every day among individuals, families, organizations, neighborhoods,*
> *communities, and businesses and between citizens and their*

government(s). And it is the quality, and fairness, of these relationships that largely determines how effectively any given society is able to pursue its collective survival enterprise. [...]. Thus fairness is an inescapable problem and an important part of the solution for every viable society. (Ibid., p.12)

A sole reliance on markets to solve this problem is, as we have already discussed, not a viable strategy, because markets alone simply do not work to solve such problems. Sustainability is not simply an economic problem, nor a problem solved by each individual firm acting to make itself sustainable. It is a moral, and thus, political problem. The current premise that accounting contributes to solving this problem merely by providing information to enable rational economic decisions in the marketplace, based on a belief that so-called market solutions are preferable to political or ethical ones, is not a serious approach. After nearly fifty years of this approach to reporting failing to improve the situation, suggests something different needs to be tried.

Conclusion

Concerns for sustainability are recognition that human activities are having effects on the Earth that cannot continue. Mankind must find alternative ways to make a living and, according to the scientific consensus, the time for doing that is short. Nearly 50 years ago the development of systems began to evaluate the behavior of corporations in moving toward becoming more focused on ameliorating the effects they are having on contributing to the unsustainable nature of our current economic system. Starting as the movement for CSR during the 1970s, a parallel development was the creation of systems of reporting on the expanded responsibilities of corporations. CSR became corporate sustainability because the circumstances that prompted the responsibility movement had not improved, but gotten worse. Had effective systems of monitoring and reporting corporate social performance been devised, we could have expected progress in our economic systems becoming more sustainable.

It is argued in this chapter that the failure to develop effective accounting systems is attributable to the false premises upon which their development has thus far been based. Accountants have, since at least the mid-1960s, based reporting systems on the assumption that the purpose of accounting is to provide information to individual economic actors to enable them to make economically rational decisions. The justification for this strategy is the faith that the organized profession has in the idealizations of neoclassical economic theory of how markets work. The supposition is that markets are an ideal mechanism for shaping society so long as they are provided with sufficient information. Thus without explicit consideration of how information about sustainability actions on the part of corporations might imply a different view of how decisions about corporate behavior should be made, and by whom, sustainability reporting has been advocated as more or less analogous to the financial reporting model. If markets provide optimal resource allocations in an economic sense, then providing them with sustainability information will lead them to optimal solutions for the problem of unsustainability, as well.

The contention in this chapter that efforts to develop systems of accounting for sustainability have progressed so little, is because markets do not actually work the way accountants believe they do. Issues of corporate social and environmental responsibility are not issues that can be resolved by markets, but are issues that require moral and political action. It is argued that the major implication for developing sustainability reporting systems is that the decision useful information metaphor is inadequate. Instead, advocacy is offered for a return to a more traditional understanding of what the function of accounting has been throughout most of its history—providing for the effective consummation of accountability relationships in society. Society is a collective survival enterprise whose effective functioning depends upon systems that maintain fairness within the society. A shift in focus from considering reports of corporate sustainability actions as information, to markets considering them as reports to society and its political institutions about fulfillment of corporate obligations, is recommended.

References and Bibliography

Adams, C.A. (2004). The Ethical, Social and Environmental Reporting-Performance Portrayal Gap. *Accounting, Auditing and Accountability Journal,* Vol. 17(5), 731–57.

American Institute of Certified Public Accountants. (1977). *The Measurement of Corporate Social Performance: Determining the Impact of Business Actions on Areas of Social Concern.* New York, NY: AICPA.

Archel, P., Husillos, J., Larrinaga, C., and Spence, C. (2009). Social Disclosure, Legitimacy Theory and the Role of the State. *Accounting, Auditing and Accountability Journal,* Vol. 22(8), 1284–1307.

Basu, K. (2011). *Beyond the Invisible Hand.* Princeton, NJ: Princeton University Press.

Bauer, R.A., and Fenn, D.H. (1972). *The Corporate Social Audit.* Social Science Frontiers, Vol. 5. New York, NY: Russell Sage Foundation.

Bayou, M.E., Reinstein, A., and Williams, P.F. (2011). To Tell the Truth: A Discussion of Issues Concerning Truth and Ethics in Accounting. *Accounting, Organizations and Society*, Vol. 36(2), 109–24.

Beaver, W. H. (1981). *Financial Reporting: An Accounting Revolution.* Englewood Cliffs, NJ: Prentice Hall.

Bradford, M., Earp, J., and Williams, P.F. *Corporate Sustainability Reporting: What Could it Mean?* Working paper. North Carolina State University.

Carpenter, G. (2014). Model Behavior. Comparing Climate Science with Economic Forecasts. *New Economics Foundation.* http://neweconomics.org/blog/entry/climate-forecasts-setting-the-record-straight?&u.

Cassidy, J. (2009). *How Markets Fail: The Logic of Economic Calamities.* New York, NY: Farrar, Strauss and Giroux.

Chang, H. (2010). *23 Things They Don't Tell You about Capitalism.* New York, NY: Bloomsburg Press.

Corning, P. (2011). *The Fair Society: The Science of Human Nature and the Pursuit of Social Justice.* Chicago, IL: The University of Chicago Press.

Danley, J.R. (1994). *The Role of the Corporation in a Free Society.* Notre Dame, IN: Notre Dame University Press.

Deegan, C., Cooper, B.J., and Shelly, M. (2006). An Investigation of TBL Report Assurance Statements: UK and European evidence. *Managerial Auditing Journal*, Vol. 21(4), 329–71.

Dworkin, R. (2011). *Justice for Hedgehogs.* Cambridge, MA: The Belknap Press of the Harvard University Press.

Foley, D.K. (2006). *Adam's Fallacy.* Cambridge, MA: The Belknap Press of Harvard University Press.

Freeman, R.E. (1984). *Strategic Management: A Stakeholder Approach*. Boston, MA: Pittman.

Gambling, T. (1974). *Societal Accounting*. London: Allen & Unwin.

Global Reporting Initiative. (2011a). http://www.globalreporting.org/Pages/default.aspx.

Global Reporting Initiative. (2011b). *Sustainability Disclosure Database*. http://database.globalreporting.org/.

Gray, R., and Milne, M.J. (forthcoming). *It's Not What You Do, It's The Way That You Do It? Of Method And Madness*. Working paper. University of Saint Andrews.

Ijiri, Y. (1975). *The Theory of Accounting Measurement*. Sarasota, FL: American Accounting Association.

International Accounting Standards Board (IASB). (2010). *The Conceptual Framework for Financial Reporting*. London: IFRS Foundation.

Kaplan, R.S., and Norton, D.P. (1996). *The Balanced Scorecard*. Boston, MA: Harvard Business School Press.

Keen, S. (2001). *Debunking Economics*. Anandale NSW, Australia: Pluto Press.

Marglin, S. (2008). *The Dismal Science: How Thinking Like an Economist Undermines Community*. Cambridge, MA: Harvard University Press.

McCloskey, D. (1985). *The Rhetoric of Economics*. Madison, WI: University of Wisconsin Press.

McCumber, J. (2005). *Reshaping Reason: Toward a New Philosophy*. Bloomington, IN: Indiana University Press.

Meadows, D.H., Meadows, D.L., Randers, J., and Behrens, III. W.W. (1969). *The Limits to Growth*. Published under the auspices of The Club of Rome. New York, NY: Universe Books.

Meadows, D.H., Randers, J., and Meadows, D.L. (2004). *Limits to Growth: The 30-Year Update*. White River Junction, VT: Chelsea Green Publishing Co.

Medema, S.G. (2009). *The Hesitant Hand: Taming Self-Interest in the History of Economic Ideas.* Princeton, NJ: Princeton University Press.

Mergen, F. (1970). (ed). *Man and His Environment: The Ecological Limits to Optimism.* Yale University: School of Forestry, bulletin 76. New Haven, CN: Yale University School of Forestry.

Milne, M.J. and Gray, R. (2013). W(h)ither ecology? The Triple Bottom Line, the Global Reporting Initiative, and Corporate Sustainability Reporting. *Journal of Business Ethics*, Vol. 118(1), 13–29.

Milne, M.J., and Grubnic, S. (2011). Climate Change Accounting Research: Keeping it Interesting and Different. *Accounting, Auditing and Accountability Journal*, Vol. 24(8), 948–77.

Milne, M.J., Tregidga, H., and Walton, S. (2009). Words not Actions! The Ideological Role of Sustainable Development Reporting. *Accounting, Auditing and Accountability Journal*, Vol. 22(8), 1211–57.

Murphy, L., and Nagel, T. (2002). *The Myth of Ownership: Taxes and Justice.* Oxford, UK: Oxford University Press.

Nelson, R. H. (2001). *Economics as Religion: From Samuelson to Chicago and Beyond.* University Park, PA: Pennsylvania State University Press.

Ormerod, P. (1994). *The Death of Economics.* New York, NY: John Wiley & Sons, Inc.

Previts, G.J., and B.D. Merino. (1998). *A History of Accounting in the United States.* Columbus, OH: Ohio State University Press.

Rodrigue, M. (2014). Contrasting Realities: Corporate Environmental Disclosures and Stakeholder-released Information. *Accounting, Auditing and Accountability Journal*, Vol. 27(1), 119–49.

Rosenberg, A. (1992). *Economics—Mathematical Politics or Science of Diminishing Returns?* Chicago, IL: The University of Chicago Press.

Schmandt-Besserat, D. (1992). *Before Writing, Volume I: From Counting to Cuneiform.* Austin, TX: University of Texas Press.

Schumpeter, J.A. (1942). *Capitalism, Socialism and Democracy*. New York, NY: Harper Torchbooks.

Smith, A. (1937). *The Wealth of Nations*. E. Cannan (ed). New York, NY: The Modern Library.

Soll, J. (2014). *The Reckoning: Financial Accountability and the Rise and Fall of Nations*. New York, NY: Basic Books.

Tregidga, H., Milne, M., and Kearins, K. (2014). (Re)presenting 'Sustainable Organizations'. *Accounting, Organizations and Society*, Vol. 39(6), 477–94. http://dx.doi.org/10.1016/j.aos.2013.10.006.

Williams, P.F. (2010). The Focus of Professional Ethics: Ethical Professionals or Ethical Profession? In C. Jeffrey (ed.), *Research on Professional Responsibility and Ethics in Accounting*, Vol. 14, 15–35.

Williams, P.F., and Ravenscroft, S. (2014). Rethinking Decision Usefulness. *Contemporary Accounting Research*, DOI: 10.1111/1911-3846.12083.

Wiseman, J. (1982). An Evaluation of Environmental Disclosure Made in Corporate Annual Reports. *Accounting, Organizations and Society*, Vol. 7(1), 53–63.

Wolfe, A. (1989). *Whose Keeper?* Berkeley, CA: University of California Press.

The Future Perspectives: What Do We Need for Market and Business Sustainability?

GÜLER ARAS

Introduction

The current economic crisis has highlighted not only the importance of governance and corporate social responsibility (CSR), it has also shown that standards and regulations for sustainability are a central part and the result of governance. The globalization of financial markets has led to an increase in the need for some international rules such as: international financial reporting standards, corporate governance, ethics, and corporate social responsibility principles. In business activity, these standards have been set forth with a view to minimizing uncertainty, and with developing an atmosphere of confidence in a web of emerging complex relations. With the impact of these developments, it is very important for financial markets and the businesses operating within these markets to accommodate and implement some necessary rules.

After markets collapsed during the 2008 financial crisis, corporate and market behavior became a crucial subject to explore. The objective of sustainable markets is to increase trust in markets in the context of investor protection, elimination of the uncertainties, and more efficient resource allocation. There are many studies conducted regarding the complex challenges of sustainable business and markets in practice. This book focuses on the perception, importance, and functions of sustainable markets and sustainable business practices. This book is intended to be largely descriptive, but also prescriptive by providing materials, when available, which are selected to be relevant for an international audience.

Are Financial Markets Sustainable?

As we mention many times in this book, the definition and measurement of sustainability is still subject to debate. However, sustainable financial institutions and markets address many key points, including creating sustainable value, achieving the institutions' and markets' goals, and maintaining a balance between economic and social benefits with a long-term perspective. In fact, sustainability offers long-term benefits to markets and institutions such as reducing risk and attracting new investors. Stigson (2002) highlights that sustainable development, in a broad sense, is about ensuring a better quality of life for now and for generations to come. One of the three pillars of sustainable development is the financial markets, which are the drivers of the sustainability engine. Financial markets, to a great degree, drive sustainable development. Indeed, if the markets do not reward sustainable behavior, progress will be slow (Stigson, 2002). When considering sustainability in the markets and institutions, we are generally confronted with a more complicated system and more problems. The reason for this stems from the very nature of finance, and of course, financial services and instruments. These may include intangible services, and risky instruments and transactions. The characteristics and functions of finance, financial services, and these instruments are rather complex, and when they are combined with insufficient information on the part of customers or consumers of these systems, and their differentiation of expectations, this can lead to skepticism, disappointment, and extreme reactions. Often, there are suitable opportunities for abuse by financial service providers under such conditions.[1] When all these combine, customers can readily claim that they are deceived, and this in turn contributes to the bad reputation of finance in terms of ethics and ethical behavior (Aras, 2008).

We have learned from elementary economic theory that the enterprise is concerned with taking risk, and that rewards accrue to those taking risks if they are successful. Risk, of course, means that success is uncertain and that failure is a possible outcome. It therefore follows that the higher the level of risk which is taken, the higher the level of rewards for success. Finance theory was developed in order to quantify the relationship between success and failure, and to make the rewards commensurate with the risk. This quantification ensured that arbitrage would occur to equalize the risk and reward relationship across various enterprises in a freely operating market system. These are things that we all learn as part of the introductory economics course. There has been

---

1   There are many examples of such misbehavior—in the UK and the USA and in other countries—which have received a high profile.

surprisingly little comment about this since the 2008 financial crisis, even though it seems clear that the reestablishment of the risk and reward relationship is an essential component of creating an economic climate in which crisis will not reoccur. It is our argument that this is a matter which needs to be raised and addressed in order for any form of sustainable economic activity to take place. Without such a change, theft is simply legitimated, yet legitimate theft cannot occur in a sustainable economy (Aras and Crowther, 2011). The question of standards for sustainable activity is one which has been in existence for a long time and gradually some standards for reporting are beginning to emerge. In many ways the development of sustainability reporting standards parallels the development of accounting standards. The harmonization of common standards is the main issue to consider. This is in distinct contrast to the end of the twentieth century when the emergence of common standards, for either accounting or sustainability, looked no better than a remote possibility (Aras and Crowther, 2009a).

Market Misbehavior and the Causes of Financial Crisis

The financial and economic crisis of 2008 has shown that there are failures in governance and problems with the market system. These have been the main issues depicted as representative of systemic failures of the market system and the lax application of systems of governance and regulation. Thus, many people are arguing for improved systems to combat this. Naturally many people have discussed these failures, and the consequent problems, and will continue to do so into the future. It is not, of course, the first such crisis and the market economy has been proceeding on a course of boom or bust for the last 20 years. This is not dissimilar to that of the 1960s and 1970s which neo-conservatives claimed to have stopped. The main differences are that recent cycles are driven by the financial markets, and the era of globalization means that no country is immune from the effects felt in other countries (Aras and Crowther, 2012). Globalization should stifle one of the debates concerning the crisis, which is the prevention of future occurrences through the introduction of an enhanced regulatory regime. Regulators are bound by their terms and areas of reference, whereas finance and trade are increasingly without boundaries. So the only form of regulation which would be effective would be a global system of regulation (Aras and Crowther, 2009a). At present this does not appear to be a viable option because of vested interests in other forms of control.

The financial and consequent economic crises which we have experienced are a direct consequence of activities that have been occurring over the years.

They have been discussed frequently and have been depicted as representative of systemic failures of the market system and the lax application of systems of governance and regulation, as depicted in Figure 11.1.

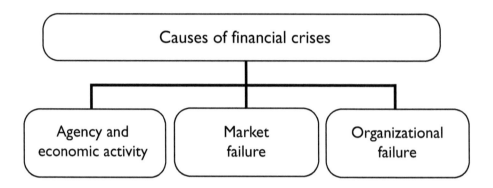

Figure 11.1   Causes of financial crises
Source: Aras and Crowther, 2012.

Thus, many people are arguing for improved systems to combat this. Others have been more concerned to allocate blame to the banks, the financial markets, the regulators, or to governments according to their personal prejudices. Still others would say that it is an inevitable consequence of greed, ignorance, and irresponsibility. All the evidence shows that most individuals are ready and willing to believe that abnormal rewards are possible for them personally, without the need to take abnormal risks, and that this situation can be perpetuated. The evidence also shows that as long as we are personally benefiting like this, then we are happy not to ask questions and to accept lax regulation. After all, regulation is to protect others rather than us. The lessons that are readily apparent, although not really talked about, are that it is not acceptable to blame others when we are personally culpable, and it is not possible to look for social responsibility in organizations when this misbehavior is happening. Put simply, social responsibility demands individual responsibility (Aras and Crowther, 2012). However, individual responsibility affects all levels of management in institutions and society at large.

There are three causes of crisis which are all interconnected — the problem of agency and economic activity, market failure, and organizational failure. These are explained below.

AGENCY AND ECONOMIC ACTIVITY

The basic assumption of economic activity is that it should be organized by profit-seeking firms, each acting in isolation and concerned solely with profit maximization, justified according to classical liberalism and the utilitarian philosophy of John Stuart Mill. This inevitably results in management which is organization-centric, seeking merely to measure and report upon the activities of the firm insofar as they affect the firm. Any actions of the firm which have consequences external to the corporation are held not to be the concern of the firm (Aras and Crowther, 2009b, 2009c). Indeed enshrined within classical liberalism, alongside the sanctity of the individual to pursue his own course of action, was the notion that the operation of the free market mechanism would mediate between these individuals to allow for an equilibrium based upon the interaction of these freely acting individuals, and that this equilibrium was an inevitable consequence of this interaction.[2] As a consequence, any concern by the corporation about the effect of its actions upon externalities was irrelevant and not therefore a proper concern for its management.

MARKET FAILURE

Regulators inevitably must, according to their requirements, focus upon the local market while finance escapes them through its ability to migrate around the world. Effectively, this means that any realistic form of regulation does not and cannot exist. One consequence of this regulatory failure is that contamination spreads, and the dubious practices developed in one financial market become the norm in other markets. When the inevitable crisis appears, this too spreads from one country to another, as all economies are affected by both the consequences of dubious lending practices and the ensuing crisis of confidence.

The only barriers to financial transactions are national regulations (Tobin, 2000). However, it can be seen that regulation is not enough to regulate and control international transactions and capital flows in developing countries and transitional economies, or to effectively regulate global financial companies. Risk has been effectively ignored and corporate governance principles flouted (Aras and Crowther, 2008a, 2009d). The principles of governance and the principles of sustainability are inextricable interrelated and the ignoring of governance principles shows that such firms have scant regard for sustainability.

---

2   This assumption, of course, ignores the imbalances in power between the various parties seeking to enact transaction through the market.

Indeed, the behavior of financial institutions still continues to have no regard for sustainability, for themselves, for national economies, or for the global economic system. It seems that they have learned nothing from previous crises which have been a regular occurrence in the Western economic system. The only difference this time round in 2008 was the global nature of the effects arising out of the local US cause. The financial crisis expanded into an economic crisis and many sound businesses perished in this climate. Others are, however, prospering and it is our argument that a large part of the difference between survival and failure, in the current climate of economic downturn, is a proper understanding and assessment of risk being based upon an understanding of the principles of sustainability (Aras and Crowther, 2009d). The evidence to support this assertion is still accumulating as the crisis continues to unfold.

ORGANIZATIONAL FAILURE

It is often stated that two features, globalization and the free market, can be considered to describe the modern world. It has been widely accepted, almost unquestionably, that free markets will lead to greater economic growth and that we will all benefit from this growth. Around the world people, especially politicians and business leaders, have argued that restrictions upon world economic activity, caused by the regulation of markets, are bad for our wellbeing. In one country after another, in one market after another, governments have been seen to capitulate and relax their regulations to allow complete freedom of economic activity. The world is rapidly becoming a global market place for global corporations, increasingly unfettered by regulation. While this argument remains unchallenged, we have seen the effects of the actions of some of these corporations within the United States—the champion of the free market—itself. We have seen the collapse of the global accounting firm Andersen, and we have seen the bankruptcy of major corporations such as Enron and WorldCom with the result that thousands of people have been thrown out of work and many people have lost their savings for their old age which they have worked long and hard to gain. More recently we have seen the devastating effects of untrammeled and unregulated free market behavior. This is best described as greed, corruption, and the kind of plundering most commonly associated with pirates of age-old eras. The economic collapse, triggered as a direct consequence of this behavior, has caused some rethinking and so perhaps the free market model might not become so ubiquitous.

In considering why this situation has arisen we must acknowledge that there are problems with accounting, with auditing, and with peoples' expectations. We must remember that the myth of the free market is grounded in classical liberal economic theory which subsequently developed into utilitarianism and the foundation of the capitalist economic system. This was proposed by thinkers such as John Stuart Mill in the nineteenth century, and states that anything goes as long as the consequences are acceptable. The regulatory regime of accounting has changed over time to serve the interests of businesses rather than their owners or society. Thus, no longer is it expected that the accounting of a business should be undertaken conservatively by recognizing potential future liabilities while at the same time not recognizing future profit. Instead, profit can be brought forward into the accounts before it has been earned while liabilities, such as the replacement of an aging electricity distribution network, can be ignored if they reduce current profitability. A study of the changes made in accounting standards over the years (Aras and Crowther, 2009a) shows a gradual relaxation of this requirement for conservatism in accounting, as these standards have been changed to allow firms to show increased profits in the present. This, of course, makes the need for strong governance procedures even more paramount.

The management of an organization tends to be treated as a discrete entity[3] and it is important to remember that this entity actually comprises a set of individuals with their own drives, motivations, and desires. Thus, every individual has a desire to fulfil their needs and one of these is self-actualization (Maslow, 1954). This need is the one at the top of Maslow's classical hierarchy of needs, and consequently perhaps the one most considered in terms of motivation. The next two most important needs which are the need for esteem—as reflected in self-respect and the respect of others—and the need for belonging—as reflected in the need for being an integral part of a community—are, however, more important for an understanding of the behavior of the members of the dominant coalition of management within an organization. These two needs help explain why managers, in common with other individuals, need to feel important, skilled, and essential to organizational performance.

Problems with Governance, Social Responsibility, and Regulations

Enron, WorldCom, Qwest, Parmalat, Tyco, ImClone, Madoff, QUALCOMM and various other corporate failures highlight governance and CSR issues, and have increased attention on the role of business ethics. Managers and CEOs of these companies must be considered responsible for all of these failures and these are cases of "corporate irresponsibility". Many people are of the

---

3   Or rather as a coalition which acts in unison.

opinion that if corporations were to behave responsibly, corporate scandals would stop. This applies particularly to financial corporations after the latest crisis. CSR protects firms against some long-term loss. When corporations have social responsibilities, they calculate their risk and the cost of failure. A company must have responsibility to shareholders and stakeholders which means that it has responsibility to all society. In particular, big scandals such as Enron have sharply affected the market and the economy, both for people in the United States and other countries. Various stakeholders, for example, employees, customers, consumers, suppliers and so on, as well as shareholders and regulators of the firm, have a responsibility to ensure good performance. Therefore, CSR is not only related to firms but also to the entire society. Therefore, changing the role of corporate responsibility shifts the focus away from the real problem that society needs to address.

One of the reasons for this outcome is increasing competition between the company and the market. Managers tend to become much more ambitious than before in their behavior and status in the globalized world. Thus, we have to focus on corporate and managerial behavior. The question is how to behave as a socially responsible manager and how to solve this vital problem in business life and in society. In the business world there are always some rules, principles and norms, regulations, and some legal requirements. However, to be socially responsible we must be more than simply law abiding—we have to be capable of acting and being held accountable for decisions and actions. The problem is the implication of these directions for company and managerial behavior. On the other hand, one perspective is that a corporation is a *legal person* and has the rights and duties that go with that status, including social responsibility. In the case of Enron, managers were aware of all the regulations. They were aware of all the irresponsible and unethical problems with company management, yet they did not change their approach or behavior.

Good governance is also important in every sphere of society regardless of whether it is the corporate environment, or general society, or the political environment. Good governance levels can, for example, improve public faith and confidence in the political environment. When the resources are too limited to meet the minimum expectations of the people, it is a good governance level that can help to promote the welfare of society. Also, a concern for governance is at least as prevalent in the corporate world (Durnev and Kim, 2005).

Corporate governance can be considered as an environment of trust, ethics, moral values, and confidence. It is a synergic effort of all the constituents of society including stakeholders, government, the general public, professional and service providers, and the corporate sector. One of the consequences of a concern with the actions of an organization, and the consequences of those actions, has been an increasing concern with corporate governance (Hermalin, 2005).

Corporate governance is, therefore, a current buzzword that is used extensively in the world. It has gained tremendous importance in recent years. Two of the main reasons for this upsurge in interest are the economic liberalization and deregulation of industry and business, and the demand for a new corporate ethos and stricter compliance with the law of the land. Another factor that has been responsible for the sudden exposure of the corporate sector to a new paradigm for corporate governance that is in tune with the changing times, is the demand for greater accountability of companies to their shareholders and customers (Bushman and Smith, 2001). According to Aras and Crowther (2009b), it is possible to say that good corporate governance will address this but that not all firms recognize it. It is equally possible to state that a firm which has a more complete understanding of the relationship between social responsibility, sustainability, and corporate governance will address these issues more completely (Aras et al., 2010). By implication, a more complete understanding of the interrelationships will lead to better corporate governance, better CSR, and therefore a better economic performance and level of sustainability.

The principles of governance and the principles of sustainability are inextricably interrelated, and ignoring governance principles shows that such firms have scant regard for sustainability—indeed the behavior of financial institutions still continues to show no regard for sustainability. It is equally possible to state that a firm which has a more complete understanding of the relationship between social responsibility, sustainability, and corporate governance, will address these issues more completely. By implication, a more complete understanding of the interrelationships will lead to better corporate governance and therefore to better economic performance. However, this is not really the reason why governance has become so important, rather that investors are recognizing that good governance leads to better financial performance. The relationship is direct and the evidence is overwhelming. The evidence is so great that it is clear that investors are increasingly willing to pay a premium to invest in a company with good governance procedures. This is because they recognize that this will lead to expected improvements in sustainable performance which will, over time, be reflected in future dividend streams (Aras and Crowther, 2012). It is also more profitable for an investor to invest in a well-governed company as the benefits will accrue both in the short and long term. However, governance may be a necessary condition for ethical and socially responsible behavior, but we cannot say it is sufficient to solve all problems in this area.

Standards, rules, and regulations are important to control businesses' and markets' activities. However, it is not always possible to control behavior and corporate activity with regulations, governance principles, rules, and norms. Therefore, another question arises in this situation: "If managers and policy makers do not know their responsibilities and how to act socially responsibly, then who will control this problem in business life and in the market?" The concern is that the social responsibility aspects of the company cannot be controlled through legal means. The only social contract between managers, society, and stakeholders is for responsible and accountable behavior.

Therefore, we can say that sustainable economic activity is dependent upon sustainable businesses, while sustainable businesses are equally dependent upon stable and sustainable markets. Equally the sustainability of national economies is dependent upon both, as is the global economy. If regulatory control of these interrelationships is problematic then this means that governance is also problematic.

Durable Strategy for Sustainability: Key Indicators

Globalization should stifle one of the debates concerning the global crisis. This is the one concerning the prevention of future occurrences through the introduction of an enhanced regulatory regime. Regulators are bounded by their terms and areas of reference, whereas finance and trade are increasingly without boundaries. So the only form of regulation which would be effective would be a global system of regulation (Aras and Crowther, 2009a). At present this does not appear to be a viable option because of vested interests in other forms of control. Of vital concern to all forms of business and also to leaders in governments, NGOs, and financial institutions is the question of sustainability and the conditions under which sustainable development becomes possible. Although environmental effects are an important part of sustainability for businesses and for economic or financial activity mediated through the markets, sustainability is actually much more complex than this and requires the balancing of a variety of different factors (Aras and Crowther, 2009a).

Sustainable markets must provide confidence to all institutions and business organizations. This should be done in terms of proper standards, good governance principles, necessary regulation, and all other market rules. The sustainable corporation needs to invest in all of its stakeholders in order to maintain and improve relationships, and that investment in stakeholder relations should be returned to the company by being recycled. So a stakeholder who is well-treated receives benefit from the company and returns benefit to that company. This continuous chain in the economy creates a great interaction with sustainability, and this causality between the market and the corporation feeds the entire global system. Therefore, for sustainable and sound markets in the longer term, further serious action is necessary.

We have all known that a significant part of the problem is related to the governance of the system, markets, and businesses. The main part of the problem is caused by failures in regulation and governance brought about by the nature of global markets and, more significantly, local governance. Consequently, external verification is also important as a part of the process of reassuring and safeguarding stakeholders in the market. Standards for reporting are obviously important as they enable comparison and benchmarking, as well as the tracking of change over time. From the corporate side, it is also essential that the approach to sustainability be embedded into the long-term strategic planning of the corporation, with implementation being an essential part of this planning. As we have seen, there are many aspects which need to be considered in assessing sustainable activity much of which is focused upon the relationship between the corporation and its stakeholders.

We have discussed in this book that we need to focus on long-term future strategy instead of only short-term benefits. We also realized the importance of responsible behavior in the markets and the business world. It may start from shareholders, but it covers all stakeholders, society, the environment, and our future (Figure 11.2). The global financial crisis in 2008 has raised several questions with respect to the corporate and financial markets' governance and social responsibility. It is fairly clear that the most important component of a sustainable market and business is good governance and responsible behavior. Every kind of business, financial or non-financial, every size of business— SME or big firm—needs long-term and durable strategies for achieving a sustainable and sound future. Some key factors in creating durable strategies are:

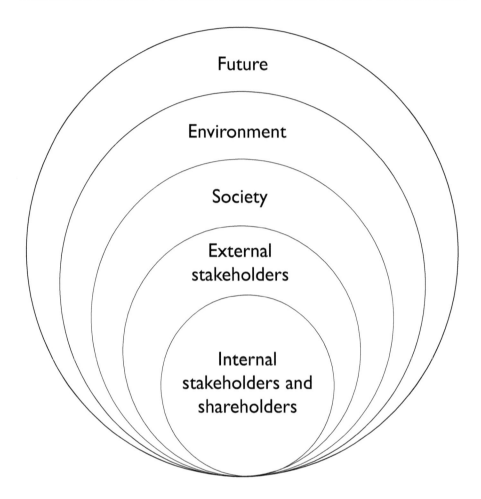

Figure 11.2   Stakeholders of the organization
Source: Aras and Crowther, 2012.

- thinking for the long term;

- implementing the necessary standards and regulations;

- controlling and avoiding market misbehavior;

- not taking or allowing excess risk;

- implementing governance principles and CSR;

- respecting stakeholders' rights;

- considering the environment and acting to protect it;

- collaborating instead of competing;

- being trustworthy and credible;

- trying to create sustainable value.

We have to consider that misbehavior is more costly than good business and market behavior. It is important to create an understanding of where and how business can best contribute to sustainable markets not only among the developed countries but more in middle and lower income countries. The answers to such questions, as listed below, are important for an understanding of where to contribute:

- What is the current state of play?

- What are policymakers, investors, and corporates most interested in regarding financial markets and business sustainability?

- What are the most important problems to solve?

- How should we approach these issues?

- Do we have enough information and data?

- What kind of research is necessary to understand the problem and find a solution?

- Where are the most significant gaps in creating solutions for sound markets?

Conclusion

In the economy, trust is extremely important. Informal, unwritten guarantees are preconditions for all trade and production (Akerlof, 1970). On the other hand, international rules and principles may have been protecting investors and stakeholders from the uncertainty in the market. Markets contain complex instruments and risky transactions. The uncertainty created by this situation makes it difficult for organizations to create confidence in the segments concerned.

Legal provisions, control mechanisms, and sanctions introduced by them alone are not sufficient to ensure the sound operation of the system and to create confidence.

Moreover, as the world's governments and markets inch closer to putting a price on environmental impact and a value on eco-system services, companies with a better understanding of eco-system services—and how they both impact and rely on them—could be better placed to operate if those services were less available and more expensive (Westervelt, 2014).

We realize that sustainability offers long-term benefits for markets, businesses, and institutions and provides strength and longevity. Sustainable markets are creating sustainable value, achieving the institutions' and markets' goals, and maintaining a balance between economic and social benefits in a long-term perspective. Therefore, corporate and market sustainability reform is at the center of the global world and considers the nature of its development.

In this book we have discussed the market and business sustainability issue, which is clearly vital for a sound economy and its sustainable development. We have also shown that sustainability is a complex issue, with many ramifications, affecting all aspects of corporate activities and its relationship with society, the environment, and all stakeholders. We still have a long way to go.

References and Bibliography

Akerlof, G. A. (1970). The Market for Lemons. *The Quarterly Journal of Economics*, Vol. 84, 488–500.

Allen, F. (2001). Do Financial Institutions Matter? *Journal of Finance*, Vol. 56(4), 1165–75.

Aras, G., and Crowther, D. (2012). *Governance and Social Responsibility: International Perspective*. Palgrave McMillian.

Aras, G., and Crowther, D. (2011). Governance and the Management of Global Markets. In G. Aras and D. Crowther (eds), *Governance in the Business Environment*. Emerald Book Series: Developments in Corporate Governance and Responsibility.

Aras, G., and Crowther D. (2010). Analysing Social Responsibility in Financial Companies. *International Journal of Banking Accounting & Finance*, Vol. 2(3), 295–308.

Aras. G., Kutlu O., and Aybars, A. (2010). Managing Corporate Performance: Investigating the Relationship between Corporate Social Responsibility and Financial Performance in Emerging Markets. *International Journal of Productivity and Performance Management*, Vol. 59(3), 229–54.

Aras, G., and Crowther D. (2009a). *The Durable Corporation: Strategies for Sustainable Development*. Farnham: Gower.

Aras, G., and Crowther, D. (2009b). Making Sustainable Development Sustainable. *Management Decision*, Vol. 47(6), 975–88.

Aras, G., and Crowther, D. (2009c). Introduction: Corporate Governance and Corporate Social Responsibility in context. In G. Aras and D. Crowther (eds), *Global Perspectives on Corporate Governance and Corporate Social Responsibility*. Farnham: Gower.

Aras, G., and Crowther, D. (2009d). Corporate Sustainability Reporting: A Study in Disingenuity? *Journal of Business Ethics*, Vol. 27, 279–88.

Aras, G. (2008). Corporate Governance And The Agency Problem in Financial Markets. In D. Crowther and N. Capaldi (eds), *Ashgate Research Companion to Corporate Social Responsibility*. Aldershot: Ashgate.

Aras, G., and Crowther, D. (2008a). Evaluating Sustainability: a Need for Standards. *Issues in Social & Environmental Accounting*, Vol. 2(1), 19–35.

Aras, G., and Crowther, D. (2008b). Developing Sustainable Reporting Standards. *Journal of Applied Accounting Research*, Vol. 9(1), 4–16.

Aras, G. (2006). The Ethical Issues In The Finance And Financial Markets. In D. Crowther and K. Caliyurt (eds), *Globalization and Social Responsibility*. Cambridge: Scholars Press.

Baums, T., and Scott, K.E. (2005). Taking Shareholder Protection Seriously? Corporate Governance in the United States and Germany. *Journal of Applied Corporate Finance*, Vol. 17(4), Fall.

Bushman, R.M., and Smith, A.J. (2001). Financial Accounting Information and Corporate Governance. *Journal of Accounting and Economics*, Vol. 32, 237–333.

Durnev, A., and Kim, E.H. (2005). To Steal or Not to Steal: Firm Attributes, Legal Environment, and Valuation. *Journal of Finance*, Vol. 60(3), 1461–93.

Friedman, M. (1970). The Social Responsibility of Business is to Increase its Profits. *New York Times Magazine*, September 13, 122–6.

Hermalin, B. E. (2005). Trends in Corporate Governance. *Journal of Finance*, Vol. 60(5), 2351–84.

Jensen, M.J. (2005). Agency Costs of Overvalued Equity. *Financial Management*, 5–19.

Jensen, M.J. (1989). Organization Theory and Methodology. *The Accounting Review*, Vol. 58(2), April, 334–5.

Jensen, M., and Meckling, W. (1976). Theory of The Firm: Managerial Behavior, Agency Costs, and Ownership Structure. *Journal of Financial Economics*, Vol. 3, 305–60.

Maslow, A.H. (1954). *Motivation and Personality*. New York: Harper & Row.

Stigson, B. (2002). Pillars of Change: Business Is Finally Learning That Taking Care of the Environment and Meeting Social Responsibilities Makes Good Business Sense. *Forum for Applied Research and Public Policy*, Vol. 16(4), 23.

Tobin, J. (2000). Financial Globalization. *World Development*, Vol. 28(6), 1101–4.

Westervelt, A. (2014). Science and Sustainability Goals: What Researchers Want Businesses To Know. *The Guardian*. http://www.theguardian.com/sustainable-business/2014/aug/29/environment-climate-data-science-sustainability-goals-business-targets, August 29.

Index